FOCUS ON WHAT

FIELD BOOK FOR EFFECTIVE OKRs
A Hands-on Guide for Managers and Teams

Gerard Chiva

Published by Aktia Solutions SL

FOCUS ON WHAT MATTERS: Field Book for Effective OKRs

Copyright © 2024 by Gerard Chiva. All Rights Reserved.

All information, techniques, ideas, and concepts contained within this publication are of the nature of general comment only and are not in any way recommended as individual advice. The intent is to offer a variety of information to provide a wider range of choices now and in the future, recognizing that we all have widely diverse circumstances and viewpoints. Should any reader choose to make use of the information contained herein, this is their decision, and the contributors (and their companies), authors and publishers do not assume any responsibilities whatsoever under any condition or circumstances. It is recommended that the reader obtain their own independent advice.

Publisher: Aktia Solutions SL, aktiasolutions.com

Author and Illustrations: Gerard Chiva

First Edition 2024

ISBN: 979-8-8757246-4-0

All rights reserved in all media. No part of this book may be used, copied, reproduced, presented, stored, communicated, or transmitted in any form by any means without prior written permission, except in the case of brief quotations embodied in critical articles and reviews.

Published by Aktia Solutions SL

Praise for Focus on What Matters

"This book is a game-changer for professionals across all roles and company sizes. By providing a comprehensive exploration of OKR definitions, it serves as a masterclass in shaping corporate vision, refining product strategy, and enhancing team management. Packed with practical examples and insightful canvases, this is a resource that I look forward to revisiting frequently. I genuinely recommend it, especially if you're seeking powerful tools to effectively communicate and advocate for the implementation of OKRs within your senior management team."

— **Samuel Lacarta,** MarTech Director at Imagin.
Former Digital Business Director and CIO at Vueling Airlines

"A transformative read for anyone navigating the world of OKRs. It brilliantly demystifies the alignment of OKRs with business strategy, offering practical insights on overcoming implementation challenges. A must-read for managers seeking a transformative guide to creating an organization that can drive strategic objectives with precision."

— **Peter Kerschbaumer,** Enterprise Agile Coach

"Focus on What Matters" provides a wealth of valuable insights and practical guidance for individuals and organizations looking to grasp, implement, and navigate OKRs within the realm of strategy and goal-setting.

Gerard through its structured approach and actionable advice make it an indispensable resource for anyone seeking to make the most of OKRs in their strategic planning and execution."

— **Ivan Font,** CSO at Travelgate

"Gerard's book is the missing manual companies need to successfully implement OKRs. Whether you're a CEO, a manager, or a team member, there is so much practical wisdom that readers can benefit from: the key role strategy and product roadmaps play in successful OKRs, how to choose the right number of OKRs for your team, and how the wrong incentives can backfire OKRs even with the best intentions. Gerard's hands on experience shines through on every page: "Focus on What Matters" is a must read for those looking to roll out OKRs and succeed at transforming their organization."

— **Sam Sgro,** SVP, Chief Architect and Head of Consumer Engineering at LendingClub

Other Books by Gerard Chiva

Kanban Fundamentals

Lean Product Management

Product Discovery

The Art of Strategy

Product Roadmapping in Practice

Strategy Design Sprint

Contents

Foreword: Luis Gonçalves i
Preface iii
Lessons from an Exceptional Leader ix

SECTION 1 – ON STRATEGY 1
    Chapter 1: The Imperative of a Product Strategy 3
    Chapter 2: The Seven Pitfalls of Strategy 15
    Chapter 3: Decalogue of a Great Strategy 27
    Chapter 4: Introduction to Wardley Maps 39
    Chapter 5: Strategy and OKRs 49
    Chapter 6: Common OKRs Pitfalls 57

SECTION 2 – OKRS FOR MANAGERS 61
    Chapter 7: A Plan is not a Strategy 63
    Chapter 8: Bridging the Gap 75
    Chapter 9: OKR Guidelines for Managers 85
    Chapter 10: OKRs and Team Structure 91
    Chapter 11: OKRs and Strategy Review 95
    Chapter 12: Performance Appraisals and Economic Incentives 107
    Chapter 13: The Leader as Coach 111
    Chapter 14: The Goal-Setting Tyranny 121

SECTION 3 – OKRS FOR TEAMS 125
    Chapter 15: Setting Up Effective OKRs 127
    Chapter 16: Blueprint for Creating Team-Level OKRs 137
    Chapter 17: How Many OKRs Are Enough 147
    Chapter 18: Turning Strategy into Action 153
    Chapter 19: OKRs and Wardley Maps 165
    Chapter 20: OKRs vs KPIs 173
    Chapter 21: OKRs and North Star Metrics 179

Chapter 22: OKRs and Roadmaps 185
Chapter 23: OKRs for Product Launch 191

SECTION 4 – OKRS GOVERNANCE 195
Chapter 24: Managing Frequently Changing OKRs 197
Chapter 25: Alignment with OKRs 201
Chapter 26: Navigating Shared OKRs Across Teams 207
Chapter 27: Evaluating OKR Progress 215

NOTES 229

Foreword: Luis Gonçalves

In an era where the noise of relentless change is the only constant, finding clarity and direction is not just a necessity but a lifeline for organizations striving for excellence. "FOCUS ON WHAT MATTERS," emerges as this much-needed compass, guiding leaders and teams through the dynamic labyrinth of modern business practices with one of the most powerful tools in today's corporate arsenal: Objectives and Key Results (OKRs).

Gerard Chiva, an expert in business strategy and operational efficiency, brings to the table a wealth of experience and insights in this compelling read. His expertise in harnessing the transformative power of OKRs is not just theoretical but steeped in a profound understanding of the practical challenges and opportunities organizations face in the contemporary business landscape.

"FOCUS ON WHAT MATTERS" is not merely a book; it is a journey. A journey that takes you through the intricacies of setting, implementing, and achieving objectives that resonate deeply with the core mission and vision of your organization. Gerard's nuanced approach to OKRs transcends conventional wisdom. It delves into the art and science of aligning organizational efforts towards impactful and measurable outcomes, making it an indispensable resource for leaders, managers, and teams.

This book stands out in its ability to demystify OKRs, presenting them not as a rigid framework but as a flexible, adaptive tool that can be molded to fit the unique contours of any organization. Gerard's narrative is refreshingly candid, dotted with real-world examples, practical tips, and insightful anecdotes, making the concept of OKRs both accessible and engaging.

As you turn the pages of "FOCUS ON WHAT MATTERS," you will find yourself equipped with more than just knowledge on OKRs. You will gain a perspective that encourages you to look beyond the horizon of mundane tasks and short-term goals. You will be inspired to embrace a mindset that prioritizes strategic focus, encourages relentless pursuit of excellence, and cultivates a culture of continuous improvement.

In a time where prioritizing and focusing on what truly matters can be daunting, this book is a beacon of clarity. It encourages us to cut through the clutter, to elevate our sights, and to steadfastly march towards objectives that not only drive organizational success but also foster personal growth and fulfillment.

"FOCUS ON WHAT MATTERS" is more than a guide; it's a catalyst for change – a change that begins with OKRs and transcends to redefine the essence of success in business and beyond.

Luis Gonçalves

ADAPT Methodology® Founder and Author Bestseller

Preface

Welcome to a practical and insightful journey through the intricacies of implementing Objectives and Key Results (OKRs) in your organization. This book is not just another theoretical treatise on OKRs; it is a field guide, crafted to address the real-world challenges you face in making OKRs work within your company.

For those who are well-acquainted with the concept of OKRs and are seeking to refine their implementation strategies – whether as a manager or a team member – this book is tailored for you. It's filled with practical examples, useful anecdotes, and a collection of practices and techniques that have been tested and proven in various organizational landscapes.

However, if you are new to the world of OKRs, you might want to familiarize yourself with the basics first, as this book assumes a foundational understanding of what OKRs are and delves directly into the nuances of effective application and troubleshooting.

A unique aspect of this book, and one that often goes unaddressed in most OKR literature, is the exploration of the relationship between strategy and OKRs. The initial section aims to demystify the often-misunderstood connection between an organization's overarching strategy and the role of OKRs in actualizing that strategy. We delve into how OKRs should not only stem from but also reinforce and drive the strategic objectives of your company.

As you navigate through the chapters, you will gain insights into aligning OKRs with your business strategy, ensuring they are more than just a set of goals, but a dynamic tool that propels your organization forward. This book is designed to be your companion in transforming OKRs from a conceptual framework into a powerful, strategic asset that galvanizes your team and drives tangible results.

Embark on this journey to master the art and science of OKR implementation and lead your team to new heights of success and organizational excellence.

Why This Book?

You might be thinking, "Gosh, not another book on OKRs!" It's true, OKRs have become a buzzword in the business world, with countless resources discussing their potential and application. But herein lies a paradox – despite the abundance of information, there remains a gap. A gap filled with misunderstandings, misapplications, and pains, especially within product teams trying to implement and use OKRs effectively.

This book is crafted to bridge that gap. While many resources provide a theoretical overview of OKRs, they often leave teams grappling with the practicalities of implementation. "How do we adapt OKRs to our specific context?" "What are the common pitfalls, and how do we avoid them?" "How do we ensure our OKRs are not just another set of goals but a tool that drives real impact?" These are the questions at the heart of this book.

Navigating the OKR Landscape – Beyond Basics to Real-World Challenges

Objectives and Key Results (OKRs) present a deceptively simple façade. Their basic principles are straightforward, yet their successful implementation is a journey fraught with psychological, organizational, and cultural hurdles. These barriers often result in either suboptimal adoption or, worse, counterproductive outcomes.

For those new to OKRs, foundational texts like John Doerr's 'Measure What Matters' or Christina Wodtke's 'Radical Focus' offer excellent starting points. However, this book is crafted for a different journey – one that delves into the nuanced, often challenging scenarios that you, as a reader, might be encountering.

Are you a development team grappling with OKR definitions? A manager navigating HR's push for OKRs in performance evaluations and compensation? Perhaps you are part of a product team handed down a revenue target or struggling with a roadmap aligned with your OKRs. Maybe you're trying to weave product metrics into effective product OKRs or integrate OKR reviews with quarterly product strategy sessions. These, and many other real-world challenges, are the focus of this book.

This is the book I yearned for when I embarked on my own OKR journey eight years ago. While classic texts laid the foundation, they fell short in addressing the practical challenges I faced as a manager, coach, and business owner. Here, I've distilled all my experiences, anecdotes, client case studies, tips, and tricks. This book is your guide to sidestepping the pitfalls I encountered and overcoming the obstacles I faced.

While rich in practical advice, tools, templates, and techniques, this book also anchors itself in a solid theoretical framework. The first section, which I debated including, tackles a frequently overlooked aspect in OKR literature: the concept of strategy. There's a common misconception that goal-setting is tantamount to strategy formulation – a dangerous and erroneous belief.

This initial section on strategy and OKRs is indispensable. It clarifies the distinction between setting goals and defining strategy. It elucidates how OKRs fit into the broader strategic framework of a business, bridging the gap between other critical techniques like roadmaps and product discovery. As Kurt Lewin aptly put it, "there is nothing as practical as a good theory." This section will prove foundational in your understanding and application of OKRs.

In essence, this book is more than a guide; it's a compass navigating the complex, often misunderstood terrain of OKRs in the real world of business and product management.

Practical Advice Based on Field Expertise

My approach is grounded in practicality and field expertise. This book distills the essence of OKRs through a lens of real-world application, particularly focusing on product teams. It's not just about setting OKRs; it's about making them work effectively within the unique dynamics of your team and aligning them with your strategic vision.

We dive deep into common challenges faced by teams, from misalignment and lack of engagement to the struggle of measuring impact. More importantly, we offer practical solutions and advice, backed by expertise and experiences from those who have been in the trenches of OKR implementation.

A Guide for Transformation

Consider this book as your guide to transforming the way your team sets and achieves goals. It's a pathway to turning the concept of OKRs from a buzzword into a powerful catalyst for strategic alignment, clarity, and results within your product team.

Whether you're starting from scratch or looking to refine your existing OKR process, this book aims to provide you with the insights, tools, and confidence needed to leverage OKRs effectively and drive meaningful change in your organization.

Understanding OKRs

At their core, OKRs are a goal-setting framework used by organizations to define measurable goals and track their outcomes. The philosophy behind OKRs is not just to set ambitious goals but to align these goals across the organization, thereby ensuring everyone moves in the same direction with clarity and purpose.

Objectives define what is to be achieved. They are significant, concrete, and action-oriented. Key Results, on the other hand, are specific measures used to track the achievement of these objectives. The beauty of Key Results lies in their ability to be quantifiable and verifiable - at the end of a period, there should be no dispute as to whether a Key Result has been achieved.

Key Learnings

Embarking on the journey through this book, you will unlock a wealth of knowledge and practical insights on the multifaceted world of OKRs. Here's what you can expect to gain:

- **Clarity on Strategy and OKRs**: Delve into the intricate relationship between strategy formulation and OKR implementation. Understand how these two critical elements of business planning complement and enhance each other.

- **Strategic OKR Applications Across Contexts**: Gain insights into how OKRs are applied strategically in various organizational settings. The text includes tailored examples from different industries, showcasing the versatility and adaptability of OKRs.
- **Navigating OKR Challenges and Best Practices**: Whether you're a manager or part of a team, this book provides comprehensive guidance on overcoming common hurdles in OKR implementation. Discover best practices that can streamline your OKR journey.
- **Integrating OKRs with Other Tools**: Learn about the synergy between OKRs and other management methodologies and tools. This overview will help you integrate OKRs seamlessly into your existing management framework.
- **Practical Implementation Through Case Studies**: The book is rich with real-life case studies, examples, and tips, offering you a hands-on perspective on implementing OKRs effectively. These practical insights will guide you in applying OKRs within your own organization.

Navigating the Book

The book is structured to take you through a logical progression in understanding and applying OKRs. Each chapter builds upon the last, gradually enhancing your comprehension and application skills.

You are encouraged to engage with the material, reflect on your current practices, and envision how OKRs can be tailored to your unique organizational needs.

However, recognizing the diverse needs of its readers, it also serves as a field book. Whether you are a manager or a team member, you can directly jump to specific chapters that address your immediate challenges and questions about OKRs.

Organization of the Book

The book is thoughtfully divided into four sections, each with a distinct focus and purpose:

1. **Section 1 – On Strategy**: This section lays the foundation for understanding the critical relationship between strategy and OKRs. It starts with the imperative of having a solid product strategy, explores common strategic pitfalls, and offers guidance on crafting a great strategy. The section culminates with a focus on integrating strategy with OKRs and addressing common OKR pitfalls for success.

2. **Section 2 – OKRs for Managers**: Tailored for managers, this section delves into the nuances of using OKRs at a managerial level. It covers the distinction between a plan and a strategy, the bridging of gaps in strategic execution, and specific guidelines for managers using OKRs. It also touches upon important

aspects like team structure, strategy reviews, performance appraisals, economic incentives, and the role of a leader as a coach.

3. **Section 3 – OKRs for Teams**: Focused on team dynamics, this section provides a blueprint for setting up effective team-level OKRs. It guides teams on how many OKRs are enough, optimizing OKR performance, and translating strategy into action. This section also elaborates on the integration of OKRs with North Star Metrics and product roadmaps, including their application in product launches.

4. **Section 4 – OKRs Governance**: The final section addresses the governance aspect of OKRs. It offers insights into managing frequently changing OKRs, ensuring alignment, navigating shared OKRs across different teams, and evaluating OKR progress effectively.

Thank You and Let's Continue the Conversation

As we close this preface, I extend my heartfelt gratitude to you, the reader, for embarking on this enlightening journey through the world of OKRs with me. Your engagement and willingness to explore this dynamic methodology are both inspiring and deeply appreciated. Remember, this book is not just a one-way transmission of knowledge, but a platform for ongoing learning and discussion.

I am genuinely interested in hearing your thoughts, experiences, and insights as you navigate the chapters of this book. Your feedback is invaluable, not only in enhancing your own understanding of OKRs but also in enriching the collective wisdom surrounding this powerful tool. Whether you have comments, suggestions, or recommendations, please do not hesitate to reach out.

My email is always open. I look forward to hearing from you and learning about the unique ways in which you apply the principles and practices discussed in this book. Your input could very well shape future editions or inspire new content that can benefit others in our community.

Thank you once again for choosing this book as your guide. May it serve as a catalyst for transformation and success in your managerial and team endeavors.

Here's to mastering the art and science of OKRs together!

Enjoy!

Gerard Chiva

January 2024

Lessons from an Exceptional Leader

When teaching Objectives and Key Results (OKRs), I often initiate the learning process with an insightful video[1] from David Marquet, author of *"Turn the Ship Around."* This serves as a cornerstone for understanding the transformative power of OKRs within any organization.

The video sets the stage, illustrating the profound impact OKRs can have on leadership and management. As product leaders, our dual responsibilities are to chart a strategic course and to ensure this course is dynamically pursued and adjusted. OKRs are instrumental in achieving these objectives.

Leadership transcends the conventional act of issuing directives. It's fundamentally about cultivating an environment that encourages independent thought and decision-making. In his compelling narrative, David Marquet, a former captain in the U.S. Navy, recounts his transformative experience aboard a submarine, moving his crew from being mere executors of orders to proactive leaders.

Marquet's epiphany was the realization that traditional leadership models, particularly in the intricate and fluid realm of submarine operations, were obsolete. To thrive in such a complex environment, he needed to empower his crew to independently think and decisively act.

His approach involved decentralizing authority, aligning it with the locus of information. This paradigm shift required granting his officers greater autonomy and placing trust in their judgment.

Marquet's approach to leadership also focused on creating a safe environment where taking risks and trying new ideas were encouraged. He encouraged his crew to question existing practices and challenge conventional wisdom, fostering a climate of continuous improvement and learning.

The transformation was profound. Marquet's crew evolved into one of the most efficient and effective units in the Navy, characterized by agility, rapid decision-making, and adaptability — essential traits for gaining a competitive edge.

The story of David Marquet serves as a powerful testament to the essence of true leadership: it's not about maintaining control, but about nurturing an environment where individuals can excel and innovate.

Key insights from Marquet's leadership approach include:

1. Aligning authority with information: Empower those with the most relevant information to make decisions.
2. Cultivating a risk-friendly culture: Encourage experimentation and learning from failures.

3. Promoting critical thinking: Foster a culture where questioning and challenging norms are valued.
4. Trusting your team: Have confidence in your team's capacity to make sound decisions.

By integrating these principles, leaders can forge high-performing teams capable of extraordinary achievements. The application of OKRs complements this leadership style, providing a structured yet flexible framework to set objectives, measure progress, and adapt strategies, thereby ensuring that teams not only envision success but actively participate in its realization.

ON STRATEGY

SECTION 1

Chapter 1: The Imperative of a Product Strategy

In the first chapter I want to address a critical topic often overlooked - the importance of a solid product strategy. I frequently see teams diving straight into product discovery or, even more precipitously, into development, without a strategy to guide, limit, and focus their efforts. And there are those who believe strategy only becomes apparent once the product reaches market traction.

But let me be clear: it's crucial to understand that neglecting this step is not only unproductive but potentially catastrophic. By skipping it, we risk squandering both time and resources. Let's explore this subject in-depth to understand the full implications of this oversight and the reasons why it should be avoided.

Understanding Strategy

Firstly, let's begin by defining what strategy is and its significance. Strategy transcends mere planning or goal-setting; it is the underlying force that shapes their formation. It embodies a cohesive set of actions thoughtfully crafted to tackle and overcome specific challenges.

At the heart of a strategy lies a clear diagnosis of the situation, a guiding policy, and a series of coherent actions targeted at overcoming identified obstacles. Moreover, an effective strategy often involves the difficult choice of saying no to many tempting initiatives.

It's not a matter of luck or intuition, but a product of deliberate design and focused intent.

To illustrate this concept further, Richard Rumelt highlights four key elements of a strategy[2]:

1. A challenge, which could be a problem to solve or a goal to achieve.
2. A diagnosis that clarifies the nature of this challenge.
3. A guiding policy.
4. A set of coherent actions to confront it.

Consider the analogy of a doctor assessing a patient: the challenge is the symptoms presented; the diagnosis is their clinical judgment; the therapy is their guiding action; and the prescriptions are the specific, coherent steps taken in response.

In a business context, the challenge often involves navigating change and competition. We diagnose the specific nature of this challenge, select a general approach, and then meticulously design actions to implement this policy.

Business Strategy vs. Product Strategy

While both business and product strategies are aimed at achieving organizational goals, they operate at different levels and have different scopes. Business strategy provides the overall framework defining the company's mission, vision, and goals. On the other hand, product strategy operates within this general business strategy. It defines how a specific product or line of products will contribute to business goals.

Take, for instance, a microprocessor company choosing to specialize in areas like IoT (Internet of Things), AI (Artificial Intelligence), or Communications. This choice represents a strategic business decision. Following this direction, the company must then define its product strategy. Questions such as whether to develop 5G modems, create mobile platforms, or enter into competition with major players like NVIDIA in the AI sector come into play. These decisions are crucial tasks for the product teams.

The Need for a Product Strategy

I vividly recall collaborating with a B2B SaaS product team in the industrial sector. The challenge was immense: develop a groundbreaking product from scratch. However, we soon realized a crucial ingredient was missing: a defined product strategy. And we wondered, how will we know where to navigate without a map?

So, we embarked on a strategic design process involving all parties. After intense work, we presented two potential routes: energy management and electrical maintenance. After internal discussions, we opted for electrical maintenance, aligning it with the corporate strategy and enhancing the company's value proposition.

With electrical maintenance, the aim was to unify all the company's hardware products under a single Cloud platform and boost sales by offering added value to the hardware. Furthermore, the company was planning to open a new line of specialized customer service, making this strategic option a great asset to propel this business unit.

From there, we began the product discovery process to determine the solution to be built. Thanks to the discovery process, we realized that the initial idea of moving towards predictive maintenance with AI was far from the market's maturity, still using pen and paper. So, the team decided to focus on preventive maintenance with alarm and incident management.

The first Minimum Viable Product (MVP) was launched successfully in the market for electrical substation maintenance. This segment, identified as early adopters during our discovery process, showed significant potential and welcomed our product with great enthusiasm.

This real case underscores the importance and function of a product strategy:

- Aligns us with the business strategy.
- Secures buy-in and commitment from stakeholders.
- Provides context and limits to the discovery process.
- Determines what is important and what is not.

We also observe the evolving nature of strategy; it's a journey rather than a static plan. It isn't set in stone indefinitely. In fact, as previously mentioned, while strategy guides the discovery process, the insights gained from discovery can, in turn, refine and reshape the strategy itself.

Strategic Development Principles

What principles should we follow when developing a product strategy? Firstly, recognize that strategy is akin to a design process. It's a complex challenge that demands a thorough understanding of both the market and the organization. It's similar to how a doctor needs to make an accurate diagnosis before prescribing treatment.

Secondly, strategy is an ongoing journey. It's not a single milestone, but a continuous process of adapting and learning, much like navigating a mountain with its various challenges.

Lastly, the execution of a strategy is as vital as its design. Without effective execution, any strategy remains merely a concept. Therefore, the design and implementation of a strategy must work in tandem.

Components of a Product Strategy

Let's review the key elements that make up a product strategy:

- **Product Vision:** The overarching goal or dream that the product aims to achieve.
- **Playing Field:** The specific market or domain where the product will compete.
- **How to Win:** Strategies and tactics to outperform competitors in the chosen field.
- **Capabilities:** The skills, technologies, and resources required to execute the strategy.
- **Management Systems:** The processes and structures needed to support and manage the strategy effectively.

In the concluding section of this chapter, I'll tie everything together with a real-world example. I'll share a case study from my work with a client in automated sports video production, showing how these various elements we've discussed are applied in practice.

Product Vision

The vision serves as our guiding star, our aspiration to win, not just compete. It's about envisioning success in a clear, impactful way. I often advise product teams to craft a vision that's a bit more encompassing than usual.

To do this effectively, they should answer these key questions:

- *What exactly is our product or service?*
- *What purpose does our product serve?*
- *Who are we serving, and in what way?*
- *How will we recognize success: What does 'winning' look like for us?*

Where to Play & How to Win

We now come to the crux of the strategy: deciding where to play and how to win.

- **Where to Play:** This aspect focuses on identifying target customers, determining the geographies to operate in, and choosing the channels for distribution.
- **How to Win:** This involves defining your unique value proposition and developing a robust business model.

It's possible that consumers might adore your product, and the technology behind it could be groundbreaking. However, neither technology nor product excellence alone guarantees success, especially in the face of intense competition and substantial capital costs.

Rather than simply launching a new technology and bracing for the inevitable competitive backlash, it's crucial to consider various strategies for success in this arena. This means thinking beyond the product – exploring innovative business models and considering creativity across the entire business spectrum.

Capabilities

After establishing the core strategy, it's crucial to assess our capabilities. We need to understand what we currently possess and what additional skills and resources are required to achieve success.

- **Identifying Key Capabilities:** This step is about pinpointing the specific abilities and resources the product team must develop to thrive in chosen markets.
- **Implementation and Execution:** This is where we determine the exact skills, knowledge, processes, and assets needed for effective strategy execution. The focus should be on areas where the product can generate the most value.

- **Product-Related Capabilities:** These include functionalities, go-to-market strategies, onboarding processes, design, and user experience.

In essence, these are critical tasks that the product teams need to excel at.

Management Systems

The final piece involves establishing the management systems and processes that underpin and facilitate the product strategy.

- **Designing Organizational Frameworks:** This involves creating structures, governance processes, and performance management systems that align the business's activities and resources with its goals. The focus here is on fostering an environment conducive to achieving the company's winning aspirations.
- **Flexibility and Adaptability:** These systems should be versatile, allowing the business to constantly evolve, learn, and improve.
- **Components of Management Systems:** This term encompasses a broad range of elements, including skills, personnel, processes, organizational structure, software, and tools.

Essentially, these are the aspects that product leadership must effectively manage and execute.

Strategy Design

While developing your product strategy using our strategy design method[3], the process entails two unique stages: formulation and validation.

The initial stage concentrates on enhancing strategic consciousness and pinpointing plausible trajectories by formulating strategic themes.

These themes arguably form the most crucial component of the strategy design method, consisting of a strategic hurdle, an opportunity, and a solution. This solution is characterized by a *'Where to Play'* and *'How to Win'* choice, which in unison shape the foundation of the strategic theme.

Strategic Theme

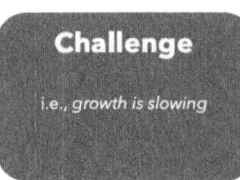

Challenge	Opportunity	Solution
i.e., growth is slowing	i.e., offer new services	i.e., diversify customer base by expanding into residential using a B2B model

Figure 1 - Strategic Theme Example

After the evaluation and selection of strategic themes for implementation, the latter part of the strategy design sprint involves pinpointing suppositions and conducting tests to confirm them, thereby choosing a victorious strategy.

To encapsulate your strategy and correlate it with your product vision, product mission, and enduring product principles, you can utilize the Strategic Intent Canvas shown below.

This canvas aids in illustrating your product strategy and ensuring its alignment with your overarching vision and mission.

Strategic Intent Canvas

Vision (Descriptive long-term ambition)

- How does news headline / cover story about our product 3-5 years from now look like?
- Bigger is better; "Aim for the stars, land on the moon" - we can achieve more, even if we don't reach our full vision
- Our vision is meant to give us sense of direction and guide our decisions
- Our vision should be tangible and measurable

Mission (Why do we exist? - our purpose)

- What impact do we want to make in the world?
- What do we want to be known / remembered for?
- Inspiring, simple & memorable

Playing Field (What value we provide to whom?)

- Where do we compete? (market, product category, industry)
- What do we do and to whom (and as such what we don't do)?
- Customer segments
- Channels
- Geographies
- Product category

How to Win (How do we create value to win in the marketplace?)

- Value proposition & Business Model
- Revenue/Costs
- Market strategy (dominant, disruptive, breakthrough)
- What unique value we bring? (pricing, image, brand, quality)
- What resources & capabilities we utilize? (technology, skills, reputation, partners, assets, brand, etc.)
- How do we sustain our position? (fastest, most agile, innovative, cost efficient, network effects, etc.)

Product Principles

- What makes us different from other companies?
- Where do we look for guidance in difficult situations?
- How do we make decisions?

▲ AKTIA
SOLUTIONS

Figure 2 - Strategic Intent Canvas

Business Model

The pinnacle of a successful product strategy is realized in a sustainable business model. It's important to note that the business model isn't the core of the strategy, but rather the outcome of it.

As we progress in the product strategy development, establishing the business model becomes critical. To do this effectively, we adopt the method of asking *'What needs to be true?'*.

This approach helps us identify the essential assumptions and constraints that will shape both the development and implementation of the business model.

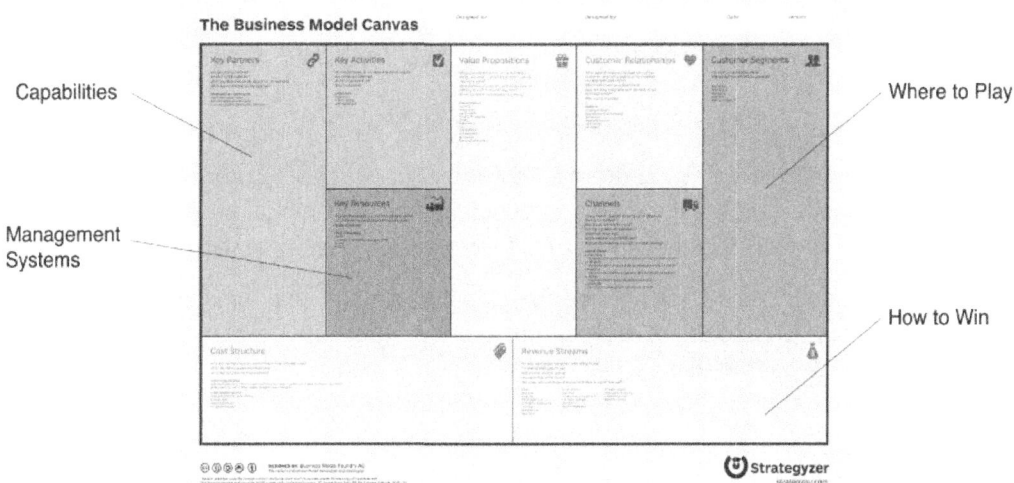

A resource such as the Business Model Canvas[4] can be of immense help, as it simplifies the depiction of the integral aspects of the strategic flow together: the marketplace, value proposition, principal activities (capabilities), resources (management systems), and the income and expenditure model.

Case Study: Sportmatic

Sportmatic, a pseudonym for confidentiality, specializes in creating automated sports video production, broadcasting, and tactical analysis solutions. They approached us for guidance on adapting their high-end market solutions to appeal to the second-tier market, including universities, high schools, and second-division clubs.

Figure 3 - Sportmatic camera system installation

Their technology involves an on-premise camera system and a sophisticated computer running AI-based software for video production and broadcasting. This system can stream content live to social networks or OTT platforms, or store videos for later use.

The videos produced are primarily used by coaches and tactical analysts for match and training analysis, broadcasters for content delivery, and sports clubs' marketing and communication departments to engage fans on social media.

Product Vision

Our goal is to become the premier provider of sports video solutions worldwide, serving both clubs and broadcasters. We aim to simplify the production, streaming, sharing, and technical analysis of sports events, from amateur to professional levels, using automated technology.

We are committed to continually enhancing the customer experience. Our focus includes improving image recognition and processing, expanding video sharing and distribution capabilities, and providing better tools for tactical analysis.

Our objectives:

- Integrate video and data into daily sports tactical analysis.
- Assist sports clubs globally in reaching a wider audience.
- Empower individual athletes in promoting their own skills and careers.

Situational Awareness

The market for automatic sports video production is shifting. There's a growing trend towards more standardized products and an increased focus on value-added services like tactical analysis and content sharing for monetization purposes.

For SportMatic to tap into new market segments, simply offering a lower-cost, scaled-down version of our premium product isn't enough. Instead, we need to enhance its value to address the significant unmet needs of customers in these segments.

Competition:

- The market is crowded with numerous competitors and a wide array of products.
- Alternatives include more affordable, easy-to-install, user-friendly, and portable options.
- Competitors are also addressing additional user demands, such as providing statistics, summaries, easy content consumption, and sharing capabilities.

Evolution of the Industry:

- There's a trend towards the commoditization of automated sports video production.
- There's a growing demand for detailed technical analysis.
- The need for video editing and sharing on social networks is increasing.

Opportunities

After our initial strategy design sessions, we pinpointed SportMatic's main challenge and identified several strategic opportunities to address it. The key opportunities we found to tackle SportMatic's central challenge include:

- *Enhancing the experience for technical staff.*
- *Facilitating content sharing for fans, family, and friends.*

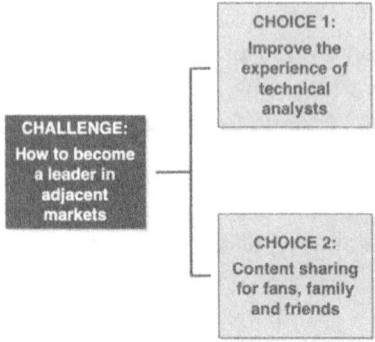

Figure 4 - Sportmatic case study: challenge & options

Strategic Themes

Once we established our strategic direction and secured buy-in, the next phase involved formulating strategic hypotheses. This entails defining our strategic themes or solutions, primarily focusing on our 'where to play' and 'how to win' strategies.

For SportMatic's case, the key strategic themes identified are:

1. Developing an integrated solution for technical staff in Tier-2 segments.
2. Creating a solution for amateur sports video production and sharing, targeted at fans, family, and friends.
3. Innovating a 'GoPro-like' product specifically designed for automated video production in amateur sports.

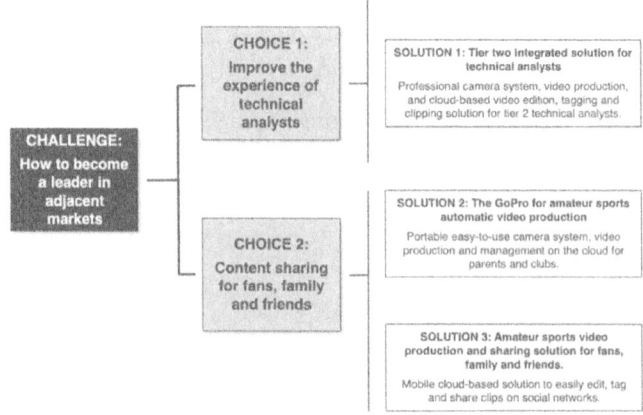

Figure 5 - Sportmatic Case study: challenge, choices, and opportunities

After careful deliberation, the team chose to focus on the first strategic hypothesis, recognizing its potential and challenge. The other two hypotheses were put on hold, earmarked for future exploration.

With our direction set, we proceeded to draft the initial business model, using the Business Model Canvas as our guide. This involved pinpointing the key assumptions and initiating the product discovery process. Our aim here was to define a compelling value proposition and fine-tune the various elements of the business model.

Chapter 2: The Seven Pitfalls of Strategy

A pervasive issue in many organizations is the premature leap to solutions without adequately grasping the problem or making an accurate diagnosis.

This rush to action often leads to discussions about plans, roadmaps, features, objectives, and KPIs that are disconnected from the core issues at hand. At the strategic level, this can have grave consequences, steering the future of products and organizations off course.

It's essential for companies to eschew blind operation, avoid setting unrealistic goals, and refrain from attributing failures solely to poor execution. A clear understanding of problems through proper processes and strategic tools is critical, as strategic blindness can prevent the recognition of actual challenges and opportunities.

The Seven Pitfalls of Strategy

Ineffective strategy is rife with lofty objectives yet lacks actionable policies. It operates under the false premise that goals alone are the blueprint for success, leading to a disjointed set of aims that are often unrealistic. Such strategies are shrouded in grandiose language that obscures a lack of true leadership and vision.

Let us now scrutinize the seven pitfalls that often undermine strategic integrity:

1. Strategic Myopia
2. Evading the Core Challenge
3. Superficiality and Jargon
4. Confusing Goals with Strategy
5. Misaligned Objectives
6. Disconnect Between Planning and Execution
7. The Secrets of Success

1 - Strategic Myopia

A common challenge for many businesses is operating with limited situational awareness, often leading to poor decision-making. Traditional tools like SWOT analysis, Porter's Five Forces, PESTLE, and the Business Model Canvas are undoubtedly useful, but a more effective approach involves adopting a strategic direction grounded in comprehensive situational awareness. This is where Wardley Maps come into play.

Wardley Maps[5] serve as a vital tool, providing crucial context and strategic positioning, much like a detailed map used by a general in warfare. Unlike conventional business tools, these maps offer dynamic insights into the competitive landscape. They enable businesses to accurately pinpoint their strategic position, identify potential challenges, and strategize effectively.

This tool proves invaluable in boosting situational awareness, guiding strategic decisions, and creating an environment where leadership can communicate and refine strategy more effectively.

In chapter 4, I'll offer a comprehensive introduction to Wardley Maps, complete with multiple examples. For now, let's focus on why they are crucial in fostering strategic awareness, especially when compared to traditional, more static and narrow approaches to strategy development.

Space Has Meaning

Picture this: a general heading into battle without a landscape map, relying solely on a SWOT analysis. This scenario mirrors how many businesses navigate today's competitive environment.

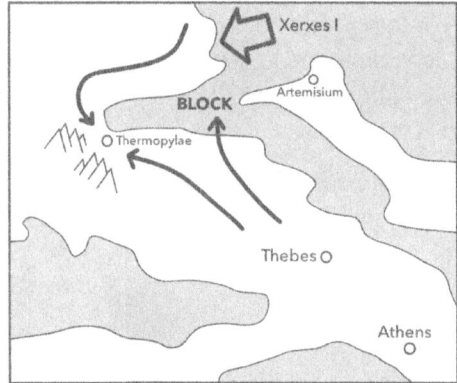 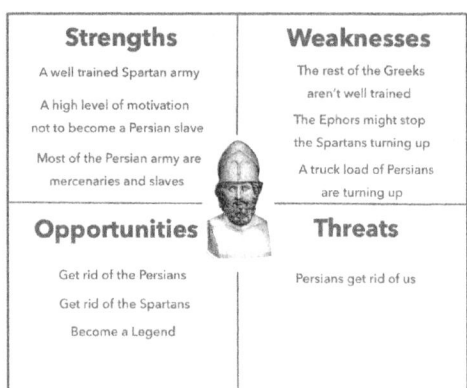

Figure 6 – Map vs SWOT: Image adapted from Wardley Maps book

Consider how space gains significance on a map. Movement of any element alters the entire context, thanks to established anchors and relative positioning.

Business strategies often lack this 'map' quality, missing crucial anchors and awareness.

Strategic thinking should mirror chess, where position and movement are key. Wardley Maps fill this gap, focusing on situational awareness and dynamic planning. They're not static like SWOT or Business Model Canvas but living frameworks that adapt to real-world scenarios.

This tool empowers leaders to navigate with clarity, addressing pivotal questions:

- *What challenges are on our path to success?*
- *Where should we focus our efforts?*
- *What strategies will lead us to victory?*

Wardley Maps transform strategy from a visionary abstract into a tangible, actionable roadmap, encouraging engagement and continuous improvement from all organizational levels.

2 - Evading the Core Challenge

The lack of a strategic 'map' in business can lead to a poor understanding of one's current position, missed opportunities, and an inability to anticipate competitors' moves.

This raises critical questions about the challenges your business currently faces and those it may encounter in the next 3-5 years. Unlike a poor strategy, which fails to recognize or define these challenges, a robust strategy emerges from the need to address specific problems or obstacles.

Strategic planning is not just about setting goals or budgets; it's a carefully charted course through challenges. Long-term plans and unrealistic goals are pitfalls to avoid. Instead, a strategy should clearly define problems, provide diagnoses, and establish guiding policies, coupled with continuous review mechanisms to adapt as situations evolve.

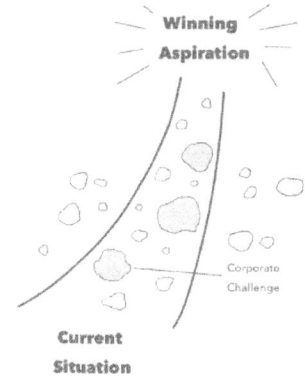

Figure 7 - Strategic Challenges

At different levels in the organization strategies cascade down and the challenges for the superior level become objectives or constraints for the subsequent level.

Consider the analogy of a football club with the ambition to be the world's best in ten years. This club must analyze its current situation and challenges, like budget constraints or talent acquisition, and strategically respond, perhaps by focusing on grassroots development.

This strategic intent then cascades through the organization, shaping the objectives at every level. For instance, the club's coach must adapt his strategy for each match, analyzing opponents and deploying the best lineup and tactics. This approach mirrors how businesses should operate – with clear intent, adaptability, and keen situational awareness.

Let's delve deeper into the football club analogy to illustrate various decision-making levels:

1. **Club's Strategic Vision (Top Level)**: The club's board sets the long-term vision to become the world's best club in a decade. This involves analyzing financial constraints, talent acquisition strategies, and overall club development.
2. **Mid-Level Strategy (Technical Direction)**: The technical team, including the coach, translates this vision into a seasonal goal – winning the league and cup. They focus on leveraging talent from junior teams and scouting for affordable, skilled players, all while aligning with the club's overarching strategy.
3. **Operational Tactics (Team and Coach)**: For each game, the coach and players prepare with a specific focus on winning. They analyze opponents, using a tactical board to plan formations and strategies, highlighting how they can exploit weaknesses and bolster strengths.
4. **Individual Player Goals**: Each player has specific objectives aligned with the team's strategy. These might include personal performance targets, fitness goals, and skill development, all contributing to the team's success.

By cascading the strategic vision down through these levels, the club ensures alignment and coherence in its approach, from broad aspirations to specific match-day tactics.

3 - Superficiality and Jargon

Fluff in strategy is akin to a mirage: grand in appearance yet lacking substance. It's often a superficial restatement of what's already known, peppered with buzzwords to mask a lack of genuine leadership insight. This pseudo-strategic chatter employs lofty, abstract language and seemingly profound concepts, creating an illusion of depth and acumen.

Need a quick, effortless strategy without delving into your company's actual position or understanding the competitive landscape? Just sprinkle in buzzwords like "digital-first," "agile," "innovative," and "customer-focused," among others, and you have a strategy in name only. This approach, recognizable to many professionals, lacks actionable direction, hindering decision-making and goal-setting.

Those adept in fluff use it to camouflage their indecision and inability to articulate a clear, concise path forward.

4 - Confusing Goals with Strategy

In the realm of strategy, confusion between goals and strategy is a common misstep. Goals are not the product of spontaneous brainstorming but emerge from a structured strategic thinking process.

Strategy goes beyond merely defining objectives or adhering to a formulaic plan that starts with vision and mission statements. It's a response to a challenge, requiring a diagnosis, a guiding policy, and a set of coherent actions, often implemented through methodologies like OKRs.

Consider the concept of strategic intent, as coined by Gary Hamel[6]. It's about setting ambitious goals that push organizations to innovate and lead.

Strategic intent involves a management process focused on winning, motivating, and maintaining flexibility. It requires building new advantages faster than competitors can imitate existing ones.

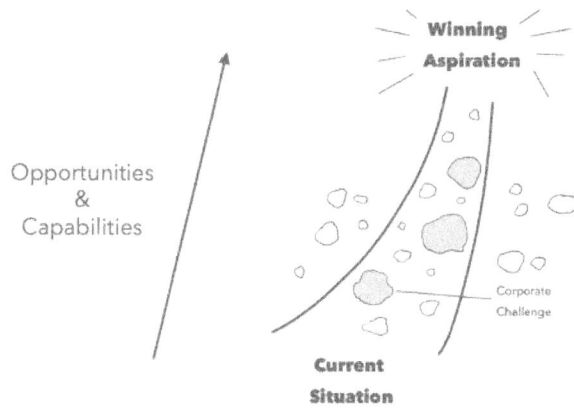

Figure 8 - Opportunities & Capabilities

Challenges are the obstacles or problems that emerge on the path to strategic success. They translate into sprints that lead to competitive advantage through capability development or opportunity exploitation.

Strategy, therefore, is a coherent response to a significant challenge. It's simple and obvious in retrospect and involves identifying critical issues to focus resources effectively. Strategy is about coordination and focus, not just setting goals and expecting execution.

True strategy requires leaders to recognize and bridge the gap between lofty goals and practical actions.

Strategy Building Blocks

In dissecting the essence of strategy, we must distinguish between three pivotal concepts: Strategic Intent, Challenge, and Strategy itself.

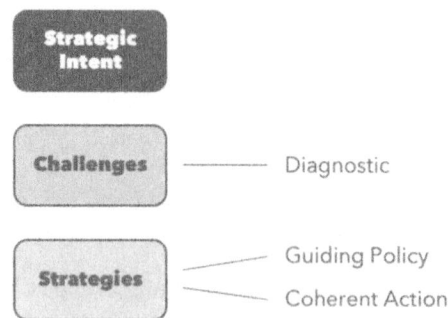

Figure 9 - Strategic concepts

Strategic Intent: It's about presenting a series of corporate challenges to guide the organization towards achieving its winning aspiration. These challenges vary annually, focusing on different aspects like quality, customer service, market expansion, or product innovation. This approach is key to developing new competitive advantages and maintaining a competitive edge.

Challenges: Defining what winning means for a company leads to identifying various challenges. These challenges, envisioned as medium-term sprints, are opportunities to develop unique capabilities and seize unseen opportunities, forming the bedrock of strategic thinking.

Strategy: Contrary to just setting objectives, a strategy is a comprehensive response to critical challenges. It involves a nuanced set of analyses and actions aimed at addressing high-stakes issues. The hallmark of a good strategy is its simplicity and clarity, focusing on a few pivotal problems and marshaling resources to address them effectively. The leader's role is crucial in identifying and responding to these strategic challenges.

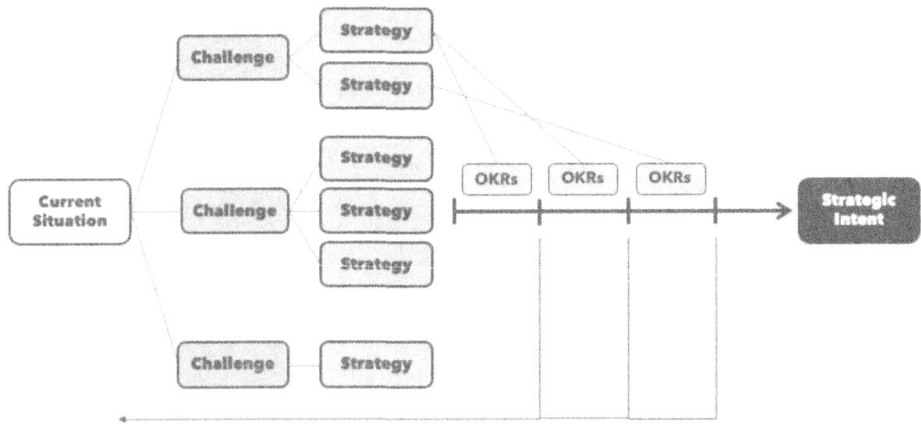

Figure 10 - Putting it all together (Intent, Challenge, Strategy, OKRs)

In Summary

Strategy transcends mere goal-setting, encompassing a broader vision to create and leverage competitive advantages. It's a dynamic process that aligns intent with action, addressing challenges with innovative and focused responses.

Simply being ambitious is not a strategy. A good strategy recognizes the nature of the challenge and offers a way to overcome it.

A good strategy includes a consistent set of actions. They are not "implementation" details.

Executives who complain of "execution" problems have generally confused strategy with goal setting. When the "strategy" process is basically a game of setting performance goals, then there is still a huge gap between these ambitions and actions.

Of course, a leader can set goals and delegate the work of figuring out what to do to others. But that is not strategy. If that's how the organization works, let's be honest: call it goal setting.

5 - Misaligned Objectives

Strategic objectives are pivotal in bridging the gap between lofty aspirations and practical actions. However, they become counterproductive when treated as ends in themselves or when they fail to address the crux of the problem.

The peril lies in setting arbitrary objectives that lack a strategic backbone.

Effective leaders see objectives as signposts along a strategically charted path, not as arbitrary checkpoints.

Inconsistent Objectives: The Jumble of Directionless Efforts

A frequent misstep in strategic planning is the creation of a sprawling list of tasks, mistakenly labeled as strategies or objectives. This leads to a scattered focus, often causing different teams or business units to pursue conflicting goals.

A well-crafted strategy concentrates efforts on a select few pivotal objectives, ensuring that energy and resources are channeled for maximum impact.

Illusory Objectives: The Trap of Unattainable Goals

A robust strategy addresses and overcomes significant challenges. However, it must bridge the gap between these challenges and attainable actions. Goals set by a sound strategy should be realistic, considering available resources and capabilities.

Illusory objectives, on the other hand, merely restate the desired outcome without a feasible plan to get there.

A leader's role is to propose achievable strategic objectives that provide a clear and practical pathway to overcome key challenges, avoiding the trap of setting goals as daunting as the challenges themselves.

6 - Disconnect Between Planning and Execution

In traditional management, three core principles have long been considered foundational:

- **Comprehensive Knowledge for Planning:** The belief that all necessary information can be known and used to formulate precise plans.
- **Separation of Planners and Doers:** A clear division is maintained between those who plan and those who execute the plans.
- **The Singular Correct Method:** The conviction that there is only one right way to approach and execute tasks.

Under this paradigm, managers function akin to programmers of robotic workers, meticulously crafting plans and dictating exact actions and methods.

This approach, however, is fundamentally flawed in many business contexts, particularly those involving complex, non-repetitive tasks where situational knowledge is crucial.

The dynamic nature of business environments often renders traditional strategic plans unreliable. Despite meticulous planning, unforeseen variables inevitably emerge, throwing plans off course.

Yet, direction and objectives are still necessary. The key realization here is that individuals are capable of self-regulation when committed to certain objectives, and these objectives must be established somehow.

This led experts to a consensus: Instead of detailed plans, businesses need a clear, compelling direction, alignment, self-organization, and a mechanism for rapid adaptation based on results.

Executing Strategy in Unpredictable Environments

Strategy execution is the process of planning actions to achieve desired outcomes and ensuring these actions are completed. In stable, predictable environments, thorough planning based on information analysis can be effective. We can predict the impact of our actions, set objectives, and use supervision and incentives to guide behavior until desired outcomes are achieved.

In contrast, in unpredictable environments, this approach often fails. However, there's a way to effectively connect strategy and operations even amidst uncertainty. This involves three interdependent principles:

- **Providing Intent:** Clearly communicating the overarching goals and the rationale behind them.
- **Ensuring Alignment:** Aligning team and individual goals with the broader organizational objectives.
- **Enabling Autonomy:** Empowering teams and individuals to make decisions and adapt their approach based on evolving circumstances and feedback.

The surge in popularity of Objectives and Key Results (OKRs) is arguably a response to this need for better alignment and autonomy.

With operational agility largely addressed in many organizations, the focus shifted to ensuring everyone is aligned with and actively contributing towards the organizational goals.

OKRs have emerged as a powerful tool in bridging the gap between high-level strategic objectives and day-to-day operational activities, thereby addressing the disconnect between planning and execution in today's dynamic business environment.

7 - The Secrets of Success

The allure of replicating the "secrets of success" of renowned companies like Spotify, Netflix, or Toyota is strong, yet misleading.

This approach is fundamentally flawed. While operational excellence and tactics can be mimicked, they do not equate to strategy.

The success stories of leading companies aren't just a collection of well-executed tactics but are the culmination of years of capability building, driven by a clear strategic intent and a deep understanding of their competitive landscape and its evolution.

The Folly of Imitation in Strategy

Take IKEA, for instance. Its strategy is well-known, but the secret to its success lies in what Richard Rumelt describes as "chain-link logic" in his book "Good Strategy/Bad Strategy." IKEA's unique coordination of policies creates an integrated system unlike any other in the furniture industry. For a competitor to effectively challenge IKEA, they would need to start from scratch, disrupting their existing business model. Even after five decades, no company has truly replicated IKEA's approach.

Similarly, consider Apple. Comparisons with Samsung or Microsoft often focus on products, markets, or industries. However, Apple's strategy transcends these aspects. Over time, Apple has built an interconnected ecosystem, underpinned by its brand and core competencies in quality, design, and customer service. This ecosystem is not merely a collection of products but a comprehensive experience that is difficult to replicate.

Strategic Uniqueness Cannot Be Cloned

The key takeaway is that strategic success cannot be easily copied. The effectiveness of a strategy lies in its uniqueness and the specific context in which it was developed and executed.

Each successful company's strategy is tailored to its unique circumstances, resources, capabilities, and understanding of its market. Attempting to clone another organization's strategy is like trying to fit a square peg into a round hole – it's unlikely to yield the desired result.

Instead of seeking to copy the strategies of successful companies, organizations should focus on developing their own strategic paths. This involves understanding their unique strengths, weaknesses, competitive environment, and customer needs. It requires building capabilities that align with their long-term strategic goals and continuously adapting to the changing market dynamics.

In essence, the true "secret" to success is not found in mimicking others but in crafting a strategy that is as unique as the company itself, leveraging its own strengths and positioning it effectively in its competitive landscape.

Conclusion

This chapter encapsulates the essence of formulating an effective strategy within an organization, highlighting its complexities, potential pitfalls, and the critical role it plays at every level of a business.

Understanding these aspects is crucial in navigating the complexities of strategic planning and execution.

In the following chapter, we will explore the attributes of a sound strategic approach and provide examples to illustrate these concepts in action.

Chapter 3: Decalogue of a Great Strategy

In this pivotal chapter, we delve into the core principles that underpin a successful strategy, laying the foundation for my unique approach to strategy design and implementation, as explored in my previous book, 'Strategy Design Sprint'.[7]

These foundational principles are essential not only for understanding the effectiveness of my strategic methodology but also for applying it meaningfully in various contexts.

These principles aren't just guidelines; they are the bedrock of all remarkable strategies. They encompass:

1. **Intent** – *The driving force behind every decision.*
2. **Facing Challenges** – *Navigating through obstacles.*
3. **Situational Awareness** – *Understanding the playing field.*
4. **Design Process** – *Crafting a strategic blueprint.*
5. **Leverage** – *Maximizing available resources.*
6. **Focus** – *Concentrating on what matters most.*
7. **Planning and Execution** – *Bridging the gap between idea and action.*
8. **Adaptivity** – *Evolving in response to change.*
9. **Simplicity** – *Clarity over complexity.*
10. **Shared** – *Uniting everyone.*

Let's embark on a detailed exploration of each tenet. Understanding these principles is crucial not only to grasp the effectiveness of our strategic method but also to apply it effectively in your own context.

1 - Intent

The concept of intent is more related to the concept of directive than to the concept of objective. An objective is the outcome or result you are attempting to achieve, whereas a directive indicates not only the outcome, but the reason behind pursuing that outcome and very importantly a guiding policy or a guideline of how to achieve it.

Strategic intent is the business adaptation of the military mission command.

We can take over military principles in formulating strategic intent. Such a statement needs to contain the following:

1. **A short statement of the overall intent**. This is classically stated as an objective plus a purpose. In other words, what we need to achieve now and why. This will represent a step toward the overall end-state. This is the real focus. Achieving it defines success. It answers the question everyone in the organization can and should ask of their leaders, the one which is hardest to answer.

2. **An account of the situation**, highlighting the essential characteristics that influence the course of action to be taken. The description of the situation should make it clear what the implications are for what the organization must do.
3. **An extrapolation of the more specific objectives implied by the intent.** These will have to be turned into responsibilities for the next level in the organization.
4. **Further guidance about boundaries, in particular the constraints to be observed.** This helps people to think ahead and warns them of things on the horizon of which they may not be aware. Constraints do not only define boundaries but help to clarify what is wanted by making explicit what is not wanted.

In summary, strategic intent is a directive expressing long-term success, why that is important, including a guideline of how to achieve it and objectives and boundaries for lower organizational units.

2 - Facing Challenges

At the heart of every strategic endeavor lies a challenge – a catalyst that demands a response, manifesting as problems, obstacles, or goals. For instance, consider the personal goal of maintaining good health in old age. The challenge might be overcoming a habit like smoking 20 cigarettes a day, coupled with the hurdles of finding time and discipline for diet and exercise.

In the business realm, challenges are diverse and multifaceted. They can range from leveraging a new technology patent to addressing underserved consumer needs, combating shrinking margins due to fierce competition, strategizing market entry, fostering growth post product-market fit, or identifying future capabilities for industry leadership.

The crux of strategy lies in the focus of your attention and the time horizon considered. Are your strategies aimed at immediate problem-solving, or do they take a visionary approach, anticipating the landscape a decade ahead? While short-term strategies might secure immediate gains, like a year-end bonus, they could also inadvertently pave the way to long-term setbacks, such as bankruptcy. Conversely, long-term strategies, though more complex and uncertain, are instrumental in securing enduring leadership and success in a rapidly evolving business world.

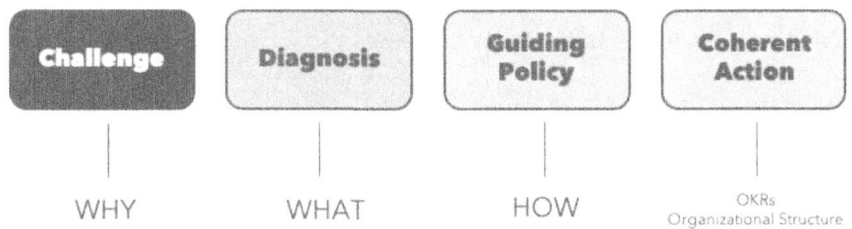

Figure 11 - The Kernel of a Good Strategy from the book "Good Strategy/Bad Strategy"

For a physician, the challenge appears as a set of symptoms accompanying a medical record. The doctor makes a clinical diagnosis, identifying a possible disease or pathology. The chosen therapy is the doctor's guide. The doctor's specific prescriptions for diet, therapy, and medication are the coherent set of actions that must be taken.

In business, the challenge is often dealing with change and competition. The first step toward an effective strategy is diagnosing the specific nature of the challenge. The second step is to choose a general guide to dealing with the situation that is based on some type of leverage or advantage. The third step is the design of actions and resource allocations that implement the chosen guidance policy.

To accurately interpret your current situation, pinpoint the precise challenges to tackle, and offer a well-informed diagnosis, a heightened level of situational awareness is essential. This critical skill enables you to understand the nuances of your environment, ensuring that your strategic responses are both relevant and effective. It sets the stage for the next crucial aspect of strategy formulation.

3 - Situational Awareness

On a sunny Sunday morning, imagine taking a family hike in the mountains. Initially, the path is clear, but suddenly, a dense fog engulfs you, disconnecting you from the outside world. The temperature drops, and anxiety sets in; you're lost, with no map or signposts in sight, akin to being pursued by an unseen threat.

This scenario mirrors how some companies approach strategy. They lack awareness of their current position, direction, and external challenges.

Effective strategic planning, as emphasized by Gary Hamel, requires more than aspirational vision statements; it necessitates industry foresight. This foresight involves understanding:

- Your current position and the path to your destination.
- The whereabouts and movements of competitors.
- Anticipating future conditions and trends.

Answering two critical questions aids in building this foresight:

- What new customer benefits should we aim to provide in the next five to fifteen years?
- What competencies must we develop or acquire to deliver these benefits?

Industry foresight is grounded in analyzing trends in technology, demographics, regulation, and lifestyle shifts. It's about creating new competitive spaces by understanding and harnessing these trends. True foresight combines creativity with a strong factual foundation, distinguishing it from mere hallucinations of success.

Industry Foresight

To get to the future first, leadership must either see opportunities not seen by other firms or must be able to exploit opportunities, by virtue of consistent capability-building, that other companies can't.

The obvious question at this point is where does industry foresight come from? How is it possible to develop industry foresight when the world seems to be in perpetual turmoil? How can one distinguish between foresight and fantasy? How is it possible to validate industry foresight when the future hasn't happened yet?

The cues, weak signals, and trend lines that suggest how the future might be different are there for everyone to observe. There are little data critical to the development of industry foresight that are possessed by only one company.

How then is it possible that some companies can craft a view of the future and other companies cannot?

One of the main causes of this problem is trying to predict the future based on the myopia of the current served market. Often, what prevents companies from imagining the future and discovering new competitive space is not the unknowability of the future, but the fact that leaders tend to look at the future through the lens of existing served markets.

Another reason is trying to predict and plan the future rather than trying to imagine how the future could be.

In "unstructured" industries the number of future permutations is countless, thus any traditional scenario-planning process would be ineffective in trying to represent the range of potential outcomes.

Scenario building and forecasting typically start with what is, and then project forward to what might happen. The quest for industry foresight often starts with what could be, and then works back to what must happen for that future to come about. That's the reason we start our strategic thinking process from the strategic intent and then we walk backwards.

Industry foresight must be informed by deep insight into trends in lifestyles, technology, demographics, and geopolitics. But to create the future a company must first be capable of imagining it. To create the future a company must first develop a powerful visual and verbal representation of what the future could be.

Amplify the Opportunity Space

To expand the opportunity space, it's crucial for companies to break free from the narrow vision confined by their present market and the limitations imposed by existing concepts of products or services, as well as traditional value-cost associations. Failing to do so may render much of the future and its potential opportunities invisible to them. It's about looking beyond the present constraints and envisioning where the market can go, not just where it currently is.

Gary Hamel argues that to increase the opportunity space leadership must conceive the company as a portfolio of core competencies rather than a portfolio of individual business units or products. Business units are typically defined in terms of a specific product-market focus, whereas core competencies connote a broad class of customer benefits.

Any company that defines itself in terms of a specific set of end product-markets ties its fate to the fate of those particular markets.

To see the future a company must be capable of escaping a narrow and orthodox view of *"What business are we in?"* and *"What is our product or service?"* Just as it is necessary to abstract away from business units to underlying core competencies, it is necessary to abstract away from traditional product and service definitions and focus on underlying jobs customers are trying to get done.

This is where methodologies such as Wardley Maps, Blue Ocean Strategy[8] or Jobs to be Done[9] allow us to get out of our legacy thinking and spot new opportunities of growth either by changing the rules of the game or by spotting untapped market segments.

4 - Design Process

Viewing strategy as a design challenge rather than mere planning or goal-setting is crucial. In design, various elements are meticulously organized, adjusted, and coordinated to address a specific problem or challenge. A robust strategy isn't just about choosing from a list of options; it's about creating coherence, aligning actions, policies, and resources to accomplish a significant objective.

The most effective strategies are akin to intricate designs rather than mere decisions. They are carefully constructed to meet identified challenges.

Think of strategy more like engineering a high-performance aircraft rather than merely deciding on a car purchase. A master strategist, therefore, is akin to a designer, harmonizing various elements to build a winning strategy.

This approach is often missing in many organizations, where goals may be multiple and disjointed, lacking the cohesive design of a well-thought-out strategy.

5 - Leverage

An effective strategy acts as a powerful lever, channeling focus, energy, and action where they are most needed, at the opportune moment and location.

Think of strategy as a lever amplifying force. It's possible, though strenuous, to move a massive rock using sheer strength, ropes, and sheer will. However, it's far more intelligent to employ levers and wheels for the task.

Three crucial leverage points in a sound strategy include:

- **Anticipation:** Foreseeing and preparing for future challenges and opportunities.
- **Pivot Points:** Identifying and acting upon critical moments that can change the course of action.
- **Concentration:** Focusing resources and efforts intensely in targeted areas for maximum impact.

Anticipation

Anticipation is about predicting shifts in consumer demand and competitors' responses.

Effective strategy stems from the ability to perceive what others have overlooked or undervalued, thereby revealing a strategic lever that can be used to gain an advantage.

The strength of a successful strategy often comes from a unique perspective on competitive advantage, reevaluating market dynamics, foreseeing future trends, or redefining the boundaries of the industry.

Pivot Points

To get leverage you need to find a pivot point that will amplify the effects of concentrated force. These points are natural or created imbalances in a situation: for example, unserved demand in one market, a robust capacity developed in one context that can be applied in another, or a cost asymmetry with respect to a rival.

In the book *"7 Powers: The Foundations of Business Strategy"*[10] you can find seven fundamental leverage points that create imbalances in the competitive landscape:

1. *Scale Economies – The quality of declining unit costs with increased business size is referred to as Scale Economies. This situation creates a very difficult position for possible competitors. If they offer the same product their P&L will*

suffer. If they try to remediate this by offering less features or raising prices, customers will abandon their service and they will lose market share.

2. **Network Economies** – the virtuous cycle where the value of the service to each customer is enhanced as new customers join the "network." The value of a product to a customer is increased by the use of the product by others. A company in a leadership position with Network Economies can charge higher prices than its competitors and makes it unattractive for competitors to try to get a piece of the cake.

3. **Counter-Positioning** – a new business model is superior to incumbents' models due to lower costs and/or the ability to charge higher prices. The incumbent does not replicate due to anticipated damage to their existing business or inertia.

4. **Switching Costs** – Switching Costs arise when a consumer values compatibility across multiple purchases from a specific firm over time. These can include repeat purchases of the same product or purchases of complementary goods. A company that has embedded Switching Costs for its current customers can charge higher prices than competitors for equivalent products or services. This benefit only accrues to the Power holder in selling follow-on products to their current customers.

5. **Branding** – Branding is an asset that communicates information and evokes positive emotions in the customer, leading to an increased willingness to pay for the product. A business with a strong brand can charge a higher price for its offering but a strong brand can only be created over a lengthy period of reinforcing actions.

6. **Cornered Resource** – A unique and powerful capability no one else possesses. The Cornered Resource can take many forms, offering uniquely different benefits. It might be a patent, a cost-saving production manufacturing approach or a talented leadership team like Intel, Apple or Pixar had at a time.

7. **Process Power** – A company with Process Power can improve product attributes and/or lower costs as a result of process improvements embedded within the organization. For example, Toyota has maintained the quality increases and cost reductions of the TPS over a span of decades; these assets do not disappear as new workers are brought in, and older workers retire. Hence, Process Power advances are difficult to replicate, and can only be achieved over a long period of sustained evolutionary advance.

If your business model fails to incorporate at least one key strategic power, you are likely to encounter significant challenges.

Example: Apple

A paradigmatic example of a company successfully implementing several of Hamilton Helmer's "Seven Powers" is Apple Inc. Apple has effectively used these strategic powers to establish and maintain its market dominance:

- **Scale Economies**: Apple's large-scale operations in manufacturing and distribution allow for lower per-unit costs and higher efficiency.
- **Network Economies**: The ecosystem of Apple products and services, like the App Store, iCloud, and Apple Music, creates a network where the value increases with more users.
- **Counter-Positioning**: Apple has repeatedly positioned itself against the norms of the tech industry, from its early personal computers to the iPhone, disrupting existing market leaders.
- **Switching Costs**: The unique operating system and integrated nature of Apple products create high switching costs for users.
- **Branding**: Apple's brand is known for innovation, quality, and design, creating customer loyalty and allowing for premium pricing.
- **Cornered Resource**: Apple's control over its proprietary technology and software, as well as key supply chain partnerships, acts as a cornered resource.
- **Process Power**: Apple's efficient and secretive product development process gives it an edge in innovation and time-to-market.

Apple's mastery in applying these powers has been central to its success and industry leadership.

Concentration

Concentration is most effective when we channel our efforts towards a select number of objectives, thus amplifying our potential for greater profits.

In this pivotal process, OKRs (Objectives and Key Results) play a crucial role by steering concentration, ensuring that focus is maintained and aligned throughout the organization. They help us to not only identify our primary goals but also to commit to them with the full force of our collective resources.

6 - Focus

A compelling strategy is not just about setting goals; it's about the intricate coordination of actions, policies, and resources to achieve a significant objective. Many organizations miss the mark in crafting focused strategies.

Focus is two-fold: it's about the synergy of policies that amplify their collective impact and applying this enhanced power precisely. It means zeroing in on a market segment with a business model that outshines competitors in delivering value to that segment.

Success in the market isn't solely about dominance; it's about profitability. Achieving this requires a strategy that distinctly sets you apart from other players in the same arena.

Example: Apple

By September 1997, Apple was two months from bankruptcy. Steve Jobs, who had cofounded the company in 1976, agreed to return to serve on a reconstructed board of directors and to be interim CEO.

Within a year, things changed radically. Steve shrunk Apple to a scale and scope suitable to the reality of being a niche producer in the highly competitive personal computer business. He cut Apple back to a core that could survive.

Jobs cut all the desktop models—there were fifteen—back to one. He cut all laptops to just one model. He completely cut out all the peripherals. He cut development engineers. He cut software development. He cut distributors and cut out five of their six national retailers. He cut out virtually all manufacturing, offshoring it to Taiwan. A new online store sold Apple's products directly to consumers, cutting out distributors and dealers.

The power of Jobs' strategy came from directly tackling the fundamental problem with a focused and coordinated set of actions. He did not announce ambitious revenue or profit goals; he did not wallow in inspirational visions of the future. He redesigned the whole business logic around a simplified product line sold through a limited set of channels.

That's focus!

7 - Planning and Execution

Industry foresight doesn't guarantee competitive success. The most foresightful firms aren't always the most profitable. All the foresight in the world, if not matched by a capacity to execute, counts for little. On the other hand, terrific executional ability, in the absence of industry foresight, is not enough to guarantee future success.

Creating industry foresight and achieving operational excellence are both challenging tasks. However, often times what are described as today's implementation failures are really yesterday's foresight failures in disguise.

The quality deficit, which cost U.S. automakers so much market share in the 1970s and 1980s, was more than just "poor execution." Detroit didn't suddenly get careless, and Japanese car makers didn't start out with a quality advantage. Japanese auto companies (and Korean a few years later) realized decades ago that new and formidable competitive weapons would be needed to beat U.S. (and European) car companies in their home market. The new weapons they set about developing were quality, cycle time, and flexibility. Twenty years later, Toyota's foresight had become GM's implementation nightmare.

Two Sides of the Same Coin

Planning and execution are two inseparable facets of a successful strategy. They are like two sides of the same coin, each critical and dependent on the other. The organizational structure and processes should be a direct response to a meticulously crafted strategy, with the flexibility to adapt operations in response to strategic shifts.

A robust strategy encompasses not just the "what" of objectives but also delves into the "why" and "how" of achieving them. It combines insightful diagnosis with the formulation of guiding policies to tackle challenges and a suite of coherent actions for a competitive edge.

To actualize your product or organizational goals, it's essential to establish appropriate organizational structures, alignment mechanisms, and rapid feedback loops. These components ensure continuous evaluation of progress and facilitate strategic adaptations as necessary.

8 - Adaptive

The strategy process is dynamic and iterative, not a linear path. It's a cycle where various factors interplay: the climate influences your intent, environmental shifts impact your strategy, and your actions resonate across the competitive landscape.

In the realm of business, the landscape is never static. Competitors maneuver, new players emerge, and unforeseen tactics unfold. Our knowledge has limits, control is often elusive, and outcomes can be unpredictable.

Strategy is more than a plan on paper; it's a living process that demands action, learning, and adaptation. Like Nokia, which evolved from a paper mill in 1865 to a technology giant, a company's purpose is subject to change, driven by shifts in its landscape and strategic actions.

This necessitates a vigilant approach to strategy, constantly updating not just the strategy itself but also the organizational structure and operations. Regular reviews of OKRs are vital, but they must be coupled with ongoing assessments to ensure their continued relevance. As a leader, focusing on the future is crucial, as the capabilities you build today are the foundation for tomorrow's victories.

9 - Simple but not Simplistic

An effective strategy should be concise, actionable, and retrospectively obvious. It serves as an accessible tool for real-time decision-making, allowing individuals to act independently without constant consultation.

Simplicity in strategy is key, but it must not veer into oversimplification. A simplistic approach may overlook essential complexities, leading to superficial goals or vague visionary statements. Conversely, a simple strategy provides clear, actionable guidance without unnecessary complexity.

Frameworks such as Wardley Maps, Blue Ocean Strategy and Jobs-to-be-done balance simplicity with depth, covering crucial strategic planning aspects in an easily digestible format, empowering any business professional to apply them effectively.

10 - Shared

It's surprisingly common to hear executives hesitate to share their strategy company-wide, fearing it might reach competitors if employees leave. However, this mindset is counterproductive. A strategy that isn't shared widely within the company hinders employees from making informed decisions, necessitating excessive controls and frequent updates, which can slow down processes.

Consider the transparent strategies of Apple, Amazon, or IKEA, which are well-known yet remain unchallenged. While certain strategic details might require confidentiality, the overall intent should be communicated clearly to employees. Effective communication channels, often determined by the organizational structure, are crucial for disseminating this strategic message. In cases where reporting lines obstruct effective communication, addressing these barriers is essential for strategic success.

A Strategic Roadmap Checklist

Whenever you embark on the journey of creating a new strategy, whether you're a team member, product manager, business owner, or executive, this checklist will guide you towards a comprehensive and effective strategy.

1. **Winning Aspiration**: Define your primary goal. What is the utmost achievement your organization or product must attain?
2. **Purpose**: Understand the reasoning behind this goal.
3. **Current Status**: Assess where you stand now.
4. **Challenges Ahead**: Identify potential obstacles on your path.
5. **Nature of Challenges**: Analyze the characteristics of these challenges.

6. **Guiding Principles**: Outline your approach to overcome these hurdles.
7. **Communication**: Plan how to effectively disseminate your strategy.
8. **Incorporating Feedback**: Establish mechanisms for feedback integration.
9. **Alignment**: Ensure that all levels of the organization are working towards common objectives.
10. **Adaptation and Review**: Create a process for regularly updating your strategy based on results and environmental changes.

Remember, a successful strategy is concise, clear, and shared, fitting on a single page, yet rich enough for everyone to connect their role to the broader organizational goals.

Chapter 4: Introduction to Wardley Maps

As discussed in the previous chapter, Wardley Maps serve as an antidote to strategic myopia. This section provides a brief introduction to the Wardley Maps framework, highlighting its importance and contributions to strategic development.

Created by Simon Wardley, Wardley Maps offer a dynamic, effective, and practical approach to strategy design and evolution. Unlike other methodologies, which offer static snapshots, Wardley Maps are grounded in situational awareness and movement. It is a tool for strategic thinking, distinct from strategic planning tools like OKRs, focusing on crafting strategies based on a deep understanding of the situation.

To design a winning strategy using Wardley Maps, several elements are crucial: a clear purpose (strategic intent), an understanding of the competitive landscape, awareness of climatic patterns affecting the landscape, and universally applicable principles known as doctrine. These elements enable leadership to address the essential strategic questions: where to play and how to win, a concept Simon Wardley refers to as 'gameplay,' which represents the action component of the strategy.

Wardley Maps' visual and context-specific nature allows leadership to effectively communicate strategy, fostering challenges and improvements. Many businesses, lacking situational awareness, rely solely on purpose and intuition, leading to misaligned efforts and goals.

Let's explore how Wardley Maps can transform this situation. We will discuss five key aspects of strategy and how Wardley Maps can enhance each:

- Strategy
- Maps
- Communication
- Patterns
- Anticipation

1 – Strategy

Richard Rumelt distinguishes between good and bad strategy. A good strategy is not just a set of objectives, or a vision filled with fancy words, which Rumelt refers to as 'fluff.' Instead, it's a clearly defined guiding policy and action plan designed to address specific business challenges.

When conceptualizing strategy, it's more effective to adopt the mindset of a chess player rather than that of visionaries or storytellers. To confirm the soundness of a strategy, you must confidently answer five key questions:

- *We are we going and why?*
- *What is our current situation?*
- *What are the main challenges in the way?*
- *Where do we want to play?*
- *How are we planning to win?*

Answering these questions requires a map to identify potential moves and navigate the landscape. Like in chess, strategy is fundamentally about understanding position and movement.

Merely copying 'Secrets of Success' from others, like the Spotify Model, the Netflix model, or any generic agile framework, does not constitute a good strategy. Effective strategic planning is tailored to the unique context and needs of your organization.

Good Strategy vs Bad Strategy	
Visual	Story telling
Context specific	Secrets of success
Position and movement	Magic frameworks
High situational awareness	Low situational awareness

The Strategy Cycle

Simon Wardley, in his book, emphasizes three critical aspects of strategy to consider:

1. The strategy process is not linear, but an iterative cycle. Various factors like climate, environment, and actions can influence your purpose, strategy, and outcomes.
2. Action is a vital component of learning. The insights gained from taking steps are integral to refining strategy.
3. Your purpose is dynamic, not static. It evolves as the landscape and your actions change. There is no permanent 'core'; it's always in transition. Consider the evolution of a company like Nokia, which has transformed from a paper mill in 1865 to its current form.

These elements are interrelated and follow a specific sequence, as illustrated in Simon Wardley's Strategy Cycle.

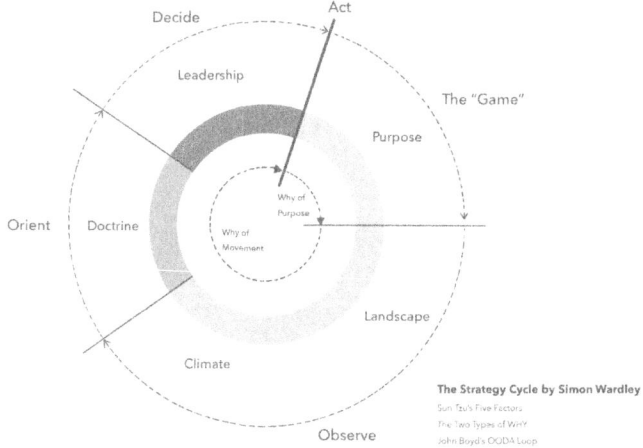

- **Purpose:** This is the strategic intent or the aspiration to win.
- **Landscape:** It involves understanding the competitive landscape.
- **Climate:** This refers to comprehending the climatic patterns – how the landscape is evolving and the rules influencing all players.
- **Doctrine:** This entails grasping the universally applicable principles and doctrines of organizations, relevant in any context.
- **Leadership:** It's about making decisions on where to play and how to win.

To effectively implement the Strategy Cycle, a map is essential – this is where Wardley Maps come into play. They provide a visual representation to navigate through these strategic components.

The Importance of WHY

Focusing solely on purpose can be limiting, as there are two distinct types of 'WHYs' in strategy:

1. **The WHY of Purpose**: This represents the overarching goal, such as winning a chess game or a war.
2. **The WHY of Movement**: This pertains to the tactical decisions within the strategy, like moving a specific chess piece or deploying infantry in a particular manner in warfare.

In chess, while the ultimate purpose is to win the game, the movement WHY involves deciding which piece to move and where. Similarly, in warfare, the purpose might be to win the war, a campaign, or a specific battle, whereas the movement could involve tactical decisions like positioning an infantry battalion, coordinating artillery and surgical attacks, or digging trenches.

Learning occurs through movement, provided we have an understanding of our environment. Without this awareness, we are left only with our overarching purpose and instinctive judgments.

2 – Maps

Space on a map carries significance. When a piece is moved on a map, it alters the map's meaning. This change occurs because of three factors: an anchor (like North on a geographical map), the relative positions of the pieces, and consistent movement patterns.

However, many business 'maps' don't function like true maps because they lack an anchor and situational awareness. In the context of business, the anchor is often the customer or the business itself.

How to Create a Wardley Map?

Consider the following example from Simon Wardley's book, which showcases a typical systems map. If you were to move an element, such as the CRM box, would it make a difference? Not really, because there's no anchor to give it context. Contrast this with a world map – if you were to move Barcelona close to New York, the map's meaning would change drastically. This is because it has a fixed reference point, like magnetic North.

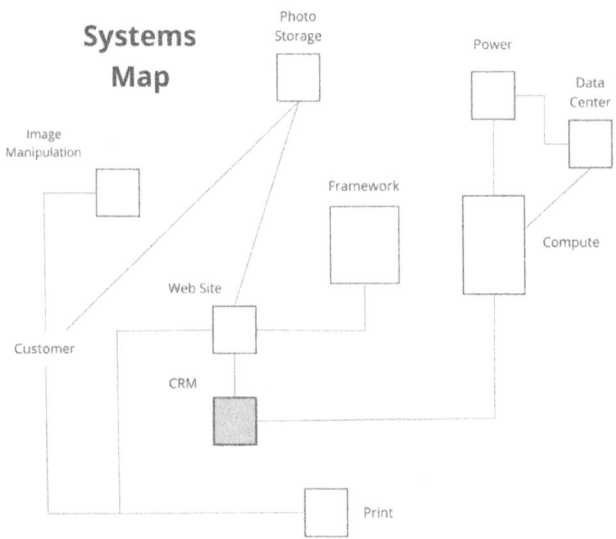

Figure 12 - Typical Systems Map adapted from Wardley Maps book

In a Wardley Map, positions are established through a chain of needs linked to a specific anchor, which is typically the business and the customer. However, it's also possible to include other stakeholders in this mapping process.

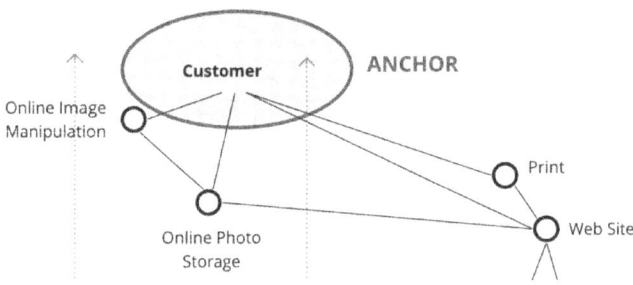

Figure 13 - Anchor in a Wardley Map

Below is the transformation of the previous systems map into a Wardley Map. In this map, the relative positions of the components to each other and the anchor are clearly visible, as well as their movement, which represents the evolution driven by competition.

The elements nearest to the anchor are those most visible to the customer. Below these are the components and subsystems necessary to meet customer needs. The components are arranged from left to right, representing their evolution from Genesis to Commodity (or Utility).

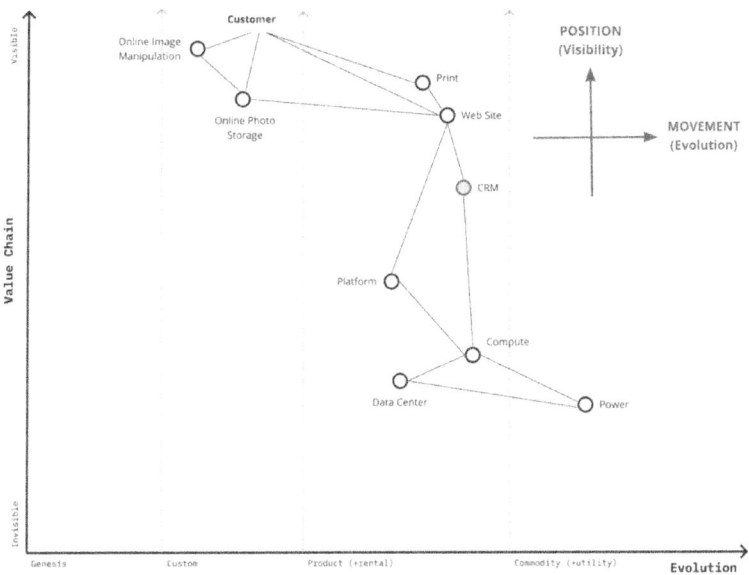

Figure 14 - Sample Wardley Map

43

Now, in the context of a Wardley Map, moving the CRM component significantly changes the landscape. The position shift has real implications due to the map's structured framework.

3 – Communication

One of the immediate benefits of presenting a map is that it invites others to challenge and critique it. For instance, imagine you're operating a tea shop.

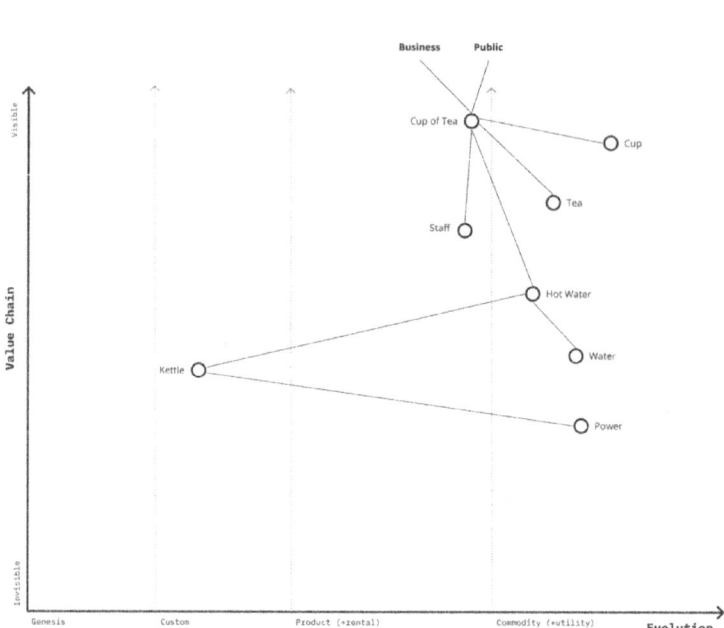

When you present your Tea Shop map to someone, it opens up opportunities for diverse perspectives. For example, in the context of running a tea shop:

- Someone might point out that staffing is a commodity.
- A finance expert could view each node as a stock of capital and each line as a flow of capital, helping to construct a basic profit and loss statement.
- An operations specialist might question the decision to custom-build kettles.
- A marketing professional could emphasize the importance of brand exclusivity.
- Another team member might highlight the significance of ethical trade and fair working conditions.

Each perspective adds depth and dimension to the strategic understanding of the tea shop's operations.

The value of a map lies in its universality. Regardless of the department or team, everyone can use the same map to discuss and understand the shared environment.

4 – Patterns

Simon Wardley identifies several economic patterns, doctrines, and context-specific strategies in his framework. He outlines 30 common economic patterns (climate), 40 patterns of doctrine, and about 100 different forms of context-specific gameplay.

Some prevalent Climatic Patterns include:

- **Competition Drives Evolution**: Everything evolves due to competitive forces.
- **Inertia from Past Success**: Companies like Blockbuster and Kodak didn't fail due to a lack of innovation; their established business models created inertia against change.
- **Efficiency Fuels Innovation**: Industrialization of practices, activities, or technologies paves the way for more advanced systems in the Genesis stage.
- **Creation of New Value Sources**: These higher order systems lead to new business opportunities.

- **Inevitability of Evolution (The Red Queen Effect)**: Evolution in any industry is unavoidable. Understanding the landscape and its dynamics is key to adapting strategy effectively.
- **No Universal Solution Due to Evolution**: Practices suitable for activities at the Genesis stage may not be applicable to those that are commodities or utilities.

Properly mapping your business or product allows identification of components for outsourcing (those on the right), those that can use off-the-shelf solutions (in the middle), and those in the Genesis phase requiring Agile and Lean techniques to minimize uncertainty and risk.

This approach corresponds to one of the doctrine patterns Wardley mentions as 'Use Appropriate Methods.'

5 – Anticipation

Anticipating change is fundamental to formulating an effective strategy. The ability to predict the movements of competitors is a significant advantage, as highlighted in the decalogue's leverage point.

A map reveals various potential areas for strategic action. It falls upon the leadership to choose the right battlefield and allocate the necessary people and resources to succeed in the game (gameplay). This decision-making process is critical to steering the organization towards victory.

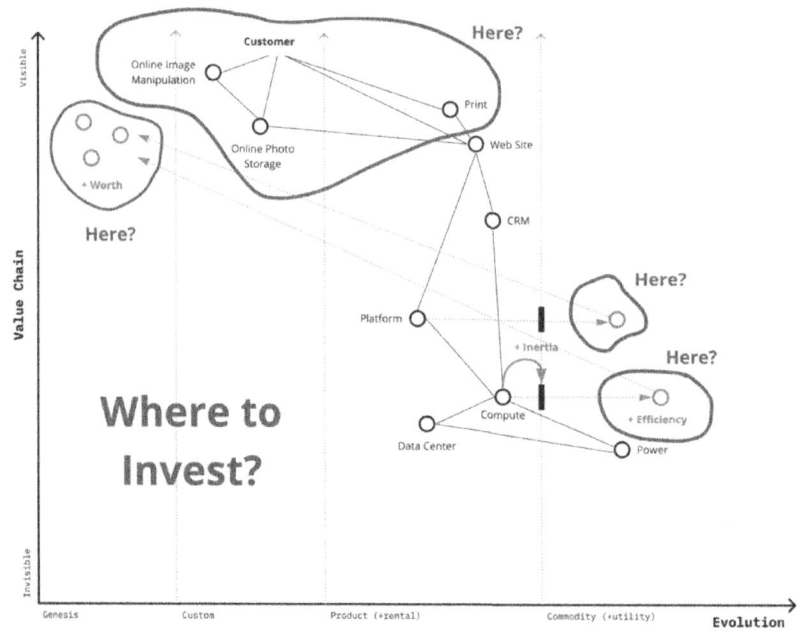

Simon Wardley highlights a common error made by organizations with low situational awareness: they focus on managing process flow rather than managing evolutionary flow. This results in making inefficient practices more efficient, instead of concentrating on necessary evolution.

This error is evident in numerous digitalization efforts, where the digitization of activities and processes is pursued for its own sake, diverting resources from more critical areas.

This ties back to a fundamental premise established at the beginning of the book: operational effectiveness or business agility alone does not constitute strategy. They are aspects of doctrine, and while important, they are not sufficient for leading companies in the 21st century.

Conclusion

The strategic advantage of using Wardley Maps in defining effective OKRs is unmistakable. With these maps, a comprehensive view of the business landscape emerges, allowing for the identification and prioritization of key focus areas. This clarity in visualization helps target the most impactful areas for action, ensuring that OKRs are not only in line with strategic goals but are also sharply focused on driving real progress and innovation.

Wardley Maps act as essential guides through the complexity of the business environment, focusing efforts where they are most needed. Integrating these maps into strategic planning enhances the ability to set OKRs that are ambitious, achievable, and deeply connected to the business's actual context. They provide the necessary clarity to ensure that OKRs result in tangible, forward-moving outcomes for the organization.

In Chapter 19, I delve into the synergistic power of combining the two methodologies. This is illustrated through a comprehensive example that not only demonstrates their practical application but also underscores the nuanced interplay between them. The example is detailed, providing step-by-step insights into how these methods can be seamlessly integrated into your workflow for optimal results.

Chapter 5: Strategy and OKRs

The year was 1890, and there was a party in Pittsburgh.

All the entrepreneurs, innovators, and businessmen of the day were there, including Andrew Carnegie, the founder of U.S. Steel and the richest man in the USA at the time.

At one point during the evening, Carnegie was in a corner smoking a cigar when he was introduced to Frederick Taylor, the man who was becoming famous at the time as an expert in work organization.

"Young man," Carnegie said, eyeing the consultant askance, *"if you can tell me anything about running an organization worth listening to, I'll send you a check for ten thousand dollars."*

Ten thousand dollars was a large amount of money in 1890.

The conversation stopped as people nearby turned to hear what Taylor would say. *"Mr. Carnegie,"* Taylor said, *"I would recommend that you make a list of the ten most important things you can do. And then start by doing the first one."*

And, as the story goes, a week later Taylor received a check for ten thousand dollars.

In "Good Strategy/Bad Strategy"[xi] the tale of Andrew Carnegie's hefty payment for a simple piece of advice initially struck me as absurd. Why would a titan like Carnegie find such value in a mere to-do list? But the story's essence lies not in the list but in the act of its creation. Targets don't propel us forward mechanically; the true worth came from the introspective process Carnegie engaged in. The $10,000 underscored that this was more than a daily checklist; it was a strategic exercise in identifying and tackling core objectives.

How to Select the Right OKRs

Objectives should emerge from a rigorous strategic thinking process, not merely be generated in a brainstorming session.

Crafting a strategy transcends the formulaic approach of articulating vision and mission statements followed by a cascade of strategic objectives and initiatives.

Strategic intent must be precisely defined, leading to the identification of medium-term challenges. Each challenge should be thoroughly diagnosed, addressed with a clear guiding policy, and met with a set of coherent actions. This strategic foundation sets the stage for the effective implementation of OKRs.

Frequent Problems when Defining OKRs

While OKRs may seem straightforward in theory, their practical application often entails nuanced challenges.

The crux of the matter typically lies in selecting OKRs that truly resonate with and propel the strategic objectives of the organization.

Here, we'll delve into three prevalent pitfalls encountered during the implementation phase of OKRs.

1. **Goals are set arbitrarily**, sometimes with no clear relationship to a challenge or the organization's capabilities. This is often the result of a lack of in-depth knowledge of the business, or a lack of understanding of the organization as a system, or both.
2. **Lack of focus on just a few high-leverage goals.** It is a natural tendency to commit the organization to more than it can achieve. The result is often that not much progress is made on any of the goals. This creates stress and discourages people.
3. **Selecting the wrong goals.** Without a consistent system for relating the organization's higher-order goals to operational activities, it's easy to do the "wrong" thing and engage major parts of the organization in underperforming, or even counterproductive activities.

To sidestep these initial challenges, it's essential to distinguish between strategic thinking and strategic planning.

Strategic thinking involves a deep understanding of the competitive environment, the organization's strengths and weaknesses, and long-term creative visioning.

In contrast, strategic planning is about translating this broad perspective into actionable steps, timelines, and measurable objectives. Recognizing this difference is foundational in selecting OKRs that are not only attainable but also align with the company's broader ambitions and capabilities.

Strategic Thinking

Behind every winning strategy there is a deliberate design process and explicit, coherent, and synchronized decisions.

Strategy means making specific decisions to win in the market.

The first step in making the strategy real is to discover the great revelation to gain a sustainable competitive advantage. That is, an intuition on how to win.

A great strategy comes from a combination of wisdom and design. That is why I use design tools such as *Design Thinking* to help my clients design innovative growth strategies that leverage their intelligence and knowledge of the industry.

A good strategy is a coherent action backed by a challenge, an effective mix of thought and action, whose central content is a diagnosis of the situation in question, a guiding policy to face critical difficulties and a set of coherent actions.

Think of the guiding policy as the guardrails on a highway. It steers and limits actions without detailing every step. Unlike goals or visions, good guidelines outline an approach to tackle situations while eliminating numerous potential actions.

Central to strategy is action coordination, offering a fundamental way to gain leverage or advantage. This demands concentrating efforts on a few critical areas. Here, Objectives and Key Results (OKRs) become crucial.

OKRs help maintain focus and alignment across the team. They spring from the guiding policy, helping us craft a clear, targeted roadmap.

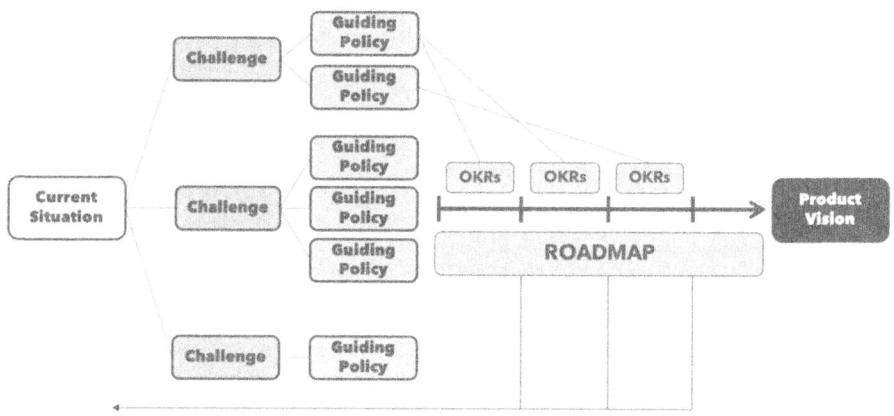

Figure 15 - Strategy framework

The image displays the complete strategic framework. At its core is our product vision, which sets our long-term goal and steers our path forward. Our first step involves understanding the current environment, followed by pinpointing the main challenges that could hinder us from reaching our vision. For each challenge, we establish specific guiding policies.

This crucial stage is where we shift from a broad strategy to tangible Objectives and Key Results.

Next, we lay out a detailed product roadmap. This roadmap outlines each step required to achieve our objectives, ultimately fulfilling our vision.

The Kernel of a Strategy

It's crucial to recognize that OKRs (Objectives and Key Results), or strategic objectives, are not synonymous with strategy. They are a vital element of an effective strategy but only represent one facet of it.

OKRs serve as a tool for strategic deployment, assisting in the planning, execution, and monitoring of your strategy. However, a frequently overlooked yet critical component is strategic design. This involves the process of discerning what matters most and what doesn't, and setting forth the guiding principles needed to achieve your strategic goals.

Strategic design forms the backbone of your strategy, shaping the direction and focus of your OKRs.

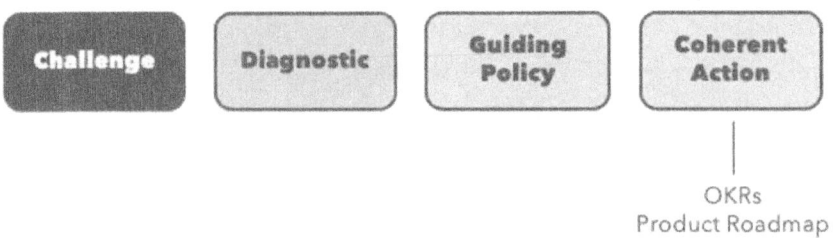

Figure 16 - The Kernel of a Strategy (by Richard P. Rumelt)

Formulating a strategy demands an in-depth analysis encompassing several critical factors. This includes evaluating competitors, understanding market trends, keeping abreast of technological advancements, and considering geopolitical influences.

The primary challenge in this process often revolves around adapting to ongoing changes and competitive dynamics.

There are three vital steps to crafting an effective strategy:

1. **Diagnosis:** This step involves a detailed assessment to pinpoint the exact nature of the challenge at hand.
2. **Guiding Policy Selection:** Based on the diagnosis, this step requires choosing a guiding policy that leverages an advantage or creates one.
3. **Action Plan and Resource Allocation:** The final step involves developing specific action plans and allocating resources efficiently to execute the chosen policy.

Strategy and OKRs: Bridging Thought and Action

Transitioning from strategy to OKRs is about connecting deep thought to actionable steps — from understanding a problem to resolving it.

Thoughtful Consideration

Albert Einstein famously said, *"If I had an hour to solve a problem and my life depended on the solution, I would spend the first 55 minutes thinking about the problem and 5 minutes thinking about the solution."* This highlights the importance of thoughtful analysis in problem-solving.

Role of OKRs

While OKRs are effective for strategic planning and organizational improvement, they are not tools for strategic thinking. They facilitate the activation and execution of a strategy but are not designed for its formulation.

OKRs keep teams aligned and focused, providing measurable, concise, and time-bound objectives.

Gap in Strategic Thinking

The challenge for many companies is not just setting a direction but also engaging in the strategic thinking necessary to design a winning strategy.

The process involves envisioning a future state, contrasting it with the present, and formulating a plan to bridge the gap. However, this approach can fall short without the foundational step of strategic thinking, which should precede the development of any strategic plan.

Executing Strategy in Dynamic Environments

The Industrial Revolution, with Frederick Winslow Taylor's "The Principles of Scientific Management," positioned the machine as the business model. Machines, designed for specific tasks, operate without cognition, fulfilling their creator's intent. Taylorism revolutionized management, enhancing efficiency significantly.

However, Peter Drucker, in "The Practice of Management" (1955), challenged Taylorism, emphasizing that planning and execution are intertwined facets of the same process. The oil crisis of the 1970s further questioned the stability of business environments, highlighting the unpredictability and inadequacy of rigid strategic plans.

Modern strategic thinking acknowledges that businesses require more than just predefined plans. In dynamic environments, strategic execution demands clear direction, alignment, self-organization, and adaptability. It's about setting objectives that foster self-regulation and adjusting swiftly to unforeseen changes, much like military strategies that value a balance of clear goals and responsive tactics.

Execution of Strategy

The execution of strategy is an intricate dance between foresight and adaptability. It involves setting forth a series of planned actions to attain specific outcomes and rigorously following through on these actions. However, when outcomes deviate from expectations, it's essential to recalibrate both goals and strategies.

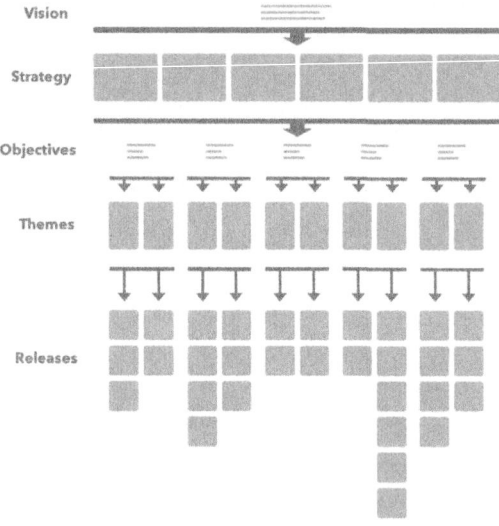

Figure 17 – Decision Levels

In predictable environments, meticulous planning based on information analysis can set a course for success. Objectives are defined, desired outcomes predicted, and structured management ensures alignment with strategic goals.

However, the unpredictable nature of today's business landscape exposes three critical gaps:

- The **Knowledge Gap**: The disparity between our desired information and our actual insights, which hampers perfect planning.
- The **Alignment Gap**: The divergence between intended actions and actual behaviors.

- The **Effects Gap**: The unpredictability of the impact of our actions, which calls for a strategy that is adaptable in the face of unforeseen outcomes.

Addressing these gaps with a rigid mindset—overemphasizing control and detailed directives—often compounds the challenges rather than mitigates them. An adaptive approach is essential, one that evolves with the unfolding reality.

Bridging Strategy and Execution in Uncertain Environments

Connecting strategy with operations amidst uncertainty requires a clear intent, alignment, and autonomy. Stephen Bungay's *"The Art of Action"*[xii] articulates these concepts:

1. **Prioritize What's Critical**: Avoid the trap of overplanning. Understand your priorities and use available knowledge to guide your strategic intent.
2. **Communicate Effectively**: Convey the core of your strategy clearly. Empower others by communicating the 'why' and 'what' and let them navigate the 'how.'
3. **Empower with Autonomy**: Recognize the unpredictability of actions and outcomes. Set broad parameters that encourage adaptability and self-guided decision-making.

While OKRs and roadmaps address alignment and effects gaps, bridging the knowledge gap is key for transitioning from strategy to effective OKRs.

Chapter 6: Common OKRs Pitfalls

The journey towards mastering Objectives and Key Results is often a challenging one, filled with common missteps that can derail the process.

This chapter delves into these pitfalls and offers practical solutions, with an emphasis on understanding, communication, and leadership. My goal is to transform your OKRs approach into a dynamic and effective tool for achieving strategic success.

1. Clarifying the Concept: Beyond a To-Do List

The true value of OKRs is often misunderstood, leading to their reduction to mere to-do lists. This common misinterpretation significantly undermines their strategic potential.

The main problem arises when OKRs are treated just as task lists, resulting in a surface-level application that misses their true strategic value.

To counter this, it's crucial to cultivate a deeper understanding of OKRs across the team. This involves training initiatives and a shift in the leadership approach, aiming to foster a culture that deeply appreciates the strategic significance of OKRs. Most importantly, coaching teams and stakeholders to transition from a focus on measuring mere outputs to measuring meaningful outcomes is key.

OKRs should represent the critical objectives the business needs to achieve in a specific timeframe, rather than just a checklist of tasks for teams.

2. Realistic Goal Setting: The Art of Balance

Setting goals is an art that hinges on finding the right balance between ambition and realism. This balance, while often challenging to achieve, is essential for the success of any strategic plan.

A common pitfall in this process is the tendency to set goals that are either overly ambitious or simply unattainable. Such goals, far from motivating teams, can lead to demotivation and even burnout.

The solution lies in establishing goals that are sufficiently challenging—those that stretch the team's capabilities and inspire them to reach new heights, yet are still within the realm of achievability.

This approach ensures teams are pushed to their limits in a constructive way, without causing undue stress or exhaustion.

To gauge whether your OKRs have hit this sweet spot, consider the validation questions detailed in chapter 14. These questions serve as a helpful guide to assess the practicality and ambition of your OKRs, ensuring they are neither too lofty nor too limited.

3. Alignment and Communication: The Cornerstones of Success

Ensuring effective communication and alignment of Objectives and Key Results with the company's strategy is crucial. Without this alignment and clear communication, OKRs risk becoming disjointed, diminishing their intended impact.

A major pitfall in this process is poor alignment and communication, which can lead to confusion and efforts being misdirected. The solution lies in making sure everyone in the organization not only understands but also aligns their OKRs with the company's broader goals. Achieving this requires clear, consistent communication, helping each team member to grasp their role within the larger organizational context.

It's important to remember that alignment happens on two levels: vertical and horizontal. Vertical alignment involves aligning your goals with those of the higher organizational levels, ensuring consistency with the company's overarching objectives. Horizontal alignment, on the other hand, focuses on synchronizing goals across different teams, fostering collaboration and coherence. The upcoming sections of the book delve deeply into these aspects, providing a comprehensive guide to effective OKR alignment.

4. Focus on What Matters: Quality Over Quantity

Embracing the principle of 'less is more' is pivotal. There's often a temptation to try and address every possible area with an OKR, but this approach can lead to scattered focus and ultimately, diminished effectiveness.

A significant pitfall in this process is the creation of too many OKRs. When there are too many goals to pursue, it can dilute the overall focus and weaken the impact of each individual objective.

The solution to this challenge is to prioritize and limit the number of OKRs to only the most critical ones. By doing so, it ensures that the focus remains sharp, and efforts are concentrated on achieving these key objectives. This streamlined approach not only enhances clarity but also boosts the potential for impactful results.

To delve deeper into this challenge and explore comprehensive strategies for addressing the issue of having too many OKRs, Chapter 16 is dedicated entirely to this topic. It provides detailed strategies and insights for resolving this common pitfall, ensuring that your OKRs remain focused and effective.

5. Consistent Tracking and Review: The Pulse of Progress

A common mistake is treating OKRs as static, unchangeable goals. In reality, OKRs are dynamic tools that require ongoing attention, monitoring, and updating to be truly effective.

One major pitfall is the neglect of regular tracking and review of OKRs. This oversight can lead to OKRs becoming outdated or misaligned with the evolving needs and goals of the organization.

The solution to this challenge lies in establishing a system for regular reviews and adjustments of OKRs. By adopting this dynamic approach, OKRs can be kept in sync with changing organizational objectives, ensuring their relevance and effectiveness.

The last chapter of this book is devoted exclusively to addressing this issue. It offers detailed guidance on how to maintain the dynamism of OKRs, ensuring they continue to serve as effective tools for organizational success.

6. Leadership Commitment: Leading by Example

The successful implementation of OKRs is deeply influenced by the role of leadership. The commitment and example set by leaders are fundamental, essentially setting the tone for the entire organization's approach to OKRs.

A critical pitfall in this context is the absence of full commitment and involvement from leadership. When leaders are not wholly engaged in the OKR process, it can lead to a lackluster implementation throughout the organization.

The solution to this challenge is straightforward yet vital: leaders must not only be actively involved but also fully committed to the OKR framework. They should serve as role models, demonstrating the significance and execution of OKRs through their actions.

Given the importance of leadership in the OKR process, Section 2 of this book is entirely dedicated to 'OKRs for Managers.' This section emphasizes how leaders can effectively champion OKRs, ensuring their successful adoption and implementation across the organization.

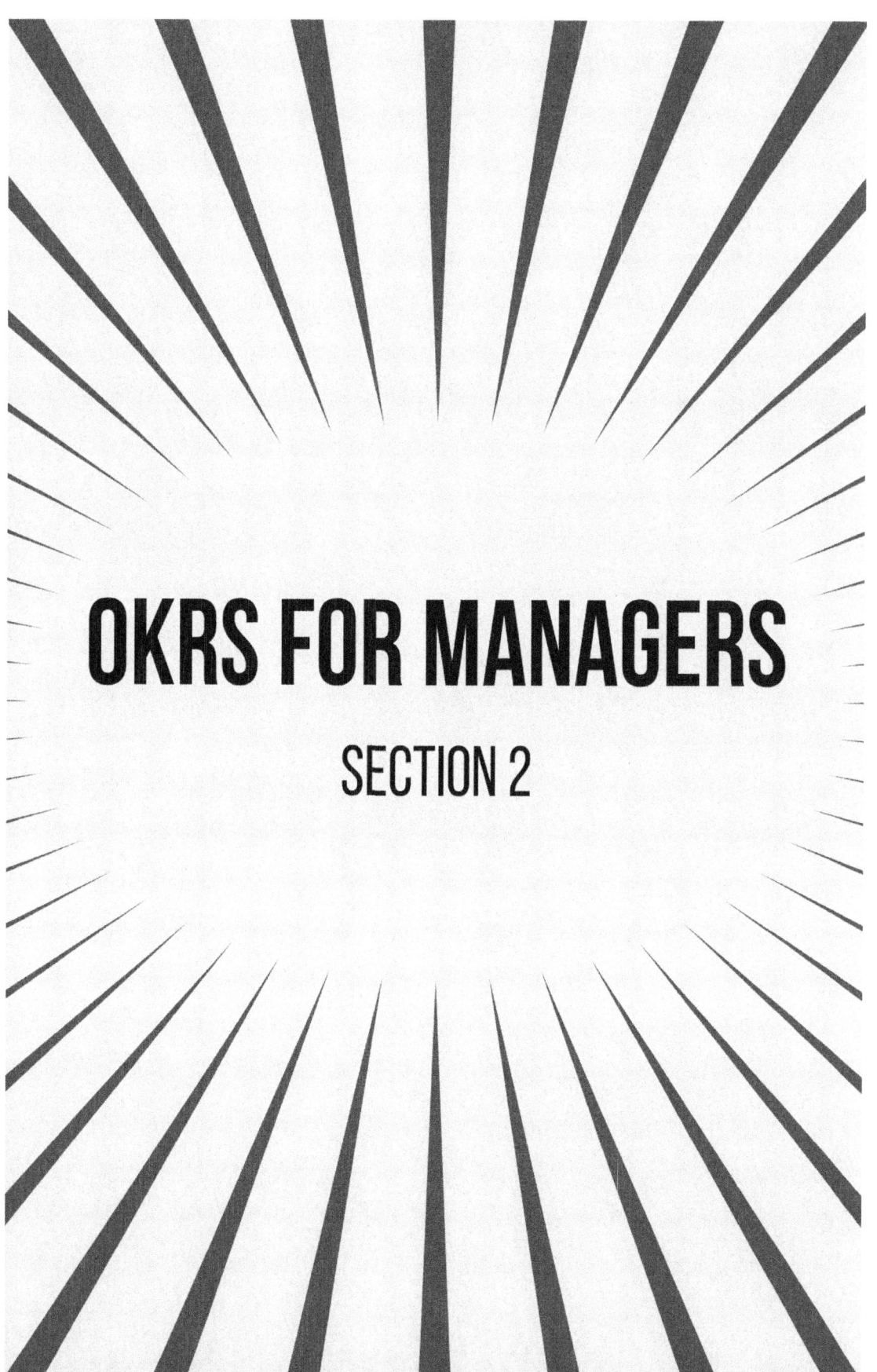

OKRS FOR MANAGERS
SECTION 2

Chapter 7: A Plan is not a Strategy

A successful business strategy is about making clear, actionable choices that enable you to excel in a chosen market segment. It's about being adaptable, continually refining your approach, and accepting the inherent uncertainty in strategic decision-making. Often, what passes for strategic planning in business is merely a list of activities. True strategy, however, is about aligning these activities towards a collective goal, ensuring internal coherence and a focused path to victory.

While companies have control over their costs, the ultimate success of a strategy hinges on customer decisions – a factor beyond direct control. This underlines the importance of not just planning, such as infrastructure expansion or staff increases, but strategizing for competitive outcomes. For instance, Southwest Airlines' strategy to become a convenient and affordable alternative to Greyhound buses involved targeted operational choices: using only 737s, omitting meals on short flights, bypassing travel agents, and adopting a point-to-point model, all aimed at enhancing efficiency and profitability.[13]

This approach contrasts starkly with companies that concentrate on operational aspects without a clear competitive angle. A compelling strategy offers unique value to a specific segment. Consider a company that outperformed major carriers by cutting costs and boosting convenience through online booking. This move wasn't just about reducing expenditures; it was a strategic decision to provide a distinct value proposition.

In conclusion, strategy is a dynamic, evolving journey. It should be straightforward, focused on areas and methods to win, and continuously adjusted based on real-world feedback. Planning, while necessary, often lacks this flexibility and is less likely to yield significant success. As a leader, embracing strategic uncertainty and clearly articulating your strategy's logic are crucial steps to move beyond mere planning and achieve greatness.

Navigating Change: Strategic Agility for Today's Market

In the fast-paced, tech-driven modern business landscape, where markets evolve swiftly, traditional strategies for planning often fall short. This dynamic environment demands more agile, responsive approaches to strategy. These conventional approaches, often rigid and linear, struggle to keep pace with the ever-evolving business landscape. Companies find themselves trapped in outdated strategies, unable to adapt quickly to unforeseen challenges and opportunities. This is where the concept of agility in strategic planning becomes crucial.

Agility in this context refers to the ability of an organization to swiftly adapt to changes in its external environment. It's about being flexible, responsive, and resilient - being able to pivot strategies when new information comes to light or when unexpected events occur. The agile approach contrasts sharply with traditional methods, where strategies are often set in stone, formulated through lengthy and inflexible planning cycles that leave little room for adaptation.

The need for agility is underscored by the reality of today's business environment. Markets are more volatile than ever; customer preferences change at an unprecedented pace, and technological disruptions can render established business models obsolete overnight. In such a scenario, clinging to a static strategic plan can be more of a liability than an asset. Agility allows organizations to embrace uncertainty as an integral part of their strategic process, turning potential threats into opportunities for growth and innovation.

Strategy isn't encapsulated in a lengthy, static document predicting a company's next five years of actions. Rather, it's a fluid interplay of various tools operating at different organizational layers, empowering individuals to make autonomous decisions and adapt flexibly.

Strategic Decision Levels

To facilitate this agile strategic approach, several tools and methodologies have emerged. Among the most effective are Objectives and Key Results (OKRs), strategic roadmaps, and product discovery.

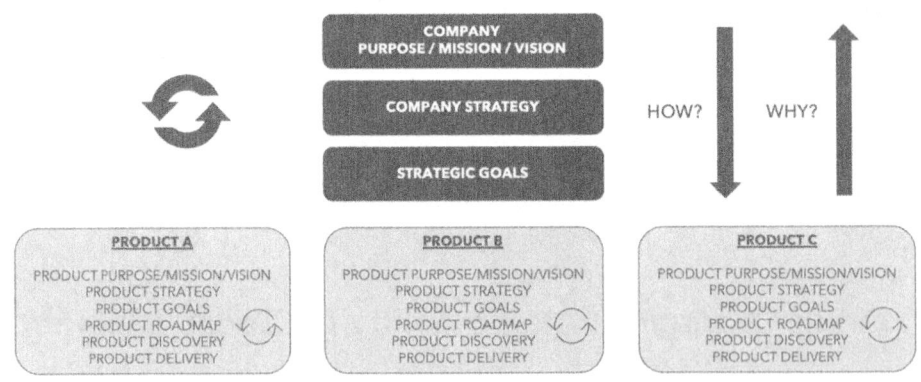

Figure 18 - Strategic Decision Levels

OKRs (Objectives and Key Results) are a goal-setting framework that helps organizations define clear, measurable objectives aligned with their overall strategy. OKRs are designed to be flexible, allowing for quick adjustments in response to change. They focus on outcomes rather than activities, driving teams to prioritize work that has the most significant strategic impact.

Product Roadmaps offer a visual representation of the path towards long-term objectives, balancing this vision with the flexibility to adapt short-term actions. They provide a broader perspective of the strategic journey, highlighting key milestones and potential pivot points, ensuring that all parts of the organization move cohesively towards common goals.

Product Discovery is a process that focuses on understanding customer needs and market conditions. It involves continuous experimentation and learning, helping organizations refine their product offerings and strategic decisions based on real-world feedback and evolving trends.

When organizations weave these tools into the fabric of their strategy-making, they can shift from a static, blueprint-focused mindset to a flexible and proactive stance, ready for today's fast-paced business climate.

This framework helps organizations cut through unpredictability and excel amidst competition.

The Role of OKRs in Strategy Execution

The introduction of Objectives and Key Results (OKRs) into the strategic planning process has revolutionized the way organizations set and pursue their goals. This framework, rooted in clarity, agility, and ambition, plays a pivotal role in translating high-level strategies into actionable, measurable outcomes.

OKRs are not just about setting goals; they are about aligning these goals with the organization's broader vision and strategic direction, ensuring that every effort contributes meaningfully to the overarching objectives.

The role of OKRs in strategy execution is multifaceted. They provide a clear, measurable path towards strategic goals, offer the flexibility needed to navigate a dynamic business landscape, and cultivate a culture where innovation and boldness are the norms.

Defining Clear Objectives

At the heart of the OKR framework is the establishment of clear and measurable objectives. These objectives are designed to be concise, understandable, and directly aligned with the company's strategic intent. Unlike traditional goal-setting methods that might focus on vague or indirect targets, OKRs demand specificity. This clarity ensures that everyone in the organization understands what needs to be achieved and why it matters.

Key Results breathe life into objectives by defining precise metrics for achievement. They go beyond simple tasks, providing quantifiable outcomes that signal the realization of the objective. OKRs thus lay out a lucid path for teams and individuals, channeling their energy towards activities that genuinely propel strategic progress.

Enhancing Agility and Adaptability

In an environment where market conditions can change rapidly, the agility afforded by OKRs is invaluable. This flexibility is embedded in the OKR cycle, typically quarterly, which allows organizations to review and adjust their objectives and key results regularly. This iterative process means that strategies are not set in stone but are living entities, evolving in response to new insights, market shifts, or internal developments.

The dynamic nature of OKRs is pivotal in diminishing strategic uncertainty. They afford organizations the flexibility to periodically re-evaluate and recalibrate their ambitions, enabling swift adaptation to shifts in the market. This level of agility is essential for maintaining relevance and competitiveness in an ever-changing business environment.

Encouraging Innovation and Risk-Taking

Perhaps one of the most transformative aspects of OKRs is their ability to foster a culture of innovation and risk-taking. OKRs encourage organizations to set ambitious, even stretch goals, pushing them to explore beyond the comfort zones of predictable outcomes. This approach breeds a mindset where innovation is not just welcomed but is actively pursued.

OKRs encourage teams to aim high, sparking creativity and opening the door to new opportunities. They infuse a collective mission and ambition, propelling teams to innovate and embrace risk thoughtfully. This ethos of aspiration and ingenuity is vital for organizations that aspire to not only adapt to market shifts but to be the vanguards, reshaping their sectors.

As we delve further into the specifics of strategic roadmaps and product discovery, the synergy between these tools and OKRs in driving strategic agility becomes increasingly evident.

Product Roadmaps as a Guide

Product roadmaps[14] serve as a critical tool in the arsenal of agile strategic planning. They are not just planning documents but dynamic guides that align long-term visions with the immediate actions required to realize them. In this section, we explore how strategic roadmaps offer a balance between long-term aspirations and short-term operational steps, and how they foster alignment across an entire organization.

Balancing Long-term Vision and Short-term Actions

Product roadmaps provide a visual representation of an organization's journey towards its long-term objectives. They lay out the major milestones and the planned path to achieve them, thereby translating strategic themes and OKRs into tangible steps. However, unlike traditional long-term plans, these roadmaps are designed with inherent flexibility. This adaptability is crucial for two reasons.

First, it allows organizations to respond swiftly to changes in the external environment without losing sight of their long-term goals. Second, it accommodates short-term operational needs that may arise unexpectedly. This dual focus ensures that while the organization is steadfast in pursuing its long-term vision, it remains nimble enough to tackle immediate challenges or capitalize on unforeseen opportunities.

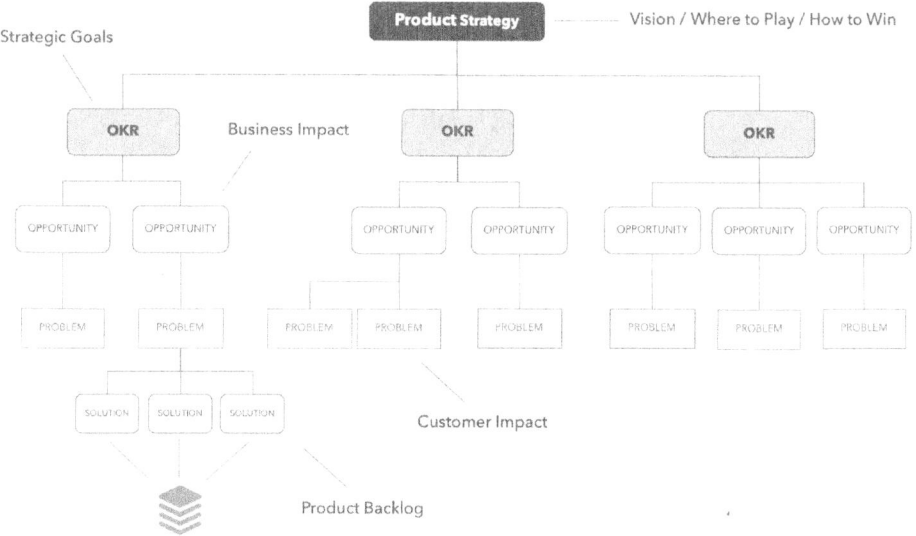

Figure 19 - Layered Approach

This balancing act is achieved through a layered approach to roadmap development. The product roadmap serves as a bridge, linking OKRs with potential opportunities, customer outcomes, and practical solutions. Regular reviews and updates to the roadmap ensure that it remains relevant and aligned with both the current market conditions and the overarching strategic goals.

Alignment Across the Organization

One of the biggest challenges in strategy execution is ensuring that different departments and teams are not just aware of the overall strategy but are actively working towards it in a cohesive manner. Here product roadmaps play a pivotal role.

Roadmaps illuminate the product's trajectory with a vision that resonates throughout the organization, ensuring every segment is in sync. They render the strategy palpable and pertinent to each team, illustrating how everyday tasks feed into wider goals. Such coherence is essential to foster collaborative synergy and prevent disjointed efforts that might weaken the strategic thrust.

Furthermore, roadmaps facilitate cross-functional collaboration. They highlight interdependencies between different teams and departments, encouraging them to coordinate their efforts and work together towards common milestones. This collaborative environment not only accelerates progress towards strategic goals but also fosters a more integrated and cohesive organizational culture.

In sum, product roadmaps transcend the role of a mere planning instrument; they provide a strategic scaffolding that imparts clarity and coherence, steering the strategic voyage. They harmonize the overarching vision with immediate flexibility and foster alignment across the company, transforming strategic goals into tangible actions.

As we move forward to discuss product discovery, we will see how these roadmaps are complemented by a deep understanding of market needs and customer behaviors, further strengthening the agile strategic framework.

Product Discovery in Reducing Strategic Uncertainty

In the realm of agile strategic planning, product discovery stands out as a critical process, particularly in its ability to minimize strategic uncertainty. This section delves into how product discovery, with its customer-centric approach and iterative learning model, plays a pivotal role in shaping and refining business strategies.

Customer-Centric Approach

At the core of product discovery is the focus on deeply understanding customer needs and behaviors. This approach marks a shift from an inward-looking, assumption-based strategy to an outward-looking, evidence-driven one. By placing customers at the center of strategic planning, businesses ensure that their decisions are not based on mere speculation but on real insights about what customers truly value.

This customer-centricity involves engaging with customers through various methods like interviews, surveys, user testing, and market research. The objective is to uncover not just the obvious needs but also the latent ones that customers themselves might not be fully aware of. This deep dive into customer psyche and behavior provides invaluable inputs for strategic decision-making.

The insights gained from product discovery help in identifying new market opportunities, refining product offerings, and even sometimes pivoting to entirely new directions. This alignment with customer needs ensures that the strategy is grounded in market reality, significantly reducing the risk of misalignment between what the company offers and what the market demands.

Iterative Learning and Adaptation

Product discovery is inherently iterative. It is not a one-time exercise but a continuous process of learning, experimenting, and adapting. This iterative nature is what makes it particularly effective in reducing strategic uncertainty.

Through ongoing cycles of hypothesis, experimentation, feedback, and learning, businesses can continuously refine their strategies. This process allows teams to test their assumptions quickly, learn from both successes and failures, and adapt their approach accordingly. It embraces the principle that not all strategies will work as planned and that failure is an integral part of the learning process.

This approach enables businesses to be agile in their strategic planning. They can pivot their strategies based on real-world feedback and emerging data trends. It allows them to evolve their products and services constantly to meet the changing needs of their customers and to respond to new market dynamics swiftly.

In conclusion, product discovery is an essential element in reducing strategic uncertainty. Its customer-centric approach ensures that strategies are aligned with actual market needs, while its iterative learning and adaptation model fosters an agile and responsive strategic planning process. As organizations navigate the complexities of the modern business environment, integrating product discovery into their strategic framework becomes not just beneficial but imperative for sustained success and growth.

Integrating OKRs, Roadmaps, and Product Discovery

The integration of Objectives and Key Results, product roadmaps, and product discovery creates a powerful, cohesive framework for agile strategic planning. This synergy amplifies the strengths of each approach, paving the way for a dynamic and responsive strategy execution. This section explores how these tools can be effectively integrated and provides practical steps for their implementation across different organizational contexts.

Creating a Cohesive Strategic Framework

Integrating OKRs, roadmaps, and product discovery begins with understanding how each component complements the others:

1. **OKRs as the Driving Force**: OKRs set the direction and priorities for the organization, defining clear, measurable goals aligned with the overall strategy.

They create a focus on outcomes rather than just activities, ensuring that efforts are strategically aligned and results-oriented.

2. **Strategic Roadmaps as the Pathway**: Roadmaps translate OKRs into a visual journey, outlining the steps required to achieve these objectives. They provide a longer-term perspective, showing how short-term actions contribute to the realization of long-term goals, and they allow for agility in adapting to changes and new insights.

3. **Product Discovery as the Feedback Loop**: Integrating product discovery ensures that both OKRs and roadmaps are grounded in real-world customer needs and market dynamics. It provides continuous feedback, enabling businesses to refine their strategies based on actual customer behaviors and emerging trends.

The integration of these tools creates a strategic framework that is both forward-looking and adaptable. It ensures that the organization remains focused on its strategic objectives while being flexible enough to adjust to new information and market shifts.

Practical Steps for Implementation

Implementing this integrated approach requires careful planning and execution. Here are practical steps to guide organizations in different contexts:

1. **Aligning OKRs with Strategic Intent**: Start by ensuring that the OKRs are in alignment with the organization's vision and long-term strategy. This alignment should be evident at all levels, from company-wide OKRs to teams'.

2. **Developing a Roadmap**: Create a product roadmap that outlines how your product plans to achieve its OKRs. This roadmap should include key milestones, timelines, and dependencies. It should be flexible enough to accommodate changes and updates as new information becomes available.

3. **Incorporating Product Discovery**: Embed product discovery processes into the strategic planning cycle. Regularly gather and analyze customer feedback and market data to inform and adjust the OKRs and the strategic roadmap.

4. **Cross-functional Collaboration**: Foster collaboration across different teams. Ensure that everyone understands how their work contributes to the strategic objectives and how it aligns with the product roadmap.

5. **Regular Reviews and Adjustments**: Implement a regular review process for OKRs, the roadmap, and product discovery insights. Use these reviews to assess progress, learn from successes and failures, and make necessary adjustments.

6. **Communication and Transparency**: Maintain open communication channels throughout the organization. Regularly share updates on progress, changes in

strategy, and insights from product discovery to ensure everyone is aligned and informed.

7. **Training and Support**: Provide training and resources to help teams understand and effectively use OKRs, roadmaps, and product discovery. Consider bringing in external expertise or assigning internal champions to guide and support the implementation process.

Adopting these measures, organizations can develop a strategic framework that resonates with their core vision while staying agile in a fluctuating business landscape. This holistic methodology guarantees that strategic planning is an evolving, continuous journey, always centered on delivering customer value and securing enduring success.

Integrating Product Roadmaps and Product Discovery

To successfully implement Product Discovery in an organization, it's essential to seamlessly incorporate it into the value chain. Product Discovery shouldn't be viewed as an occasional or extra activity, but as a standard part of how modern product teams operate. This means making sure it's visible and well-integrated with the primary strategic tool of product management: the product roadmap.

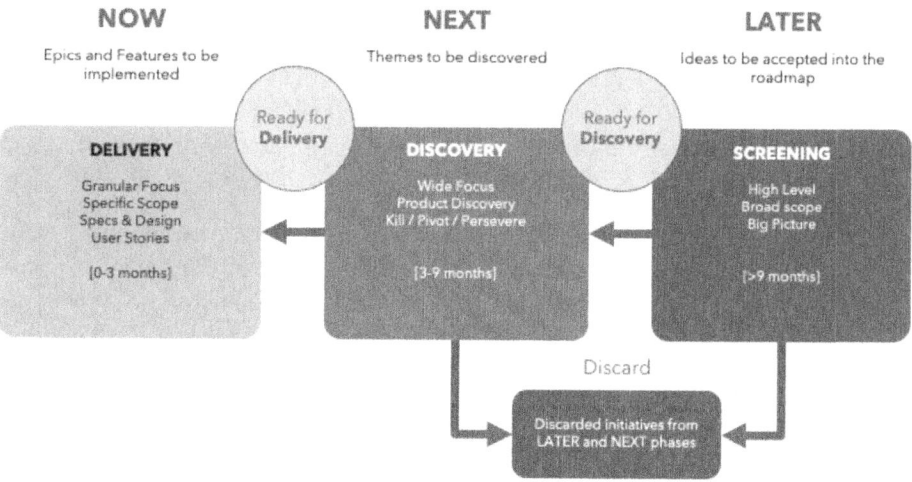

Figure 20 - Integration with Product Discovery

The figure above shows how I helped a client integrate the Product Discovery process with their product roadmap. In this approach, new initiatives first go through a screening process. This step helps decide whether to include them in the roadmap or set them aside. To make it onto the roadmap, each initiative must meet specific criteria to enter the 'Ready for Discovery' buffer. This ensures that only well-considered initiatives move forward in the process.

For this case, the 'Ready for Discovery' checklist included:

1. Opportunity Canvas
2. Mapping of Assumptions
3. Briefing on Strategy
4. Roadmap Submission Form
5. A lightweight Product Discovery Plan
6. Agreement with stakeholders

The discovery process begins with a kickoff meeting to align the product team. The outcome of this process is either to remove the roadmap theme or move it to the 'Ready for Delivery' buffer, depending on the findings.

Real-world Stories of Strategic Adaptability

Welcome to a section where the crisp lines of strategic theory blur into the vivid colors of real-world experiences. As managers and strategists, we often find ourselves at a crossroads where the best-laid plans meet the unpredictable dynamics of the market. This section is dedicated to sharing two personal stories from my career, each rich with insights and practical lessons in strategic planning and adaptability.

The first story unfolds in the high-tech automotive market of Germany, a sector renowned for its precision engineering and rapid technological advancements. Here, I navigated the challenges of a rigid strategy in an incredibly dynamic environment, learning valuable lessons about the necessity of adaptability and the risks of inflexible planning.

The second story takes us to the competitive world of e-commerce, where I played a transformative role as a product coach. This journey highlights the power of an agile, customer-focused approach in a market characterized by fierce competition and rapidly changing consumer trends. It's a testament to how strategic agility, coupled with a deep understanding of customer needs, can lead to remarkable business success.

Story 1: A Rigid Course in a Rapid Race

In Germany, known for its pioneering automotive industry, I found myself in the role of a product manager at a leading tech company specializing in automotive software solutions. Our product, a cutting-edge vehicle telematics system, was designed to revolutionize the way drivers interacted with their vehicles and the road.

The automotive sector, especially in Germany, is characterized by its rigorous engineering and precision. However, it is also a sector undergoing rapid transformation, driven by evolving technology and consumer expectations. When I took on this project, the market was buzzing with advancements in connected car technology and autonomous driving features.

Despite understanding the market's dynamic nature, our company's strategy was surprisingly rigid. I had hoped for a more adaptable approach, given the rapid technological advancements and shifting consumer preferences in the automotive tech space. We spent months perfecting our telematics system, but by the time we launched, our competitors, who had been more responsive to the market's pulse, had already introduced more advanced and user-friendly features.

This experience in the high-tech automotive market was a profound lesson for me. It highlighted the critical need for flexibility in strategy, especially in industries where technological advancements and customer preferences evolve at breakneck speed.

Story 2: Agility Wins in the E-commerce Arena

As a product coach, I embarked on a journey with a mid-sized European company entrenched in the highly competitive e-commerce sector. Their product was an innovative online retail platform that aimed to offer a unique shopping experience but was struggling to gain traction.

The e-commerce industry is known for its fierce competition and rapidly changing consumer trends. Success in this space requires not just understanding customer needs but anticipating and responding to them swiftly. When I stepped in, the company was burdened with a strategy that was outdated and misaligned with the industry's fast-paced nature.

I introduced a new approach centered around agility and customer-centricity. We discarded the old plan and adopted a strategy that prioritized understanding emerging shopping trends and customer behaviors. Through continuous product discovery and a flexible roadmap, we were able to iteratively develop features that resonated with our target audience.

The transformation was dramatic. Within months, the platform saw significant growth in user engagement and market share. This success in the e-commerce domain reinforced my belief in the power of an agile, customer-focused strategy, proving its efficacy in navigating the complexities of today's digital marketplaces.

Conclusion

In this chapter, we have journeyed through the dynamic landscape of strategic planning, underscored by the integration of Objectives and Key Results (OKRs), product roadmaps, and product discovery. These elements, when harmoniously combined, create a robust framework for agile and effective strategic execution.

The key takeaway is that true strategic mastery transcends mere planning; it involves a deep comprehension of market dynamics, an acute awareness of customer needs, and, most critically, the agility to adapt strategies in response to these evolving factors.

This integrated approach ensures that businesses are not just planning for the future but are actively shaping it, ready to adapt and thrive in the ever-evolving landscape of market challenges and opportunities.

The path to strategic mastery is, therefore, one of constant learning, adaptation, and alignment with both internal goals and external realities.

Chapter 8: Bridging the Gap

This chapter explores how Objectives and Key Results effectively bridge the gap between high-level strategy and ground-level execution, transforming lofty plans into achievable goals, thereby closing the gap between planning and doing.

Product Strategy

As previously discussed, a common obstacle in defining effective OKRs is the absence or ambiguity of a well-articulated strategy.

For managers looking to implement OKRs successfully, the starting point must be the development of a clear and comprehensive product strategy.

This chapter outlines a systematic approach for managers to craft a product strategy that provides clear guidance and measurable objectives.

Defining Core Components of Product Strategy

A robust product strategy is built upon clearly defined elements:

- **Precise identification of users and customers:** Understand who your product is for.

- **Clear value proposition and business model:** Articulate the unique value your product offers. This should address why customers should choose your product over competitors and how the product will be monetized and contribute to business goals.

- **Business benefits:** Define the tangible benefits your product delivers to the business, such as revenue growth, market share expansion, or cost reduction.

- **Distinctive factors:** Identify the key factors that set your product apart in the marketplace.

The Core of Strategy

The following checklist serves as a comprehensive guide, helping product leaders and teams to thoroughly prepare for this critical phase. It encompasses key areas such as defining your overarching goals, understanding your current market position, identifying, and overcoming potential challenges, and ensuring stakeholder alignment.

This approach is designed to provide a clear, strategic direction, enabling product teams to make informed decisions, utilize resources effectively, and ultimately, drive their products towards success in a competitive landscape.

Following this checklist ensures that your product strategy is robust, realistic, and aligned with both market needs and organizational objectives.

1 - Winning Aspiration: Defining the Overarching Goal

Determine the primary, overarching goal of your product unit. What is the single most critical achievement your product must attain?

Align this goal with market trends, customer needs, and your organization's vision.

Ensure that your product's winning aspiration resonates with your team and stakeholders.

2 - Current Situation Analysis: Assessing the Product's State

Conduct a comprehensive analysis of your product's current state in the context of the competitive landscape, technological advancements, market trends, geopolitical factors, overall business performance, and regulatory environment.

Evaluate how your internal capabilities and resources match up against these external factors.

Understand your product's position in the market and how it differentiates from competitors.

3 - Identifying Challenges: Recognizing Potential Obstacles

Identify the primary challenges that may hinder you from reaching your overarching goal, considering both internal and external factors.

Understand the nature and implications of these challenges in detail.

Analyze how these challenges could impact your product roadmap and strategic objectives.

4 - Guidelines for Overcoming Challenges: Strategy Development

Develop specific strategies or guidelines to navigate and overcome the identified challenges effectively.

These strategies should include risk mitigation plans, leveraging organizational strengths, and addressing any gaps in resources or capabilities.

Ensure that these guidelines are adaptable, measurable, and aligned with your key metrics and success indicators.

5 - Engaging Stakeholders and Ensuring Buy-in

Communicate your product vision, roadmap, and strategies for overcoming challenges to key stakeholders.

Establish mechanisms for ongoing feedback and engagement to ensure alignment and buy-in.

Regularly review and adjust your approach based on stakeholder feedback and changing market conditions.

Consolidating Findings into a Strategy Briefing Document

Once you have clarity on these strategic components, consolidate your findings and decisions into a Strategy Briefing document.

This document should clearly articulate the strategic direction and objectives to your team and stakeholders, serve as a reference point for aligning team efforts, especially when working on OKRs and developing the product roadmap, and ensure everyone understands and works cohesively towards the shared goals outlined in your product strategy.

Sharing the Strategic Plan

Effective communication is key to the success of any strategic plan. That's why I use the "Strategy Briefing" approach, which was developed by Stephen Bungay in his book "The Art of Action".

This approach involves clearly and concisely communicating the strategic plan to all members of the organization and empowering them to take ownership of their roles in executing the plan. By using the *Strategy Briefing* approach, we are able to ensure that everyone in the organization is aligned and working towards the same goals and objectives.

Strategy Briefing is a way of structuring thought to focus the mind on what matters now and leave out what does not matter. It seems deceptively simple. Briefing is difficult to do well and has a huge impact, as it essentially determines how people are going to spend their time and what results they are going to try to achieve. Few things could be more important to any business.

A strategy briefing is different from a project plan. It's important to understand that a project plan is more detailed and is created later in the process. Before the briefing, some strategic planning should already be in place, ideally including a statement of strategic intent. The main goal of a strategy briefing is to empower people to work independently towards a common objective.

The briefing aligns everyone's efforts. It focuses on achieving a specific result: each person aims for a clear end goal, which is about creating a specific change or outcome in the real world. This effort is shown through actions or tasks that each person undertakes, contributing to making a meaningful difference.

Strategy Briefing Template

The template I offer to assist clients in focusing their strategy is straightforward yet effective. It guides you through identifying key elements of your strategy in a clear and concise manner.

This template ensures that you don't get lost in details and stay focused on what's truly important. It's designed to help you zero in on the core aspects of your strategy, making it easier for you to develop a focused and impactful plan.

Strategy Briefing Template

1 – CONTEXT – What does current situation look like?

Here the keys to the internal and external situation are detailed, and what are the problems or opportunities with this situation.

2 – HIGHER INTENT - Strategic fit

We must be able to explain how our strategy fits with the strategic intent of the organization and the product.

We should reference higher order OKRs here.

3 – OUR INTENT - What do we want to achieve and why?

What do we want to achieve?

- What?
- Why?

- How will we measure it?

4 – IMPLIED TASKS

It isn't about listing every single task. Instead, it's about pinpointing the most critical elements and identifying the gaps.

- What are the biggest uncertainties?
- What capabilities and resources do we need?
- What skills do we need?
- What are the main action lines?
- What positions of strategic power do we want to conquer?

5 – BOUNDARIES - Freedoms and constraints

Providing autonomy and control effectively involves establishing clear boundaries and limitations. This balance ensures that while individuals have the freedom to make decisions and take action, they do so within a well-defined framework that aligns with the overall goals and strategies of the organization. Setting these parameters helps maintain focus and direction, while still allowing for creativity and independent problem-solving.

- What are we not allowed to do?
- What KPIS can go south as a side effect of this initiative?
- What parts of the brand or company can't we touch?
- What decisions can the team make?
- What if one of our actions could have a negative impact on another part of the business?

Condensing a comprehensive strategy into a Strategy Briefing document offers essential clarity and direction. This allows managers to effectively share their vision and lead their teams in creating OKRs and roadmaps that align with the organization's strategic objectives. This process ensures that everyone is working towards common goals, with a clear understanding of their roles and how their efforts contribute to the broader strategy.

Strategy Briefing Example

Here's a strategy outline for a video streaming company. It focuses on increasing their subscriptions by exploring a new, potentially profitable market.

STRATEGY BRIEFING - Video Streaming Company

1 – Context

Year-over-Year (YoY) revenue growth has decelerated to 20% (previously 55% in 2012, 50% in 2014, and 35% in 2016).

Analysis shows that households with an annual net income > $120K are 4x more likely to subscribe to streaming services. This indicates a significant growth opportunity in targeting the 'Golden Generation' (60+ year old viewers).

Current content and user experience may not fully appeal to the Golden Generation. This demographic is a substantial segment in traditional TV viewership, yet their presence in streaming platforms is minimal.

2 – Higher Intent

Our goal is to expand our streaming subscription business both domestically and internationally by enhancing the customer experience. This includes diversifying our content library and optimizing our user interface, with a special focus on the Golden Generation.

3 – Our Intent

Achieve a market penetration of 25% among the 60+ age group within 18 months of launching tailored initiatives. This should include customizing content and user experience to meet the specific needs of the Golden Generation, thereby increasing retention and satisfaction.

4 – Key Implied Tasks

OVERALL EXPERIENCE

- Conduct interviews with 60+ customers who have left the service vs those who remain.
- Analyze usage patterns of other streaming platforms, particularly in the 60+ demographic.

CONTENT

- Identify the most appealing content categories for the 60+ age group from our current catalogue.
- Research popular content categories from traditional TV for the 60+ demographic.
- Evaluate the integration of additional relevant content for this age group.

USER EXPERIENCE

- Conduct in-depth interviews with 60+ customers to understand their usage habits and challenges.

FEASIBILITY/VIABILITY

- Explore the feasibility and viability of partnerships with Smart TV manufacturers to enhance accessibility for the 60+ audience.

5 – Boundaries

- Operations must align with our established net income and operating profit targets.
- Changes to accommodate the Golden Generation must not adversely affect the experience and revenue generated from our primary user base. This includes ensuring that any interface and content alterations do not negatively impact current customer satisfaction and retention.

Translating Strategy into Coherent Action

At the heart of OKRs lies the ability to convert strategic guidelines into clear, actionable objectives.

Break down broad strategic themes into quarterly or annual OKRs that are tangible and measurable. This process involves distilling the essence of strategic themes (or guidelines) into specific objectives that teams can understand, embrace, and act upon.

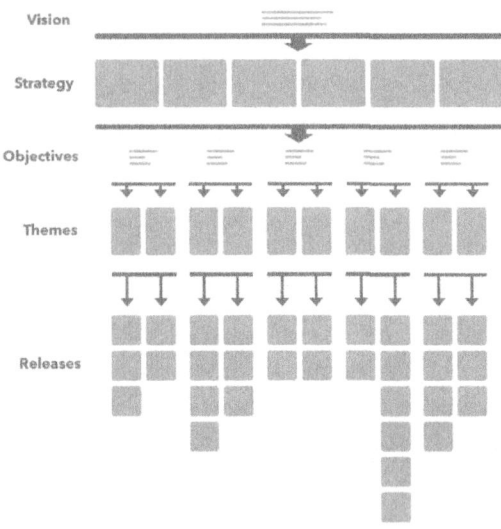

Figure 21 - From product vision to delivery

Every team should use higher level goals as a guiding star to define their own OKRs and roadmap.

Recommendations for Managers: Bridging the Gap

In managing and guiding teams, it's essential to bridge any gaps in understanding and execution. Here's a summary of key recommendations:

Ensuring Alignment Across All Organizational Levels

- **Collaborative OKR Development:** Address dependencies among teams by working together on shared or complementary OKRs. Avoid conflicting objectives to maintain a unified direction.

- **Clear Communication of Team Contributions:** Explicitly communicate how each team's OKRs support broader product or organizational goals. This clarity helps every team member understand their role in the larger picture, fostering a cohesive effort towards shared objectives.

- **Regular Monitoring and Updating:** Continuously review and update shared OKRs across teams to ensure they remain relevant and effective.

Cultivating Transparency and Commitment

- **Visibility of OKRs:** Maintain open visibility of OKRs to all team members. Celebrating achievements enhances commitment and creates a sense of collective success, motivating continuous improvement.

Adapting to Change with Agility and Flexibility

- **Regular OKR Reviews:** Conduct frequent reviews of OKRs to allow for timely adjustments in strategies and tactics. This adaptability ensures the organization stays responsive to changes, maintaining the relevance of strategic efforts.
- **End-of-Cycle Performance Review:** Evaluate OKRs at the end of each cycle to ensure alignment in future planning.
- **Customized OKR Processes:** Tailor the OKR definition and monitoring process to suit each team's unique circumstances for better adaptability and effectiveness.

Measuring Progress and Outcomes

- **Defining Key Results:** Incorporate well-defined key results in OKRs for precise measurement of progress and impact. Ensure the primary key result directly reflects the objective's success, providing a straightforward benchmark for achievement evaluation.
- **Setting Clear Targets:** Establish specific targets for each key result to clearly define expected outcomes and facilitate accurate tracking of progress.

Adherence to these recommendations enables managers to effectively close gaps in alignment, transparency, adaptability, and measurement, leading to a more coherent and successful execution of organizational strategies.

Chapter 9: OKR Guidelines for Managers

Objectives and Key Results go beyond being a simple goal-setting tool; they play a pivotal role in shaping a culture that thrives on feedback and continuous learning.

This chapter delves into preserving the strategic essence of OKRs, ensuring they effectively guide organizational direction. We explore how OKRs bolster key aspects of corporate culture, promoting growth, innovation, and mutual understanding within teams.

Avoiding the 'To-Do List' Trap in OKRs

The conflation of tasks and strategic objectives is a common misstep in OKR implementation, leading to a tactical rather than strategic focus.

Tasks are specific activities, whereas OKRs encapsulate broader strategic objectives. The key is to ensure your OKRs reflect the 'what' and 'why' of your strategic ambitions, steering clear of the detailed 'how' of operational tasks.

Key results shouldn't be a list of initiatives either, but measurable outcomes expressed in terms of leading indicators.

In case you are falling into this trap ask yourself the following questions to find out the goals and drive alignment:

- *Why are we doing this?*
- *What is the intended outcome of this initiative?*
- *If we complete this initiative, does that mean we have achieved the objective or the key result? What else would we need? Why?*
- *How will our customers be impacted by this initiative? How will we know?*
- *How will our business benefit from this initiative? How will we know?*

By reverse engineering your shopping-list you can effectively identify the objectives and key results and define whether you are cooking for Christmas Eve or for Thanksgiving.

Crafting Inspirational and Measurable Objectives

An OKR should inspire and challenge your team, pointing towards ambitious yet achievable horizons.

Aim to establish OKRs that ignite enthusiasm and motivation, focusing on measurable outcomes rather than mere tasks. This approach transforms OKRs from a mundane checklist into a powerful motivator.

OKRs should not be used as the basis for determining incentive compensation as this goes against the principle that OKRs should be stretch goals and encourage creativity and autonomy.

Setting Clear and Attainable Goals

The clarity and achievability of goals set through OKRs are essential for boosting team motivation.

Ensure that each OKR is specific, measurable, and attainable. This approach aids team members in understanding their roles and the significance of their tasks, providing a clear guidance for what needs to be accomplished and why.

Fostering Transparency

The clarity and transparency fostered by OKRs are foundational to effective communication within teams and across the organization.

OKRs ensure that each team member is not only aware of their objectives but also understands the goals of their colleagues and the organization. This openness facilitates collective understanding and alignment, making it easier to work towards common goals.

Chapter 15 highlights the importance of aligning OKRs both vertically and horizontally within teams. It's crucial for teams to collaboratively establish shared OKRs, review them together, and proactively confirm and track dependencies throughout the OKR cycle. This approach ensures that everyone's efforts are harmonized and geared towards common goals.

Instilling a Sense of Purpose and Direction

Aligning team OKRs with the organization's objectives gives team members a sense of contribution to the broader success.

It's crucial that each team's OKRs are interlinked with the overall business strategy. This alignment not only enhances a sense of purpose but also ensures that every effort contributes to the overarching goals of the organization.

In chapter 14, you'll find a dedicated section in the OKR definition template. This section is designed to guide you in correctly aligning your OKRs. It provides a structured approach to ensure that your OKRs are set up effectively, fostering collaboration and strategic alignment within your team.

Encouraging Creativity and Autonomy

A prescriptive approach to OKRs can stifle innovation and hinder the potential for creative problem-solving.

OKRs should not dictate the methods; instead, they should define the desired outcomes, leaving room for teams to innovate and find their unique paths to success. This autonomy fosters a culture of creativity and ownership.

Allow teams the freedom to devise their approach and solutions. This empowerment leads to a stronger sense of ownership and commitment, thereby boosting team engagement and productivity.

Driving Autonomy Through Alignment with OKRs

Building on the introduction of this book, where we discussed the pivotal role of alignment in driving autonomy, it's essential to explore how this concept is embodied and enhanced through the implementation of OKRs.

Alignment as the Foundation for Autonomy

When OKRs are aligned with the organization's vision and goals, they provide a clear direction for teams. This alignment ensures that every team member understands the broader objectives they are contributing towards, creating a unified sense of purpose.

Once the strategic alignment is established through OKRs, it grants teams the freedom to choose the best methods and approaches to achieve these objectives. This balance of clear direction (alignment) with the freedom of method (autonomy) is what makes OKRs a powerful tool in modern management.

Empowering Teams Through Clarity and Freedom

OKRs provide clarity on what needs to be achieved but do not dictate how to achieve it. This approach empowers teams to innovate, experiment, and find the most effective paths to their goals, fostering a culture of trust and responsibility.

When teams have the autonomy to determine their course of action within the framework of aligned objectives, it leads to greater engagement and investment in the outcomes. Autonomy is a powerful motivator that encourages creativity, problem-solving, and ownership.

Nurturing a Culture of Trust and Accountability

Leadership's trust in teams to manage their OKRs fosters a sense of accountability and ownership. This trust is crucial for creating an environment where autonomy can flourish.

Autonomy, when paired with accountability, ensures that while teams have the freedom to operate independently, they are also responsible for the outcomes of their actions. This accountability is essential for maintaining the balance between freedom and responsibility.

Embracing Dynamism through Regular Review and Adjustment

Treating OKRs as unchangeable can cause them to become outdated and misaligned with your strategy. To keep OKRs agile and effective:

- Conduct regular review cycles to check if OKRs are still in line with your strategic goals. This allows for necessary updates, ensuring your OKRs keep pace with the changing needs of your organization.
- For teams working on shared OKRs, it's important to review and adjust these goals collectively.
- At the end of each cycle, review all OKRs within a business unit together. This helps in shaping future strategy based on the insights gained.

Building a Culture of Feedback and Learning

OKRs serve as vital tools for learning and growth, functioning as platforms for ongoing discussions about progress and development. By integrating OKRs into your team's culture, you encourage an environment where feedback is not only accepted but embraced as a key element for continuous improvement and learning. This approach instills a cycle of constant feedback and timely recognition, which is critical in maintaining high team morale.

Regular reviews of OKRs are essential, as they provide opportunities for offering constructive feedback and acknowledging accomplishments. Such positive reinforcement is instrumental in enhancing team motivation and reinforcing desirable behaviors. The inherent structure of OKRs encourages periodic reviews, making them continual opportunities for feedback, essential for team development and course correction.

Moreover, these regular reviews promote an environment where feedback becomes a normalized, ongoing process. This not only helps in maintaining focus and alignment but also underscores the value of giving and receiving constructive feedback as part of the team's growth journey. Through this integrated approach, OKRs become more than just goals; they transform into catalysts for team development and strategic alignment.

Recognizing Achievements and Making Adjustments

Celebrating successes and learning from challenges are integral parts of the OKR process, contributing to motivation and valuable learning experiences.

The process of reaching or revising OKRs allows teams to acknowledge their achievements and understand areas for improvement. This recognition is not just motivational but also instrumental in identifying effective strategies and areas needing attention.

Learning through Experimentation and Review

OKRs encourage teams to explore new strategies and approaches, leading to a cycle of experimentation, learning from mistakes, and continuous improvement.

This experimental approach embedded in OKRs fosters a culture where trial and error are not only accepted but encouraged. It leads to a mindset of growth and continuous improvement, essential for adapting to changing environments and pursuing innovative solutions.

Conclusion

OKRs are more than just tools for setting and achieving objectives; they are vital instruments for building a robust organizational culture centered on learning, growth, and continuous improvement.

Through transparent goal-setting, regular feedback, a focus on learning through experimentation, recognition of achievements, and fostering autonomy, OKRs can significantly influence an organization's culture.

Leaders should leverage OKRs not just for their practical goal-setting benefits but also as a means to cultivate a more dynamic, responsive, and growth-oriented organizational environment.

Chapter 10: OKRs and Team Structure

Integrating team structures with Objectives and Key Results (OKRs) is crucial for guiding teams towards collective achievements. Successfully applying OKRs at the team level significantly influences the overall success of this approach.

Understanding how to tailor team structures to complement OKRs is vital for any organization looking to fully leverage this method's capabilities. This requires rethinking how teams are organized and interact within a company. Moving away from traditional, rigid organizational structures to more fluid, cross-functional team setups not only improves alignment but also cultivates a collaborative and shared-success culture.

Such a tailored approach ensures that OKRs become more than mere goals; they transform into drivers for profound change and continuous growth within the organization. This shift in team dynamics and structure is key to unlocking the true potential of OKRs.

Establishing Top-Level OKRs

The journey towards effective OKR implementation begins at the top. Leaders must set top-level OKRs as an exemplar for the rest of the organization. This sets the stage for lower-level teams to align their OKRs with overarching organizational goals, ensuring coherence and unity in purpose across all levels of the organization.

Rethinking Traditional Team Definitions

The traditional approach of aligning team structures strictly with the organizational chart often falls short in the context of OKRs. Experience shows that this approach can inadvertently foster silos rather than promoting cross-functional alignment. Instead, OKRs encourage a more fluid definition of teams, one that transcends conventional boundaries and fosters collaboration across different functional areas.

Approaches for Team-Level OKR Implementation

There is no one-size-fits-all solution when it comes to structuring teams for the effective implementation of Objectives and Key Results.

The diversity in organizational needs and cultures necessitates a flexible approach to determine the most suitable team structure for setting and achieving OKRs.

Here, we explore three prevalent methods that have demonstrated success in various organizations. These approaches go beyond the conventional boundaries of org charts, fostering a culture of cross-functional alignment and collaboration.

It's important to remember that these methods are not mutually exclusive; they can be adapted or combined to fit the unique context and objectives of your organization.

Let's delve into each approach to understand how they can be leveraged to optimize team-level OKR implementation.

Shared OKRs for Highly Dependent Teams

In a real-world scenario from my experience with a manufacturing company, the design and production teams initially operated under separate management structures. Each team had distinct goals and leadership, which frequently led to strong dependencies and coordination challenges. This separation often resulted in misalignments and inefficiencies, particularly when it came to meeting the company's overarching objectives.

To address these challenges, we made a strategic decision to unify the design and production teams under a single OKR framework. This approach required both teams to collaboratively define and review their Objectives and Key Results.

The integration facilitated a more harmonized workflow, ensuring that both teams were not just aligned in their goals but also in their operational processes.

This restructuring proved to be a game-changer, significantly reducing silos and enhancing overall productivity. The shared OKRs became a powerful tool for guiding collective efforts, ensuring that both design and production contributed cohesively towards the company's strategic objectives.

Leveraging Existing Cross-Functional Squads

Consider a scenario where an e-commerce enterprise abandons traditional departmental OKRs. Instead, it forms customer-centric squads such as "B2B Engagement Squad" or "Consumer Experience Squad." This pivot towards customer-focused teams aligns OKRs with the nuanced needs of diverse customer segments, enhancing the relevancy and impact of set objectives.

Many organizations, especially in high-tech and e-commerce, have found success in defining OKRs for cross-functional squads that are already in place. These squads, organized around specific customer segments or parts of the customer journey, offer a practical basis for setting and achieving OKRs.

Defining Cross-Functional Teams Based on Top-Level OKRs

When organizations lack pre-existing cross-functional squads, top-level OKRs can guide the formation of new teams. For instance, envision a scenario where a company's top-level objective is to enhance digital innovation. To achieve this, a special task force, comprising leaders from IT, marketing, and R&D, is formed. This team, dedicated to the digital innovation objective, exemplifies how top-level OKRs can directly influence the creation of specialized, cross-functional teams.

Conclusion

Integrating Objectives and Key Results (OKRs) into the fabric of an organization is a multifaceted process that, while challenging, yields significant rewards.

A transformative approach to setting and achieving objectives emerges from strategically structuring teams. The key to this transformation lies in understanding the unique needs and strategic goals of the organization, and then shaping the team structure to best support these objectives.

Insights gained from various examples highlight the significant impact team structures have on the success of OKR implementation, underscoring the profound changes this approach brings to team dynamics and goal alignment.

Chapter 11: OKRs and Strategy Review

Product strategy isn't a one-off plan that's just executed and forgotten. It needs ongoing revisions and fine-tuning.

This chapter will guide you through setting up productive strategy review meetings, bringing in the right team members, and selecting the best information to inform essential updates.

Purpose of Strategy Review

A product strategy review meeting is essential for discussing and updating a company's product strategy. Its primary aim is to ensure everyone involved in product development is aligned with common goals and objectives. During these meetings, any discrepancies or gaps in the strategy are identified and addressed, ensuring everyone is moving in the same direction.

Another critical aspect of these meetings is managing expectations. It involves setting realistic goals and clarifying each team member's roles and responsibilities. This ensures everyone knows what's achievable and what's expected of them.

Sharing key insights and learnings is also a vital goal of these meetings. The team exchanges information about the product, market trends, and the competitive environment. This shared knowledge helps in making informed decisions.

Furthermore, selecting and prioritizing initiatives is a significant part of the agenda. It involves determining which initiatives are most critical and allocating resources effectively.

Lastly, reviewing progress towards goals is crucial. It's about evaluating how well the team is meeting its objectives and pinpointing areas where progress might be slow.

Consistently following these steps is key to enhancing the effectiveness of a product strategy. It helps the team stay on track with their goals and significantly boosts the chances of success for both the product and the company. This approach ensures that strategic efforts are well-directed and aligned with the company's objectives.

Guiding Principles

Product strategy review meetings are crucial for aligning teams, shaping product direction, and driving successful outcomes. However, the effectiveness of these meetings hinges on adhering to certain guiding principles. These principles are not just best practices; they are the cornerstone of conducting productive, focused, and strategic discussions.

In this section, we delve into six key principles that define the backbone of an effective product strategy review meeting. Together, these guidelines provide a framework for productive and efficient strategy review meetings, essential for any team committed to achieving excellence in product development and management.

1. Advance Information Sharing

This principle emphasizes providing attendees with all relevant information and materials before the meeting. It ensures that everyone arrives well-prepared, with a clear understanding of the topics and issues to be discussed, leading to more engaged and focused discussions.

2. Proactive Preparation

Preparation involves doing necessary research and work before the meeting, preparing to discuss and make decisions. Effective preparation allows participants to contribute meaningfully to the discussions.

3. Structured Meeting Plan

An agenda sets a clear and organized plan for the meeting, outlining topics, objectives, and required decisions. A well-defined agenda keeps the meeting on track, focused, and ensures all attendees are aligned with the meeting's goals.

4. Effective Facilitation

A dedicated facilitator manages the meeting flow, ensuring productivity and effectiveness. The facilitator keeps the meeting on track, moderates discussions, and ensures active engagement and involvement from all attendees.

5. Managing Meeting Size

This principle involves controlling the number of attendees to keep the meeting manageable. A limited capacity ensures a focused and efficient meeting where everyone has the opportunity to participate and be heard.

6. Strategic Focus

Focusing on the big-picture issues and challenges while avoiding getting bogged down in details is crucial. This approach ensures the meeting concentrates on vital issues and decisions, aligning the team on the overall direction and goals of the product strategy.

Review Frequency

The frequency of reviewing your product strategy is largely influenced by the maturity of your product and its market. Generally, the greater the uncertainty and rate of change, the more often you should revisit your strategy. For most cases, a review cadence ranging from monthly to quarterly is appropriate.

If you're unsure where to begin, consider these suggested cadences:

- **Yearly**: Conduct a comprehensive review of your overall product strategy. This should include strategic themes, product Objectives and Key Results (OKRs), and the product roadmap.
- **Quarterly**: Focus on assessing the progress of your OKRs and updating the product roadmap accordingly.
- **Monthly**: Review the progress of key results and initiatives.

These intervals provide a structured approach to ensure your product strategy remains aligned with market dynamics and company goals.

How to Run an Effective Product Strategy Review Meeting

Begin with Strategy

The primary responsibility of a product leader is to develop and execute a well-defined product strategy. As discussed in the first section of the book, this strategy should articulate your hypotheses for tackling key strategic challenges, define the metrics for tracking progress, and outline the tactics, including initiatives or experiments, for each strategic area.

At the beginning of the meeting, spend the first 15 minutes providing a recap of the company's overarching product strategy. This is the time to outline the planned stages of your product's growth, emphasizing that these developments don't need to occur simultaneously. Instead, highlight that the product's focus will naturally evolve in phases over several years.

Attendees

The composition of a product strategy review meeting varies, primarily depending on your business's maturity and product type. Different sectors, like a SaaS startup, an eCommerce retailer, a financial service, or a hardware product company, will have distinct requirements for meeting attendees.

As previously emphasized, it's important to keep the number of attendees to a minimum to ensure the meeting's effectiveness. Typically, the participants would include:

- CEO (or Business Unit Manager)
- Chief Product Officer (or Head of Product)
- Other Executive Officers involved in product-related areas such as Technology, Marketing, Sales, and Finance
- Product Manager from each product team
- A Facilitator

On certain occasions, you might need to invite additional attendees:

- Members from other business units for specific discussions
- HR or Legal representatives for workforce or legal matters
- Engineering, Design, or Data Leads for discussions on specific technological, data, or design aspects

The Head of Product is usually the person responsible for overseeing these meetings.

Preparation Work

It's crucial for product managers to publish their work ahead of the meeting. This allows all participants to review the materials beforehand and provide their thoughts and questions online. At the meeting, product managers then focus on presenting a selection of their work, informed by these pre-meeting comments.

Active participation is expected from everyone involved. All attendees should engage thoroughly both in the pre-reading phase and during the meeting itself. Passive participation is not an option.

Before the meeting, several key documents need to be current and accessible to all participants. These include the product strategy, objectives, metrics, product roadmap, and any briefing documents. Additionally, any recent insights from product discovery, research, competitive analysis, customer feedback, and data should be available and updated. This ensures that everyone comes to the meeting with the latest information and can contribute effectively to the discussion.

Agenda

The duration of your quarterly product strategy meeting can vary significantly, primarily based on the size of your product organization. These meetings can last anywhere from two hours to a full day, depending on the number of product teams involved.

A typical meeting's agenda is structured as follows:

Introduction by the Head of Product (15 - 30 min.)

- Purpose of the meeting (clarifying meeting goals)
- Establishing meeting ground rules
- Highlighting key achievements
- Updating on overall product strategy, OKRs, metrics, and roadmap
- Identifying key focus areas
- Presenting a rolling four-quarter product plan, detailing next quarter's goals and briefly covering subsequent quarters, for each product team

Research and Insights (30 min.)

- Sharing strategic-level insights from recent research and product discovery

Product Teams (15 min. per team)

- Each product team has a dedicated slot, though not every product manager needs to present at each meeting
- Focus on highlighting achievements, progress of current initiatives, and status of upcoming projects

Parking Lot and Next Steps (30 min.)

- Keeping track of unresolved items from the meeting
- Determining next steps and their timelines towards the end of the session

Wrap Up (5 min)

- A crucial practice I've adopted through my experience as a manager, consultant, and coach is to dedicate the final 5 minutes to ensure clarity and commitment. Often, at the end of a seemingly clear meeting, individual understandings of the agreed actions can vary significantly. Thus, I recommend concluding the strategy review meeting with a round of confirmation, ensuring everyone is on the same page regarding their responsibilities and commitments.

Facilitator

In the realm of business meetings, the role of a facilitator is crucial. Having personally participated in numerous strategy review and design meetings, I've seen firsthand how vital active facilitation is. My involvement has often been key in preventing teams from going in circles or engaging in endless, unproductive discussions about trivial matters. A facilitator is not just a participant; they are the pivotal force that ensures meetings are productive, focused, and directed towards achieving specific objectives.

The Facilitator's Role in Effective Business Meetings

As a facilitator, your primary role is to guide discussions, ensure everyone has a chance to contribute, and lead the group to a decision or conclusion.

Creating a Supportive Environment

Your foremost responsibility is to create an environment conducive to open and honest communication. This involves establishing meeting rules that encourage active listening and respectful dialogue, ensuring everyone is aligned with the meeting's goals and agenda from the start.

Maintaining Focus

An essential part of your role is keeping the discussion relevant and on track. This means controlling the conversation flow, making sure the group stays focused on the main topics, and avoiding digressions.

Handling Conflicts

Effective facilitators are skilled in resolving conflicts, helping the group find common ground, and moving discussions forward in a constructive manner.

Three Tips for Effective Facilitation

1. **Start with a Clear Agenda**: Begin every meeting with a defined agenda and objectives. This sets expectations and helps participants understand their roles.
2. **Encourage Everyone to Participate**: Promote an inclusive atmosphere where all members are encouraged to engage. Use open-ended questions, prompt individuals to share insights, and create opportunities for equal participation.

3. **Drive the Meeting Forward**: Summarize key points, make decisions, assign tasks, and ensure the group remains focused on the meeting's objectives.

Effective facilitation is instrumental in achieving the group's goals and advancing its work. A facilitator's ability to foster communication, maintain focus, and facilitate decision-making processes is key to the success of any business meeting.

Empirical Insights for Quarterly Strategy Reviews

As you define OKRs for the upcoming year, a pivotal aspect to consider is the systematic review of these objectives. This section explores how an empirical approach to your quarterly strategy review can be instrumental in shaping more effective OKRs.

The Four Essential Feedback Cycles for Successful OKRs

To ensure the ongoing relevance and effectiveness of your OKRs, incorporate these four critical feedback mechanisms:

1. **Weekly KPI Review:** Focus on leading indicators for continual monitoring. This helps in early detection of trends and issues, allowing for prompt adjustments.

2. **Delivery Review:** Regular evaluations of the progress of key initiatives. This ensures that the efforts are aligned with the strategic objectives and are moving the needle in terms of results.

3. **Monthly OKR Check-in:** A dedicated time to assess whether you are on track with your OKRs and to determine if any adjustments are needed. This keeps the team aligned and responsive to changes.

4. **Quarterly Strategy Review:** The culmination of the previous cycles, where the strategic progress of the quarter is analyzed to refine OKRs and update the product roadmap accordingly.

Deep Dive into the Quarterly Strategy Review

At the heart of the Quarterly Strategy Review that we have seen in the previous section is the evaluation of strategic progress and the adaptation of OKRs and the product roadmap based on empirical data.

- **Objective and Progress of KRs:** Detailing the status and advancement of each Key Result.

- **Impact on North Star Metric (NSM):** If applicable, assess how the OKRs are influencing your primary success metric.

- **Analysis of Roadmap Themes or Opportunities:** Evaluate each roadmap item based on assumption, expected impact versus actual outcome, and action proposals (kill, pivot, persevere).
- **Status and Outcomes of Roadmap-Linked Developments:** Review the state and results of epics or developments connected to roadmap opportunities.

For further insights into the concept of opportunities in roadmaps, read my previous book *'Product Roadmapping in Practice'*[15] or visit the Aktia Solutions' blog[16] for valuable information on result-oriented roadmaps and agile product roadmaps.

Quarterly OKRs Review

As we navigate the strategic tides of product development, the Quarterly OKRs Review stands as a pivotal ceremony. It's a time to pause and reflect, to measure our strides against the grand vision we're pursuing. This review isn't just a retrospective—it's a strategic rendezvous where we connect the dots between our daily endeavors and the overarching mission of our enterprise.

In this section, we'll uncover the essence of the Quarterly Strategy Review, a periodical gathering that goes beyond mere progress check-ins. It's an opportunity to:

- **Anchor in Outcomes:** We zoom out to see how our actions align with broader initiatives, ensuring our work continues to be outcome-driven.
- **Navigate with Agility:** The results and insights gained prompt us to question whether it's time to pivot or persevere in our current direction.
- **Chart the Roadmap:** We scrutinize our learnings to see how they refine our understanding of the roadmap ahead.

Building on the approach detailed in the Product Strategy Review, I recommend a seamless integration with the OKR Review process. This unified review will not only assess strategic progress but will also adapt our Objectives and Key Results in sync with the product roadmap.

By leveraging empirical data, this integrated review enables a holistic examination of our strategic direction and operational execution. This ensures that our product strategy remains dynamic and responsive to the insights gained from our OKRs.

Reviewing Results

This template is a key tool for improving how you set and achieve goals. It's made especially for product managers, startup founders, and team leaders. It helps you check how well your Objectives and Key Results (OKRs) are doing.

Here, we offer a clear way to look at your goals and results. This isn't just about seeing if you've succeeded or not. It's more about thinking deeply, learning, and planning your next moves. When you look closely at each OKR, you'll understand what works, what doesn't, and how to adjust your plans wisely.

No matter if you're experienced or new to OKRs, this template is easy to use and fits right into your business's needs.

Instead of measuring progress through the typical scoring system, consider integrating more nuanced factors like the NSM, opportunities, and the actual impact of your initiatives. This approach provides a more comprehensive view of how your OKRs are performing and their real contribution to the organization's objectives.

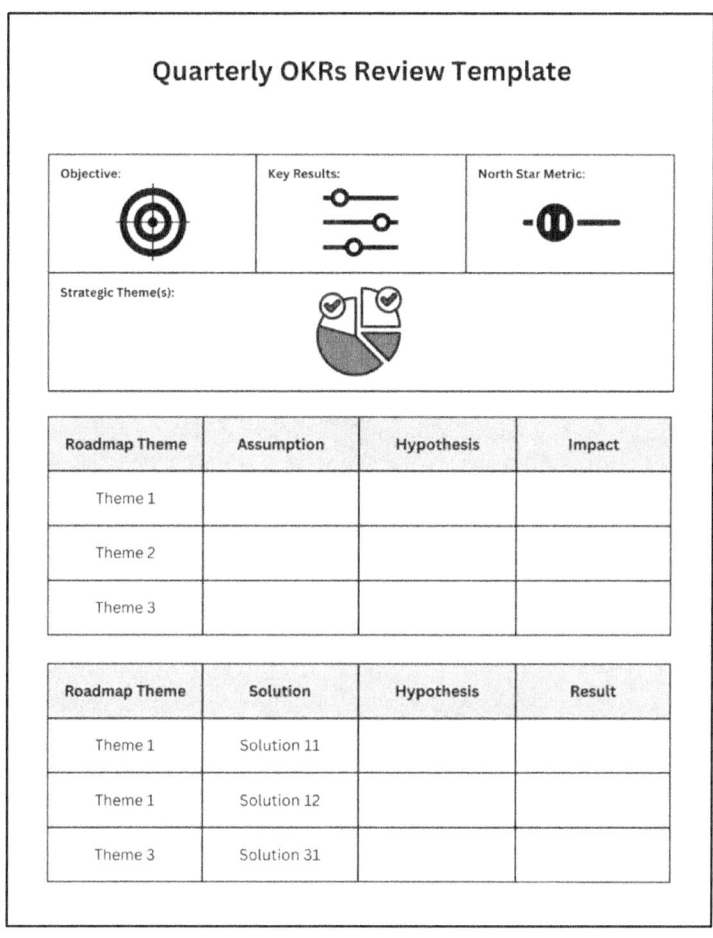

Objective:

- Define the primary goal the team set for the quarter, aligning with the company's North Star Metric.

Key Results:

- Detail the specific, measurable outcomes achieved in relation to the quarter's goal.
- Quantify the level of completion for each key result.

North Star Metric:

- Translate the key results' impact on the North Star Metric, showing the direct influence on the product's success metric.

Strategic Theme(s):

- Discuss the underlying themes that drove the quarter's strategy, such as market trends, competitive landscape, or customer feedback.

Roadmap Themes:

- List the opportunities or problems addressed in the quarter.
- For each, articulate the initial assumption and the hypothesis that guided the team's actions.
- Evaluate the impact of pursuing these opportunities on the OKR and North Star Metric.

Solutions:

- Present the specific solutions undertaken to explore the identified roadmap themes.
- For each solution, reiterate the hypothesis and assess the results against expected outcomes.

Insights and Planning

Now, it is time to reflect on the past quarter's learnings and their impact on our understanding of the opportunity space. This critical analysis informs our goals for the upcoming quarter, focusing on key opportunities and aligning our efforts with our North Star Metric.

This stage is more than just measuring progress; it's about strategically guiding our future growth and impact.

Learnings and Impact in Opportunity Space:

- Summarize key learnings from the quarter's activities and their influence on the understanding of the opportunity space.
- Adjust the opportunity space diagram or description to reflect these insights.

Next Quarter Plans:

- Set out the goals for the upcoming quarter, with expected outcomes and impacts on the North Star Metric.
- Describe the opportunities that will be focused on and the evidence supporting their importance.
- Share the planned initiatives and their intended contribution to the goals.

Chapter 12: Performance Appraisals and Economic Incentives

To fully harness the psychological benefits of OKRs, it's essential for leadership to carefully consider how they are implemented and perceived within the organization. A critical aspect of this consideration is the separation of OKRs from individual performance evaluations and economic incentives.

For OKRs to effectively motivate and engage teams, leadership must avoid directly tying them to individual performance appraisals and economic incentives. This approach not only aligns with research and expert opinion, but also fosters an organizational culture that values growth, innovation, and intrinsic motivation.

By doing so, leaders can ensure that OKRs serve as a tool for strategic alignment and team empowerment, rather than a mere metric for performance evaluation.

Avoiding the Pitfalls of OKRs in Performance Appraisals

Linking Objectives and Key Results directly to performance appraisals can compromise their effectiveness and the positive psychological impacts they're designed to offer. When OKRs are connected to evaluations or financial incentives, several unintended consequences can occur, as outlined below.

Short-Term Focus Over Long-Term Value

When financial incentives are tied directly to OKRs, employees may prioritize short-term achievements over long-term value creation. This can lead to myopic decision-making where the focus shifts to achieving immediate results at the expense of the broader, strategic objectives of the organization.

Gaming the System

In an environment where financial gains are linked to OKR attainment, there's an increased risk of 'gaming the system.' Employees might set less ambitious goals to ensure they meet them or manipulate data to appear as if they've achieved their objectives, leading to a culture of dishonesty and inauthenticity.

Undermining Collaboration

OKRs are meant to encourage collaboration and alignment towards shared goals. However, when individual rewards are at stake, employees might become more competitive, choosing to work in silos rather than collaboratively. This can lead to hoarding information, reluctance to help others, and generally putting individual success over team or organizational success.

Reduction in Innovation and Risk-Taking

The fear of failing to meet OKRs might discourage team members from setting challenging objectives and taking innovative approaches.

Diminished Focus on Learning and Development

The focus shifts from growth and improvement to merely meeting set targets, limiting the potential for professional development and organizational learning.

Destructive Competition

When an individual's income and critical life aspects, such as paying for their children's education, depend on achieving these goals can inadvertently encourage undesirable behaviors and workplace dynamics, leading to a counterproductive and potentially toxic environment.

Stress and Burnout

The pressure to meet OKRs for financial reasons can lead to excessive stress and burnout. This not only harms employee well-being but can also reduce productivity and creativity in the long run. Employees may become risk-averse, fearing the consequences of not meeting their goals, which stifles innovation.

Demotivation and Unfairness

Linking OKRs with performance appraisals and rewards can create a sense of unfairness, especially if the goals set are perceived as unrealistic or if factors beyond an employee's control impact their ability to achieve them. This can demotivate staff and lead to higher turnover.

Misalignment with Company Values

If a company values teamwork, innovation, and long-term growth, using OKRs as a basis for financial rewards can create a misalignment with these values. It encourages a culture that values individual achievement over collective success and short-term gains over sustainable growth.

The Cure is Worth than the Disease

While OKRs are a powerful tool for setting and achieving goals, using them as a primary basis for performance appraisals and financial rewards will create a competitive environment that is counterproductive to the collaborative and innovative culture that most organizations strive to cultivate.

It's crucial to design reward systems that encourage teamwork, long-term thinking, and alignment with the company's core values and objectives.

Research Supporting the Separation of OKRs from Incentives

The integration of Objectives and Key Results (OKRs) with performance evaluations and financial incentives has been a topic of extensive research. The consensus from various studies suggests that this integration can, in fact, diminish the effectiveness of OKRs, especially in terms of creativity and long-term employee engagement.

These findings collectively underscore the importance of intrinsic over extrinsic motivators in fostering creativity, productivity, and long-term engagement. Therefore, directly linking OKRs to performance appraisals and financial rewards may counteract their intended psychological benefits, underscoring the need to reevaluate such practices in organizational settings.

Impact on Creativity and Performance

A notable discussion in a Harvard Business School article[17] critically examines research by R. Eisenberger and J. Cameron on the impact of reward on creativity. This critique highlights a crucial oversight in Eisenberger and Cameron's work: they do not adequately address instances where rewarded activities exhibited lower creativity compared to non-rewarded activities. Furthermore, their evidence suggesting increased creativity under reward conditions applies more to simple human behaviors than to actual creative performance.

Intrinsic vs. Extrinsic Motivation

Intrinsic motivation, driven by internal factors such as personal interest and fulfillment, has been identified as a more potent and sustainable driver of employee engagement and productivity than extrinsic rewards. This type of motivation occurs when activities resonate with personal values, attitudes, or meaningful work. Research indicates that employees who are intrinsically motivated not only perform better but also exhibit enhanced creativity, problem-solving skills, and conceptual thinking.[18]

In contrast, extrinsic motivation is influenced by external factors like rewards and incentives. While these factors are essential for guiding efforts towards organizational goals and inducing performance, they are not as effective in differentiating performance levels as intrinsic motivators. The evidence suggests that a higher proportion of employees exceeding performance expectations are intrinsically motivated, compared to those driven by extrinsic factors.

Daniel Pink's 'Drive' and OKRs

Daniel Pink's work *'Drive'*[19] delves deep into the psychology of motivation, emphasizing the importance of intrinsic motivators – autonomy, mastery, and purpose.

Pink argues that these intrinsic motivators are far more effective in driving long-term engagement and performance than extrinsic rewards like financial incentives. This concept aligns with the philosophy behind OKRs, which are designed to provide clear goals (purpose), allow personal approaches to achieving them (autonomy), and encourage skill development (mastery).

Conclusion

OKRs can significantly influence team morale and performance, for better or worse, and much of that outcome rests on your approach. When implemented effectively and separated from performance evaluations and incentives, OKRs can foster a work environment that promotes both success and the psychological well-being of team members.

On the other hand, choosing the wrong approach can lead to the exact opposite effect.

As leaders and managers, it's crucial to consider the psychological impact of OKRs on your teams. Understanding this can provide valuable insights, helping to maximize the effectiveness of OKRs and enhance your team's overall performance.

Chapter 13: The Leader as Coach

This chapter explores how leaders can effectively facilitate Objectives and Key Results (OKRs) to foster team development and growth and delves into the three pillars of product leadership essential for transforming a product organization.

Facilitating OKRs for Team Development

At the core of successful OKRs implementation is a leader who adopts a coaching stance, guiding their team through the nuances of OKRs to promote growth and development.

Setting Meaningful Objectives

The leader's role includes helping the team set OKRs that are not only achievable but also meaningful and aligned with the company's strategic intent. Involving the team in the OKRs definition process ensures their commitment and understanding.

Empowering Autonomy and Ownership

Leaders should empower teams to make key decisions and own their OKRs. Providing direction and support without micromanagement allows teams to determine how best to achieve their OKRs, fostering a sense of ownership and accountability.

Continuous Review and Adjustment

OKRs are dynamic, requiring regular review and adaptation. Creating an environment where feedback is constant, constructive, and adjustments are part of the learning process is essential for OKRs to remain relevant and effective.

Celebrating Achievements and Learning from Challenges

Recognizing successes and learning from challenges is key. OKR review meetings should be opportunities to celebrate accomplishments and openly discuss challenges, promoting a culture of trust and transparency.

Ongoing Team Development

Utilize OKRs as a tool for both professional and personal development of team members. Identifying growth opportunities through OKRs and providing resources and training can help teams reach their full potential.

The Three Pillars of Product Leadership

Product leadership, a crucial foundation of modern product organizations, requires a strong product direction, management, and inspiration.

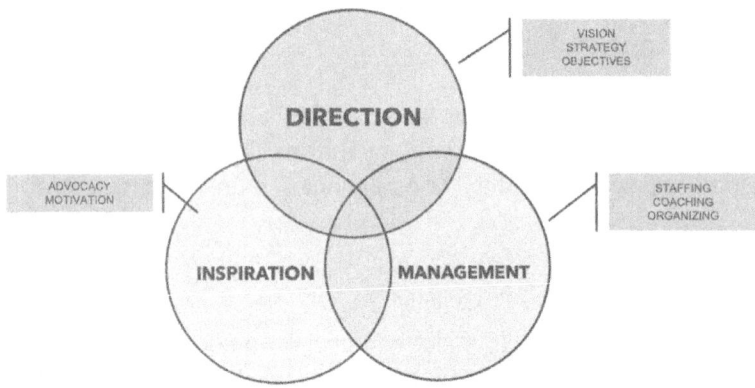

Figure 22 - The Three Pillars of Product Leadership

1. **Direction:** Setting a clear and compelling direction is the primary duty of product leadership. It involves developing a strategic direction considering the organization's strategic objectives, the competitive environment, and the organization's capabilities.

2. **Management:** Effective management is about providing and controlling the means to follow the direction. It includes understanding goals, solving problems, and organizing work efficiently to maximize resources.

3. **Inspiration:** Leading is fundamentally a moral and emotional human activity. Leaders must motivate and inspire people to pursue the set direction and perform their tasks to the best of their abilities.

What's particularly interesting about OKRs is their complexity and comprehensive nature. They intersect with all three core responsibilities of a leader.

The Role of Coaching

The three pillars of product leadership – Direction, Management, and Inspiration – form the backbone of a successful product organization. Central to these pillars, and particularly pivotal in 'Management', is the practice of coaching.

Effective leadership in the modern era is not just about setting goals and directives; it's equally about nurturing, guiding, and developing teams.

This section explores how coaching is an integral part of 'Management' and why leaders must either develop coaching skills or engage professional coaches to facilitate team success.

Direction: Setting a Strategic Course

Setting a clear and compelling direction remains the primary duty of product leadership. It's about crafting a vision that aligns with both the organization's objectives and the current market environment.

Coaches help leaders in developing clarity around their vision and strategy, ensuring that the direction set is not only ambitious but also realistic and well-communicated.

Management: Empowering Teams through Coaching

In the context of product leadership, 'Management' goes beyond traditional task delegation and resource allocation. It's about empowering teams, solving problems, and organizing work efficiently.

Coaching is central to effective management. Leaders must develop coaching skills to guide their teams through challenges, facilitate problem-solving, defining strategy and goals, and enable autonomy.

This approach helps in building a resilient team capable of navigating complex project landscapes.

Alternatively, hiring an external coach like me can provide an objective perspective, helping leaders and teams to unlock their potential, enhance collaboration, and drive innovation.

Inspiration: Motivating Towards a Shared Vision

Inspiration in leadership is about motivating teams to pursue the organization's vision passionately. It involves igniting a sense of purpose and driving engagement.

Coaches aid leaders in developing inspirational skills. Through coaching, leaders learn to connect with their teams on a deeper level, understand their motivations, and inspire them towards shared goals.

In conclusion, coaching is not a standalone activity but a crucial component of effective product leadership. Whether leaders develop their coaching skills or engage professional coaches, this practice is essential for fostering a culture of empowerment, problem-solving, and innovation.

By integrating coaching into the fabric of product leadership, organizations can ensure that their teams are not only aligned with the strategic direction but are also motivated and equipped to achieve it.

As a leader, your role in this process is invaluable, offering guidance, insights, and support to your teams as they navigate the complexities of modern product management.

Integrating Product Strategy with OKRs

Product strategy is about determining which problems product teams need to solve and is pivotal in realizing the product vision. It requires a profound understanding the current situation, identifying major challenges, and designing a guiding policy and coherent actions.

In modern product organizations, teams focus on solving problems rather than merely developing features. They are responsible for diagnosing situations, identifying obstacles, and designing appropriate approaches to overcome them.

While strategy sets the overall guiding policy, the tactics are the specific actions taken to achieve the strategic goals. OKRs play a crucial role in implementing these actions, providing coordination, concentration, and focus so teams can define an effective product roadmap.

Leaders as coaches play a vital role in guiding, motivating, and supporting their teams in the OKR journey, blending the art of leadership with the science of strategic planning.

The Leader's Role

Integrating product strategy with OKRs is a crucial task that falls under the purview of leadership. It's not just about setting strategic goals but also about creating an environment conducive to the effective implementation of OKRs.

Leaders must take active steps to empower their teams, foster continuous improvement, and ensure alignment with the organization's vision.

Leader's Responsibility in OKR Implementation

The success of OKRs hinges on the leader's ability to nurture the right environment and provide the necessary support. This involves several key responsibilities:

- **Collaboration with Executives and Stakeholders:** Leaders must effectively communicate the OKR approach to executives and key stakeholders, ensuring they understand how product teams will work towards strategic objectives. This involves clearly explaining the benefits of OKRs and how they align with broader business goals.
- **Supporting Teams with Well-Defined OKRs and Strategy:** Providing teams with clear, well-crafted OKRs and a coherent product strategy is essential. Leaders must ensure that OKRs are not only aligned with the company's vision but also realistic and achievable.
- **Coaching Through the OKR Process:** Leaders should adopt a coaching mindset, guiding and supporting their teams throughout the OKR cycle. This involves helping teams to set their OKRs, review progress, make necessary adjustments, and learn from outcomes.

Practical Recommendations for Leaders

To effectively integrate product strategy with OKRs, leaders can follow these practical recommendations:

- **Facilitate OKR Workshops:** Conduct workshops or training sessions to help teams understand the purpose of OKRs and how to set effective ones. Use these sessions to align OKRs with the overall product strategy.
- **Regular Check-ins:** Schedule regular check-ins to discuss OKR progress, address challenges, and provide support. These meetings should be a platform for open dialogue and collaborative problem-solving.
- **Encourage Cross-Functional Collaboration:** Promote collaboration between different teams and departments. This helps in ensuring that OKRs are comprehensive and take into account different perspectives.
- **Recognize and Celebrate Success:** Acknowledge and celebrate when teams meet or exceed their OKRs. This not only boosts morale but also reinforces the value of the OKR process.
- **Lead by Example:** Demonstrate commitment to the OKR process by setting and diligently following your own OKRs. Leaders' active participation sets a positive precedent for the team.
- **Provide Continuous Learning Opportunities:** Offer resources and training to help teams develop skills relevant to achieving their OKRs. This could include workshops on strategic thinking, data analysis, or specific technical skills.

In summary, the leader's role in integrating product strategy with OKRs is multifaceted. It involves clear communication with executives and stakeholders, providing support to teams, and coaching them through the process.

Leaders who adhere to these practical guidelines can foster an environment where OKRs are successfully implemented. This approach paves the way for ongoing improvement and the attainment of strategic objectives.

OKR Coaches: Catalyzing Effective OKR Implementation

In recent years, there has been a notable surge in the prevalence of OKR Coaches and related certifications, driven largely by the popularity and the challenges associated with the proper implementation of the OKR (Objectives and Key Results) methodology.

OKR Coaches, whether external consultants or internal advisors, play a pivotal role in aiding organizations to comprehend, adopt, and institutionalize OKR practices. Their primary focus is on the process, ensuring that the methodology is not only understood but also effectively integrated into the organization's fabric.

The Temporary Nature of OKR Coaching

Ideally, the involvement of an OKR Coach is transient. It's anticipated that within two to three planning periods, teams and managers should be capable of independently managing their OKRs. A reliance on OKR Coaches beyond three quarters (approximately 9 months) warrants a thorough evaluation of the situation to identify and address underlying issues.

Beyond OKR: Holistic Coaching

While OKR Coaches are instrumental in their specific domain, there are more comprehensive roles like Product Strategy Coaches, Product Coaches, and Product Discovery Coaches. These professionals not only possess expertise in OKRs, as evidenced in this book, but also offer a more holistic support covering the entire product lifecycle from ideation to market. This includes strategy, OKRs, product discovery, and even go-to-market strategies, coupled with personalized coaching for individuals or teams.

Typical Interventions by OKR Coaches

1. Deploying OKRs

For organizations aiming to enhance agility, alignment, leadership, and autonomy, the articulation of OKRs becomes crucial. In such instances, dedicated OKR Coaches are essential, especially in scale-ups or large transforming companies. They guide through the initial training, deployment, and continuous improvement of OKRs.

2. Addressing Time or Personnel Constraints

Often, parts of an organization might have successfully adopted OKRs, but there may be a lack of time or appropriate personnel to assist new teams in adopting OKRs. Here, OKR Coaches work with these new teams, aligning them with the broader company practices and policies regarding OKRs.

3. Rectifying Faulty Implementations

A common scenario is the need to rectify flawed OKR implementations. If OKRs in your organization haven't enhanced agility, strategic alignment, and decision-making, an OKR Coach is needed. They can provide a detailed diagnosis, action plan, and support through the improvement process.

In organizations where OKRs have been misapplied—for instance, for performance evaluation, or where they are defined but not effectively utilized—an OKR Coach's intervention can be particularly beneficial. They can also be invaluable in situations where specific teams struggle with effective OKR implementation due to their unique composition or context.

Case Study: Streamlining OKRs for Enhanced Focus

Background

Company XYZ, a burgeoning high-tech e-commerce entity, encountered challenges with their existing OKRs program. Leadership noted an excess of poorly articulated OKRs, leading to diluted focus and an overwhelming workload.

The Problem

The company, experiencing rapid growth, was grappling with over-ambitious projects and a tendency to pursue new initiatives without clear direction. The CEO observed that despite the hard work, the lack of focus hindered effective progress.

Our Approach

Working closely with their leadership team, we developed customized OKR guidelines that specifically addressed their unique needs. A pivotal aspect of this approach was to cap the number of objectives for each team at three. We emphasized the importance of defining clear targets for all key results, ensuring each had a measurable 'line in the sand'. Additionally, we ensured that every set of OKRs included key results focused on both quality and progress.

Case Focus: Customer Success Team

The customer success team exemplified the successful adoption of this refined OKR approach. Their process included:

1. **Development of Strategy:** The team formulated their strategy aligned with company's strategic intent.
2. **Setting Just Three Objectives:** Once the strategy was clearly defined, narrowing down to just three objectives became a straightforward task with measurable Key Results, ensuring clarity and attainability.
3. **Finalization and Publication:** The team's OKRs, after thorough consultation with the CEO, were shared with other teams. This collaborative process led to their finalization, incorporating feedback, and making necessary minor adjustments.
4. **Mid-Cycle Check-In:** A mid-cycle assessment was conducted, where the customer success team reviewed and updated their progress.

5. **Quarterly Review:** At the end of each quarter, we held a review session. This included participation from our coaching team, who provided specialized guidance and insights.
6. **Reflect and Plan:** As Q4 drew to a close, we conducted a session centered on reflection and future planning. This session particularly emphasized evaluating the achievements of key results and gathering insights for the upcoming planning period.

Conclusion

This case study underscores the effectiveness of a streamlined, focused approach to OKRs in a high-growth, dynamic environment. Through disciplined objective setting and a more strategic approach to key results, Company XYZ witnessed a marked improvement in team focus and alignment.

Chapter 14: The Goal-Setting Tyranny

In the journey of implementing Objectives and Key Results, a critical yet often overlooked factor is the inherent diversity in how individuals approach goals.

This diversity in mindset plays a pivotal role in the successful integration and efficacy of OKRs in a business environment.

Understanding and accommodating the different mindsets towards goal setting is crucial for the successful adoption and effectiveness of OKRs within an organization.

Within any team, there are those who are intrinsically goal-driven, focusing keenly on the end results. Conversely, there are individuals who are process-driven, finding their stride in the journey towards achieving these goals.

This chapter delves into the unique challenges and strengths each of these orientations brings to the table, underscoring the importance of understanding and leveraging these differences for the effective implementation of OKRs.

The Goal-Oriented Mindset and OKRs

For goal-oriented individuals, the focus is predominantly on achieving specific outcomes. They are typically driven and motivated by the end achievements, making them naturally align with the objective-setting component of OKRs.

Challenges and Solutions for Goal-Oriented Individuals

While goal-oriented people excel in setting and striving for targets, they might underemphasize the importance of processes and sustainability. To address this, incorporate process and quality Key Results (KRs) alongside outcome KRs in their OKRs.

Encourage these individuals to consider the broader impacts of their goals, including team collaboration, long-term sustainability, and adaptability.

The Process-Oriented Mindset and OKRs

Individuals with a process-oriented mindset thrive in the journey towards an outcome. They value the experiences and learning gained through task execution, focusing on the 'how' of achieving objectives.

These individuals might find it challenging to commit to time-bound, specific goals. To assist them, break down overarching goals into short-term, achievable milestones that align with their process focus.

Help them see how their focus on processes can be integrated into the OKR framework by setting KRs that measure the efficiency, quality, and effectiveness of their processes.

Effective OKR Implementation

To successfully implement OKRs, it is essential to create an environment that values both goal and process orientations. A harmonious blend of these approaches cultivates a more comprehensive and effective goal-setting culture within an organization.

Strategies for Integrating Diverse Mindsets

1. **Inclusive OKR Workshops with Interactive Elements:** Conduct workshops that are specifically designed to engage both goal-oriented and process-oriented individuals. Incorporate interactive elements like group discussions and role-playing exercises to demonstrate the significance of both outcomes and the journey towards them.
2. **Customized Coaching with Tailored Tools:** Offer personalized coaching sessions, equipped with tools and resources that are tailored to individual orientations. This ensures that each person's unique approach to OKRs is recognized, understood, and developed to its fullest potential.
3. **Dynamic Feedback Mechanisms with Structured Formats:** Implement structured feedback sessions that encourage open dialogue and exchange of perspectives between different orientations. Utilize formats such as round-table discussions or peer review systems to foster a deeper understanding and appreciation of diverse approaches within the team.
4. **Celebrating All Forms of Success with Recognition Programs:** Develop a recognition program that celebrates both the achievement of specific goals and notable advancements in process efficiency. This could include awards, public acknowledgments, or even informal recognition in team meetings, emphasizing that both goal attainment and process refinement are vital to the organization's overall success.
5. **Cross-functional Team Collaboration:** Encourage collaboration between different departments or teams, where varied goal-setting orientations can naturally intersect and complement each other. This cross-pollination of ideas and methods can lead to more innovative approaches to OKRs.
6. **Regular OKR Review and Adaptation Sessions:** Schedule periodic sessions to review and adapt OKRs, ensuring they remain relevant and effective. These sessions should be forums for both goal-oriented and process-oriented team members to provide input on how the OKRs might be evolved to better align with organizational objectives and team dynamics.

Conclusion

The varying approaches to implementing OKRs, influenced by different goal and process orientations, necessitate thoughtful integration and consideration for effective adoption.

Leaders and coaches who recognize and adapt to these differences can establish a more dynamic, inclusive, and successful framework for setting and achieving goals.

Embracing and addressing these diverse approaches not only boosts the effectiveness of OKRs but also plays a key role in fostering a robust and flexible organizational culture.

OKRS FOR TEAMS

SECTION 3

Chapter 15: Setting Up Effective OKRs

Setting clear and actionable objectives is paramount. Objectives and Key Results have emerged as a powerful tool to bridge the gap between strategy and execution. However, crafting effective OKRs is an art that requires a deep understanding of strategy, challenges, and organizational capabilities.

This chapter delves into the intricacies of setting impactful OKRs and offers insights to avoid common pitfalls.

Strategy vs OKRs

OKRs are a byproduct of a well-thought-out strategy, not its precursor. A common misconception is that goals are set first, followed by the strategy to achieve them.

If we're distinguishing between goals and objectives, this might hold some weight. A goal can be likened to a strategic intent or product vision. However, objectives aren't just brainstormed; they bridge the gap between the current situation and the overarching goal.

Strategy involves assessing the current scenario, diagnosing issues, pinpointing key challenges, and designing a roadmap to tackle these challenges. Only after this groundwork can you define objectives to provide focus, direction, and a means to gauge progress.

Bad Objectives

Did you know that to achieve the EU's Net Zero goal by 2050, we would need to build a nuclear power plant every 20 days or install 1 million solar panels a day?

This is what's called a poor objective. It's arbitrary, impossible to achieve, and doesn't simplify the challenge. It's merely the challenge, expressed in positive terms. If the challenge is that we emit too much CO_2, the objective can't be to stop emitting CO_2.

An energy transition of this magnitude requires decades, not years. In fact, there are several economies in the world, such as China or India, that have not yet completed the energy transition from coal to oil, even after more than 100 years.

Behind that Net Zero objective, as commendable and necessary as it is, there is no strategy; it's pure political propaganda that doesn't help at all.

And the same happens in many organizations. If goals are as complex as the challenge itself, they lose effectiveness.

For instance, if the issue is a very low conversion rate, setting a goal like 'increase the conversion rate' is too vague.

A better approach would be to conduct a thorough analysis of the situation to identify specific areas for improvement. These areas then become our realistic and achievable objectives, leading us toward the ultimate goal of improving conversion.

Bad objectives can derail even the most promising strategies. Let's dissect some typical traps:

- **Arbitrariness:** *Objectives set without clear ties to challenges or organizational capabilities often stem from a lack of deep business understanding or an inability to view the organization as a cohesive system.*
- **Dispersion:** *Spreading efforts thin over too many objectives can lead to minimal progress in any direction, resulting in stress and demotivation.*
- **Disorder:** *Choosing the wrong objectives can misalign organizational efforts, leading to suboptimal or even counterproductive outcomes.*

Crafting Good Objectives

Good strategic objectives emerge from the complex problem-solving process of strategy. When leaders grapple with strategy, they're essentially bridging long-term ambitions with short-term actions. Effective objectives:

- *Simplify the original challenge, making it more manageable.*
- *Are achievable, albeit challenging.*
- *Offer clear choices, narrowing focus and defining what needs to be done (and what doesn't).*

Setting Effective OKRs

To set powerful OKRs, a strategic context is essential. Without it, product objectives risk being arbitrary, misguided, or even detrimental.

It's crucial to translate overarching goals into tangible strategies, identify challenges, and then set objectives and key results to track progress.

Example

Now, imagine your head of product, following up on the company's strategic guideline, defines the following overarching goal for the year: *"to be the reference in our sector for premium customers."*

While this might seem vague, it sets a clear and compelling direction. It's now up to each product team to define their product objectives in line with this vision.

Together with your product leader, all teams develop this product vision into a set of strategic themes:

- **Personalization** - Generate content relevant to the specific situation of each client.
- **Premium attention** - Ensure that customers find quick and effective solutions to any problem they may encounter at any point in the journey, without the need to call customer service.

These two strategic themes provide a clear path forward. Now, it's time to set the milestones that will bring us closer to this vision, guided by the product's strategic themes. This is where OKRs come into play.

For instance, under **Personalization**:

- *Offer discounts in ancillaries.*
- *Reduce steps in the checkout process.*
- *Increase the offer of relevant products for each client.*

Possible Key Results:

- *Increased retention.*
- *Increased CLTV.*

For **Premium attention**:

- *Deliver personalized, real-time insights into service disruptions.*
- *Proactively offer solutions to customers in the event of service disruption.*
- *Offer contextual information at each step of the journey.*

Possible Key Results:

- *Reduced number of calls to the call center due to service disruptions.*
- *Increased NPS.*
- *Increased retention.*
- *Increased CLTV.*

Defining Key Results

An objective inherently signifies forward movement or progress. It addresses the pivotal question: *"What advancement are you aiming for, be it in your personal life or your product?"*

It's advisable to frame objectives with a verb that indicates direction at the outset. Verbs such as "increase," "decrease," "eliminate," "improve," "maximize," or "minimize" can be particularly effective.

However, there are instances where an objective might not naturally start with such a verb. In these cases, it's crucial that the first Key Result (KR) clearly delineates the criteria for success. Take, for instance, the objective *"Offer personalized information in real time."* How do we gauge its achievement?

This is where KRs come into play, providing both a metric style and a specific target value. Examples include:

- *The number of calls to the call center resulting from service disruptions.*
- *The average duration required to provide a solution to the customer following a disruption.*

Validation Tests for OKRs

To guarantee the precision and ambition of your OKRs, I employ the following validation questions to assess for any ambiguity and to ensure they are suitably challenging.

Testing for Ambiguity

- *What do you want [insert goal here] for?*
- *How will you know you've achieved [insert goal here]?*
- *What will you see when [insert goal here]?*
- *How will you know things have improved enough that you don't need to pursue this goal anymore?*
- *Suppose you achieve [insert goal here], what difference would it make for the customer?*
- *How would that be helpful for the business?*

Testing for Ambitiousness

- *Imagine that you have achieved the goal. Tell me three things that will be different.*
- *What must be true to achieve the goal?*
- *What would customers say is different?*
- *What would be the first small thing you will do to demonstrate [insert goal here]?*

OKR Definition Template

There are many templates out there for defining OKRs, all quite similar in nature. If you have one that you prefer, feel free to continue its use. However, I urge you to give my template a chance, as it requires a connection to the higher strategic level, explains why this objective is important now, identifies dependencies, limits, and necessary requirements for the objective to be achieved within the expected time span.

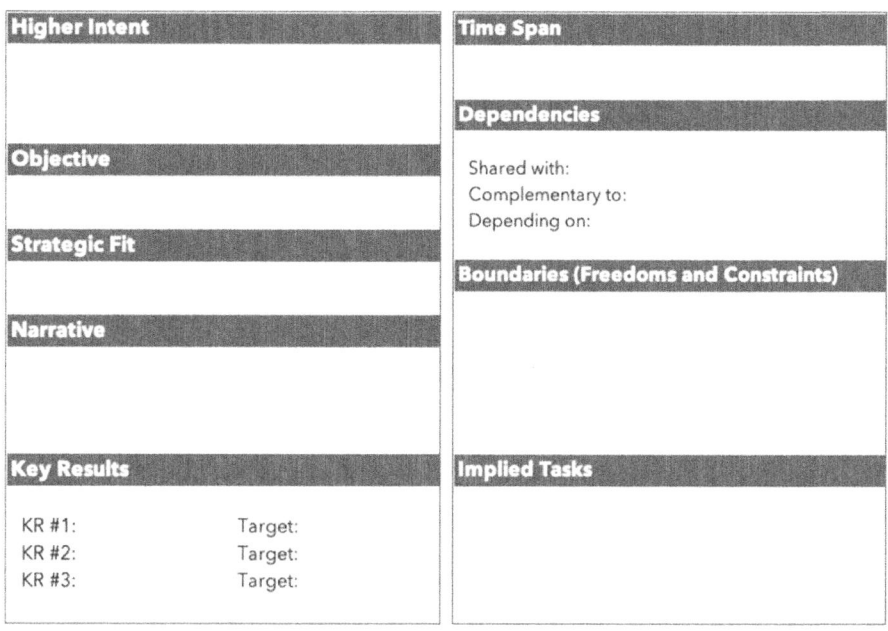

Figure 23 - OKR definition template

Next, we'll break down each element of our OKR definition template in detail. Following this, the next chapter will present a comprehensive case study, illustrating how these principles are applied in practice.

Higher Intent

We begin by outlining the strategy that informs our objective-setting process, which we refer to as 'higher intent'. This term represents our overarching strategic direction. Depending on the situation, its interpretation varies:

- For one of several product teams, 'higher intent' refers to the specific product strategy.
- For the Head of Product, it points to the broader organizational strategy.

This section is designed to offer strategic context that helps guide and shape the formulation of our objectives. It should be concise, ideally not exceeding 3-4 sentences.

Objective

A concise, one-sentence objective statement.

Strategic Fit

In this part, we detail how the objective aligns with the overarching strategy. It's important to clearly articulate how this specific objective contributes to advancing the broader strategy and meeting its goals. As discussed earlier, this section may also include the strategic themes associated with the objective.

It's crucial to clearly outline the objective's connection to higher-level goals (vertical alignment) or to the goals of other teams (horizontal alignment).

Narrative

If you've thoroughly prepared, you'll be able to justify your choice of this specific objective over others, and why it's important to tackle it now rather than later.

While the previous point clarified the strategic fit, this section is about elucidating the rationale behind the choice. Given the myriad of opportunities and challenges that could further the higher-level strategy, it's crucial to articulate the reasons for selecting this particular objective.

Key Results

In this section, we list the Key Results along with the specific target that determines their achievement.

While there are various scoring systems available, I personally prefer a straightforward approach as it avoids subjective discussions and interpretations, which can be unprofessional and simplistic. The target is either met or not. If it's achieved, great; if not, it's crucial to analyze the reasons behind this outcome. This analysis helps in deciding whether it makes sense to continue with this objective or if there is a need to revise our approach to keep pursuing it.

The simplicity of this method ensures clarity and objectivity in assessing the progress towards each Key Result. It enables a clear focus on outcomes rather than just activities, aligning efforts directly with the overarching strategic goals.

Time Span

It is advisable that objectives are time-bound. It could be a month, a quarter, or a year.

However, it's crucial to remember that we do not know when the objective will be achieved. What we are indicating here is how long we expect to work on achieving this objective.

For example, it could be a startup needing a certain ARR figure to secure the next funding round, or capturing a market segment before competition launches its new product.

Dependencies

Here we identify dependencies on other teams within the organization.

It could be a shared objective with another team, a complementary objective to another team to achieve a higher-level objective, or a dependency on another team to achieve the expected result.

Boundaries (Freedoms and Constraints)

Here you should provide any further guidance about boundaries, especially the constraints to be observed, and indicate future decisions that may have to be taken.

This assists people in thinking ahead and alerts them to things on the horizon they may not be aware of.

Constraints not only define boundaries but also help clarify what is desired by explicitly stating what is not wanted.

Questions to consider:

- *Have I covered all the boundaries, so the team understands what is off-limits?*
- *Were conflicting goals from stakeholders and other units considered?*
- *Have I made the choices that enable the team to make trade-offs?*
- *Am I clear about the decision-making authority of the team?*
- *Is it clear about how we will interact with other parts of the company?*
- *What is really outside the control of the team?*

Implied Tasks

It's important to note that we're not discussing initiatives, projects, or features at this stage; those elements will be addressed later during the product roadmap and backlog development. In this part, we're effectively communicating our needs to our higher-ups.

It's about clearly stating, *'To achieve this objective, I require your support in these specific areas.'*

For instance, this might involve requesting the hiring of a particular skill set, providing training for the team, setting up a collaboration with a partner, or engaging a service provider. Additionally, it's an opportunity to detail any necessary actions to address dependencies highlighted in the relevant section.

Strategic Context Creation for Effective OKR Definition

As discussed in the first section of this book, a common challenge teams face is the task of defining objectives without a clear underlying strategy. This situation is not only prevalent but also problematic.

Many OKR experts suggest initiating the OKR definition process by asking teams to define their mission, which then leads to the setting of objectives. However, this approach, rather than being helpful, can often be counterproductive and even hazardous. It can lead to misaligned objectives that don't truly support the organization's broader goals.

If you find yourself in this situation, it becomes your responsibility to create a strategic context that enables your team to effectively define OKRs for the upcoming period. This is where the 'DNA Canvas' tool, which we frequently use in such scenarios, becomes invaluable.

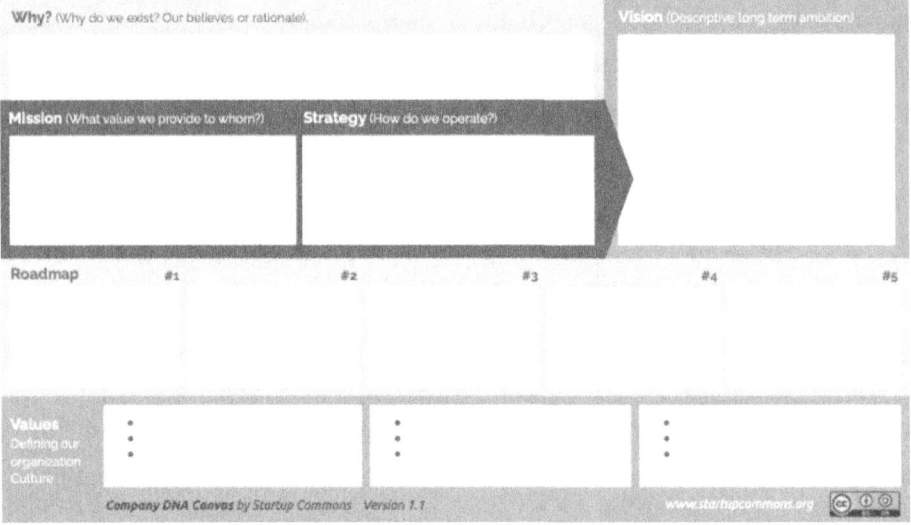

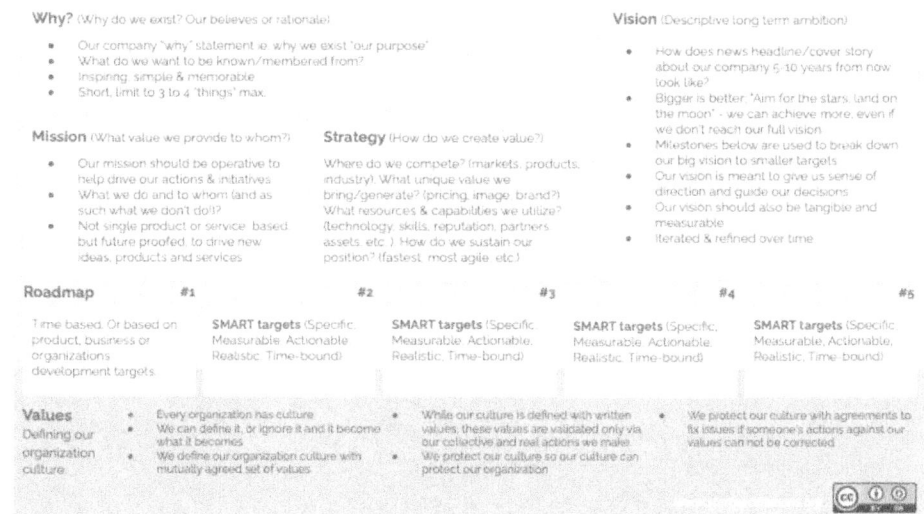

The process involves organizing a series of workshops where you, along with your manager and other key stakeholders, work to define crucial elements like the WHY, MISSION, STRATEGY, and VISION of your team. These workshops are not mere formalities but are essential in aligning the team's understanding and approach towards its goals.

Post these discussions, it's crucial to validate these elements with stakeholders and related teams. This step ensures that the defined strategic elements are not only in sync with your team's perspective but also align with broader organizational objectives and the expectations of external stakeholders.

Once you have this validation, you can proceed to define your OKRs, following the guidelines laid out in the ROADMAP section previously discussed. It's important to note that the ROADMAP referred to here is not the typical product roadmap. Instead, it pertains to the outcomes or objectives your team aims to pursue in the forthcoming period.

This approach ensures that your OKRs are grounded in a solid strategic foundation, making them more likely to be relevant, achievable, and impactful.

Conclusion

Crafting effective OKRs is a blend of art and science. It demands a profound grasp of your strategy, challenges, and the capabilities of your organization. By steering clear of typical missteps and formulating concise, actionable objectives, product leaders can elevate their products to new heights of success.

In my role as a product coach with a focus on discovery and strategy, I've witnessed the remarkable impact that well-executed OKRs can have. Embrace this approach and observe the remarkable growth and success it can bring to your product.

Chapter 16: Blueprint for Creating Team-Level OKRs

The journey from high-level organizational goals to actionable team-level OKRs is a nuanced process. It requires a deep understanding of strategic alignment, cross-functional dependencies, and a relentless focus on outcomes rather than outputs.

Drawing on insights from my previous work, including the notable case of Sportmatic, this chapter outlines a detailed process for defining team-level OKRs. Here, I'll provide practical steps, enriched with examples and tips, to ensure teams are not just setting goals but are on a path to real achievement.

In my experience, most organizations initially attempt to implement OKRs independently. Often, they aim to use OKRs to sharpen their focus but end up establishing an overwhelming number of them. Others seek to leverage OKRs for enhancing cross-functional alignment and mitigating the effects of organizational silos. Paradoxically, these organizations typically delineate teams according to their organizational structure and then isolate the OKR drafting process within these defined silos.

To guide my clients in circumventing these prevalent challenges and in crafting effective OKRs, I have refined and adapted a seven-step process for creating team-level OKRs. This approach is inspired by and diverges from the methodology presented in *'The OKRs Field Book'* by Ben Lamorte.[20] The primary distinctions in my adaptation appear in steps 1, 4, and 5, where I incorporate strategic context into the OKR formulation—a facet not explicitly addressed by Ben. Additionally, I have incorporated enhancements and insights gleaned from my professional experience into the other steps to further enrich the process.

Seven Steps for Defining and Aligning Team-Level OKRs

1. Higher Intent
2. Dependencies
3. Develop Objectives
4. Describe Strategic Fit and Narrative
5. Draft Key Results
6. Refine Key Results
7. Validate Key Results

The seven steps are not meant to be perfectly sequential. Once you draft and refine KRs it's recommended to review objective definition, and after getting feedback from management, stakeholders, and other teams it is likely that you have to go through the process again and make some minor adjustments.

Example

Here is one of the OKRs we developed with Sportmatic's Marketing Team after completing these seven steps:

Higher Intent	Sell 10,000 licenses in the US market for tier-2 clients (highs schools and universities) in 2022
Dependencies	We depend on sales, product, and customer success. Sales and finance depend on us.
Objective	Create a consistent flow of qualified leads
Strategic Fit	To successfully penetrate the tier-2 US market, the company needs to adopt a dual strategy: an outbound sales distribution model, complemented by a concerted effort in brand awareness and an online marketing strategy focused on lead generation.
Narrative	Facing formidable competitors in the US market, our strategy is to carve out a niche in the tier-2 segment by capitalizing on our robust brand presence in the premium market. We plan to achieve this by blending a traditional outbound approach with a robust online lead generation strategy.
Key Results	• Avg. new leads per month > 500 by Q3 • Keep overall cost per lead (CAC) below $200. • More than 30% of quality of leads as measured by those that convert to opportunity within four weeks of creation.

Sportmatic's Marketing Team's journey through these steps is a testament to the effectiveness of this approach. Their objectives and Key Results not only aligned with the company's strategic goals but also fostered inter-team collaboration and accountability. By focusing on qualified lead generation and brand awareness, they could address both immediate and long-term market challenges.

Next sections break down the steps we took to develop their OKRs.

1 – Higher Intent

I highly advise initiating the OKR formulation process by articulating your team's overarching intention. This 'higher intent' serves as the foundation for aligning your team's objectives with the broader strategic direction of the organization.

For leaders such as Heads of Product or Business Units, it's imperative to anchor this section in the company's broader strategy and overarching goals. This approach ensures that the team's efforts are not only synchronized with the company's vision but also contribute significantly to its strategic objectives.

On the other hand, if you are crafting OKRs for a specific product team, this segment should distinctly outline the strategy and goals specific to your product. This clarity is crucial for ensuring that the team's actions are tightly coupled with the product's strategic direction and intended outcomes.

Taking the case study of Sportmatic's Marketing Team as an example, their 'higher intent' was meticulously defined to reflect their specific role within the larger organizational framework.

> *Sell 10,000 licenses in the US market for tier 2 clients (highs schools and universities) of our new integrated solution for technical staff.*

This approach provided a clear, strategic direction for their OKRs, ensuring alignment with both the company's and the product's strategic objectives.

2 – Dependencies

In achieving exceptional results, cross-team collaboration is usually a key ingredient. While some organizations establish cross-functional squads for this purpose, others shape their team-level OKRs following the structure of their organizational chart.

Regardless of the method used to define OKR teams, it's crucial to allocate time at the onset of each OKR cycle to pinpoint and understand interdependencies among teams. When a team heavily relies on another for success, it's beneficial to involve key individuals from those external teams in the planning process. Their insights often contribute to the development of dependent key results or even shared OKRs, enhancing cross-functional alignment and cooperation.

It's a common temptation to bypass this step of alignment verification, but experience shows that spending some time to recognize external dependencies can significantly streamline the OKR process. This practice ensures that teams are not working in isolation but are attuned to the broader organizational dynamics.

Illustrating this approach, let's consider the outcome of Step 2 as applied by our case study's marketing team at Sportmatic. They invested time in this crucial step, leading to a more integrated and effective set of OKRs that not only served their team's goals but also aligned well with the company's overall objectives.

> **We depend on ...**
>
> - Product to outline the roadmap, provide dates and develop the product.
>
> - Sales to call new leads and provide intel about competitors, what clients we win and what clients we lose.
>
> - Customer success to create happy customers that agree to be featured in marketing collateral.
>
> **These teams depend on us ...**
>
> - Sales team needs us to provide qualified leads.
>
> - Finance team needs us to report cost per lead.

3. Develop Objectives

Once alignment has been established, it's time for the team to embark on drafting objectives. Leveraging the higher intent as a backdrop is instrumental in shaping team-level OKRs. However, crafting team-level objectives is an exercise in strategic thinking and requires more than just a straightforward approach.

It's crucial to move away from the direct cascade approach where higher-level key results are simply replicated as team objectives. This method tends to overlook the unique context and challenges of each team, leading to less effective and uninspired objectives.

Creating team-level objectives is as much an art as it is a science, and it benefits greatly from guided principles. To assist your clients in this creative yet structured process, we recommend adhering to these three guidelines:

- **Conciseness**: Frame each objective as a single, clear sentence. This helps in maintaining focus and clarity.
- **Action-Oriented**: Start each objective with an action verb, which instills a sense of purpose and direction.
- **Focus on Improvement**: Ensure that the objectives target areas of growth or improvement, rather than merely maintaining the status quo.

After finalizing a set of objectives, it's crucial to perform the validation tests for ambitiousness and ambiguity, as outlined in the previous chapter. This step is key to refining the objectives, ensuring they are strong, relevant, and in harmony with the broader goals of the organization.

4. Strategic Fit and Narrative

Once the objectives are set, allocate a focused period, ideally between 15 to 30 minutes, for teams to construct three to five sentences that delve into two crucial aspects: the strategic fit of the objective within the broader scope of the higher intent and the narrative that underscores its current significance.

This exercise isn't just about elaborating on the objective; it's pivotal to explicitly articulate the connections of the objective. These connections can be vertical, linking directly to overarching company goals, or horizontal, aligning with the objectives of parallel teams. This clarity in alignment helps in understanding the broader impact and relevance of the objectives.

Take, for example, the marketing team in our Sportmatic case study. Their objective was intricately woven into the fabric of the company's broader strategy, displaying a vertical alignment with the company's overarching sales goals. At the same time, it demonstrated a horizontal alignment with the sales team's objectives, particularly in the generation of qualified leads. This dual connection highlights the multidimensional nature of well-crafted objectives.

To further illustrate this, here are two additional OKRs formulated during the objective setting phase for Sportmatic's marketing team:

Objective	*Develop a strong brand awareness in the US tier-2 market.*
Strategic Fit	*Our strategy involves capitalizing on our established premium brand to position ourselves as leaders in the tier-2 market, a segment currently occupied by lower quality competitors.*
Narrative	*By building robust brand awareness, we'll not only support our sales team but also enhance both the quality and quantity of our leads.*

Objective	*Improve our online marketing readiness.*
Strategic Fit	*To penetrate the high school and university market, we need to explore new channels and implement innovative online strategies.*
Narrative	*To achieve both strong brand awareness and a steady stream of qualified leads, proficiency in the latest techniques, technologies, and channels (like TikTok, Instagram, and YouTube) is crucial. To this end, we must focus on training our team and hiring new talent with expertise in these areas.*

These examples underscore how objectives, when thoughtfully crafted, serve as vital links connecting various facets of an organization's strategy and operational goals.

Each objective definition clearly illustrates how it aligns with the higher intent of the organization, ensuring vertical integration with overarching goals. Simultaneously, it demonstrates how the objective aids other teams, highlighting horizontal alignment and fostering cross-team collaboration. Additionally, the rationale behind the importance and timing of each objective is articulated, emphasizing their relevance and urgency in the current organizational context.

5. Draft Key Results

Drafting objectives is typically straightforward, but formulating key results often presents a greater challenge, as they need to be precise and quantifiable. To illustrate, consider the following examples of draft key results. These were developed during the fourth step of our process with the marketing team in our Sportmatic case study:

1. Limit cost of leads to less than $200
2. X number of followers on TikTok by Q3
3. Reduce conversion time from 4 weeks to 3 weeks by Q4

These examples showcase how key results, when carefully crafted, encapsulate specific, measurable outcomes that directly stem from the objectives, offering clear indicators of progress and success.

Here are some valuable tips to keep in mind when defining Key Results (KRs):

- **Focus on Outcome Quality:** In the forthcoming step, we emphasize the importance of not only defining but also measuring the quality of the outcome. This ensures that the KRs truly reflect the impact and effectiveness of the efforts.
- **Specify Baselines:** When articulating a key result, go beyond simply stating an improvement goal like "Increase metric A to Y." Instead, include the starting point to give a clear picture of the intended progress. For instance, "Increase metric A from X to Y." This approach provides a more comprehensive understanding of the expected growth or change.

6. Refine Key Results

Key results should function cohesively, forming the essential set of vital metrics that collectively articulate the accomplishment of an objective. It's important to avoid redundancy; if all key results are highly correlated, they may not add distinct value. Ideally, each key result should contribute uniquely, with a well-rounded set of key results narrating different aspects of the objective's story.

Progress and Quality

Teams adept in utilizing OKRs typically craft key results that not only track progress but also assess quality. This dual focus ensures a more holistic approach to measuring success.

In our case study with Sportmatic's marketing team, an exemplary demonstration of this principle can be seen in their drafting of key results. Here are two key results they developed, one focusing on progress and the other on quality, for their specified objective:

> **Progress key result:**
>
> - *Avg. new leads per month > 500 by Q3*
>
> **Quality key results:**
>
> - *Keep overall cost per lead below $200.*
>
> - *More than 30% of quality of leads as measured by those that convert to opportunity within four weeks of creation.*

These examples highlight the team's skill in creating a balanced set of key results, each offering a unique perspective on the objective's fulfillment.

When a team concentrates solely on a progress key result, like increasing lead quantity, there's a risk of compromising the quality and cost-effectiveness of those leads. By incorporating a comprehensive set of key results, teams can maintain a balanced focus on both the quantity and quality of leads.

Leading and Lagging Indicators

Effective use of OKRs often involves defining key results that encompass both leading and lagging indicators. This concept is explored in greater detail in chapter 18. Leading indicators, typically more controllable, are often seen as inputs. They provide early insights into performance and can be adjusted more readily. In contrast, lagging indicators, generally considered as outputs, may be less controllable, especially in the short term.

Examples of lagging indicators include fundamental business metrics such as revenue, profit, and Net Promoter Score (NPS). On the other hand, leading indicators might encompass metrics like the number of new leads generated, website traffic, and conversion rates on landing pages.

To illustrate the application of this approach, let's examine how Sportmatic's marketing team might effectively balance leading and lagging indicators in their OKRs:

> **Leading indicator key result:**
>
> - *Drive conversion rate on landing pages to 5% by Q2*
>
> **Lagging indicator key result:**
>
> - *Drive marketing contribution to pipeline from $500K to $1 million.*

In this scenario, the marketing team is poised to immediately start working on developing a high-quality landing page. However, it's important to recognize that the impact of an enhanced conversion rate on the overall sales pipeline might not be instantaneous. It could take several months before these improvements meaningfully influence the pipeline metrics.

The creation of a high-converting landing page is a proactive step that is expected to drive an increase in the pipeline. In this context, the landing page conversion rate serves as the leading indicator or input. It represents an actionable metric that the team can directly influence and monitor in the near term. Meanwhile, the effect on the pipeline is the lagging indicator or output. This lagging indicator is a result of the cumulative effect of various inputs, including the improved landing page, and tends to manifest over a longer period.

Therefore, in setting their OKRs, the marketing team effectively aligns these two types of indicators – the immediate, controllable action of enhancing the landing page (leading indicator), and the subsequent, broader impact on the sales pipeline (lagging indicator). This alignment ensures a strategic and measured approach to achieving their objectives.

Assessing Key Results Effectiveness

To ascertain the effectiveness of Key Results, it's crucial to evaluate them against a set of guiding questions. These questions help ensure that the KRs are not only aligned with the objective but also comprehensive and practical. Here are three pivotal questions to consider:

- **Objective Achievement**: If all the key results are successfully met, will the associated objective be considered fully achieved? This question helps ensure that the KRs collectively cover all aspects necessary for the complete realization of the objective.
- **Simplicity and Focus**: Can the set of key results be streamlined? This question encourages a focus on essential metrics, avoiding the complexity that can arise from too many KRs. The goal is to identify the minimal yet comprehensive set of KRs that can effectively measure the success of the objective.
- **Comprehensiveness of Metrics**: Do the key results adequately capture both progress and quality? Are they inclusive of both leading (inputs) and lagging

(outputs) indicators? This ensures a balanced approach, considering both immediate, actionable metrics and long-term outcomes.

As the process of developing key results progresses, it's important to periodically re-evaluate the objective itself. The seven steps outlined for OKR formulation are not rigidly sequential; they are iterative and should be revisited to ensure alignment and relevance as the OKRs evolve. This iterative approach guarantees that the objectives and key results remain aligned with the team's and organization's evolving needs and goals.

7. Validate Key Results

Before finalizing and sharing OKRs, it's crucial to use the characteristics of effective key results as a final checklist to refine them. This checklist ensures that the key results are well-crafted, clear, and aligned with the set objectives. The characteristics of effective key results include:

1. **Specificity**: Ensure language clarity to avoid ambiguity. Specific key results provide a clear direction and make it easier to gauge progress.
2. **Measurability**: Key results should be quantifiable. The progress towards these results should be objectively measurable, not based on subjective opinions.
3. **Outcome-Oriented**: Focus on outcomes or results, not just tasks or activities. Key results should reflect the impact or change that results from completing tasks.
4. **Aspirational**: Set ambitious goals. Higher targets often inspire greater effort and lead to more significant achievements, even if the ultimate goal isn't fully met.
5. **Scorability**: Apply confidence scores and/or specific targets. This helps manage expectations and provides a quantitative measure of progress.

After refining the key results, conduct a final review to confirm their alignment with the objectives. Before publishing, we advise teams to share their OKRs with other relevant teams and senior leadership. This step is essential for ensuring vertical alignment and obtaining final approval.

Once the OKRs are approved, it's important to publish them in a single, accessible location. This practice ensures transparency and provides a reference point for all team members and stakeholders involved in the OKR process.

Chapter 17: How Many OKRs Are Enough

When it comes to Objectives and Key Results, there's a pervasive challenge that many teams grapple with—OKR overload. It's a common trap: equating more OKRs with more progress.

But here's a thought that may seem counterintuitive at first blush: having a multitude of OKRs can be less effective than having none at all. I've observed this pattern unfold time and time again.

The optimal range for OKRs is surprisingly narrow: one to three per team. Any more, and you're likely veering off course.

Why Do We Have So Many OKRs?

So, why do teams end up with too many OKRs? It typically stems from a fundamental misunderstanding of the purpose of OKRs. They aren't just another box to check; they're beacons, guiding your team toward your product vision through strategic milestones. But when they're misaligned or misunderstood, they become castles in the sky—impressive to imagine but impossible to inhabit.

Many teams create OKRs by gathering around the whiteboard, throwing ideas at it to see what sticks, and then voting for the favorites. But this method often results in a glut of OKRs that are, at best, tangentially related to the team's true purpose and, at worst, completely irrelevant.

The Fallacy of Prioritizing OKRs

Some propose a simple fix: prioritize your OKRs. Begin with the most important one, then the next, and so on. This approach might seem logical, but it's akin to applying a bandage to a deep wound—it addresses the symptom, not the underlying issue.

Prioritization doesn't work because it's based on the same flawed premise that led to too many OKRs in the first place: a lack of clear understanding of the team's primary challenges. Without that understanding, you can't effectively prioritize.

Having too many OKRs isn't a sign that your team needs better prioritization; it's a sign that your team lacks a clear, cohesive strategy. This is a diagnosis problem, not a prioritization problem. Just as a doctor diagnoses an illness before prescribing treatment, a team must diagnose its strategic challenges before setting OKRs.

Lack of Strategy: The Core Problem

The crux of the matter is that OKRs are meant to be a strategy execution tool, not the strategy itself. A sound product strategy involves defining your playing field and planning how to win. This clarity illuminates key challenges, which in turn inform your OKRs.

Without this foundation, even the most well-intentioned OKR-setting exercises are doomed to fail.

However, possessing a clear and compelling strategy is not a foolproof safeguard against missteps. The ensuing sections will delineate common errors that, if not avoided, can lead to an overwhelming proliferation of OKRs, undermining their intended efficacy.

Misguided OKRs: Confusing Goals with Plans

Another common misstep is using OKRs to articulate plans or initiatives instead of strategic goals. This confusion results from the absence of an effective product roadmap.

Strategy should lead to goals, and goals should inform the roadmap.

If your team already has a predefined delivery roadmap, I advise taking the time to reverse-engineer the OKRs based on your list of initiatives. This process can lead to insightful discoveries, such as uncovering misalignments, contradictions, or even potentially detrimental goals within your team's current pursuits.

The 'Business as Usual' OKR Trap

OKRs should focus on strategic outcomes that drive the business and product forward. They aren't meant to track routine operations or "business as usual." Your daily dashboard metrics are important, but they shouldn't all be OKRs.

Reserve OKRs for extraordinary efforts to change or improve those metrics significantly.

While your team may be equipped with a dashboard to monitor key metrics daily, it's not necessary to set OKRs for each metric.

Consider the Conversion Rate on your website, for example. Your objective might be to sustain a rate above 5%. Should the rate consistently hover around 6%, your routine processes are effectively maintaining the status quo. However, if that rate were to dip to 4%, it signals a need for strategic intervention.

In such instances, crafting a targeted OKR becomes crucial to realign efforts and steer performance back to desired levels.

Crafting Effective OKRs

If you find your team without a strategy and under pressure to define OKRs, I recommend Richard Rumelt's 'Kernel of Strategy' framework we have seen in previous chapters.

The framework consists of identifying a challenge, conducting a diagnostic, establishing a guiding policy, and then executing coherent actions. This sequence is crucial for the transition from strategy to OKRs.

Navigating the Storm - A Tale of Strategic Transformation

In the bustling world of FinTech, a mid-sized company, found itself at a crossroads. let's refer to the company as "AlphaTech," a prominent entity in the FinTech sector.

Despite having a talented team and a solid market presence, they were struggling to outpace competitors. As their newly appointed Product Strategy Coach, I recognized the urgent need for a clear, impactful strategy and effective OKRs to guide their journey.

Challenge: AlphaTech's main challenge was twofold: their product was losing market share to more innovative competitors, and internally, there was a lack of cohesive direction. The leadership team was under immense pressure to revitalize their product line and regain their competitive edge.

Diagnostic: My initial analysis revealed that AlphaTech's product development efforts were scattered, with teams working in silos, often pursuing conflicting goals. There was a palpable absence of a unifying strategic vision. Using Rumelt's framework, I conducted a series of workshops to dissect the company's current market position, internal capabilities, and the evolving needs of their customers.

Guiding Policy: From the insights gained, we formulated a guiding policy focused on *"Capturing Increased Market Share among Small to Medium-Sized Enterprises (SMEs)."*

This policy aimed to realign the company's efforts towards developing features that addressed emerging market trends and SMEs pain points, thus differentiating AlphaTech from its competitors.

Coherent Actions: To translate this policy into action, we identified three critical OKRs:

1. *Objective: Boost Market Share Among SMEs*
    - *Key Result 1: Achieve a 20% increase in SME customer base within the next year.*
    - *Key Result 2: Increase feature adoption among SMEs by 30% following the launch of new SME-tailored features by the end of Q3.*
2. *Objective: Improve User Retention and Service Usage*

- Key Result 1: Increase user retention rate by 25% over the next two quarters.
- Key Result 2: Enhance user activity, targeting a 35% increase in monthly usage per user.

3. **Objective: Innovate Product Offerings to Match SME Needs**
   - Key Result 1: Conduct comprehensive market research to identify top three SME-specific demands by the next quarter.
   - Key Result 2: Implement a feedback loop with SME clients to refine product features, aiming for a 30% increase in positive feedback.

Each of these objectives was strategically chosen to foster innovation, enhance operational efficiency, and broaden market influence, adhering to our guiding policy.

Implementation: The journey wasn't without its challenges. We had to recalibrate certain key results as we gained more insights. Cross-functional collaboration was intensified, with regular check-ins to ensure alignment with our guiding policy. The product roadmap was meticulously updated to reflect our coherent actions.

Outcome: Nine months following the implementation of our targeted strategy, AlphaTech's transformation was distinctly visible. The focused approach to capture increased market share among SMEs led to a marked improvement in our customer base within this segment. The launch of new features tailored to SME needs not only enhanced product adoption by 20% but also played a pivotal role in elevating user retention and service utilization. The streamlined product offerings, aligned with SME-specific demands, resonated well with our target audience, contributing to a substantial increase in monthly usage per user.

Reflection: AlphaTech's story is a testament to the power of a well-orchestrated strategy, underpinned by carefully crafted OKRs. By adopting Richard Rumelt's *'Kernel of Strategy'* approach, we were able to transform a directionless team into a cohesive unit, united by a common goal and clear roadmap. The experience highlighted the importance of not just setting OKRs, but grounding them in a solid, strategic foundation.

How Many OKRs are Enough?

If you've taken to heart the advice above, you'll likely find that your OKR-setting process naturally yields a handful of actionable goals. In the rare case that it doesn't, you're equipped to discern which OKRs truly matter and can postpone the rest for future planning.

Adhering to the 1-3 OKR range per team is a sound practice, ensuring that each OKR is significant and manageable.

Conclusion

In conclusion, the mantra 'less is more' holds particularly true when it comes to setting OKRs. Too many OKRs can dilute focus, misdirect resources, and muddle your strategic direction.

Recognizing common pitfalls and adopting a structured approach to defining OKRs helps teams avoid feeling overwhelmed and stay in line with their overarching product strategy.

The key focus should not be on achieving as many objectives as possible, but on realizing those that truly impact your product and business. A simple, strategic, and focused approach can significantly enhance your team's effectiveness.

Chapter 18: Turning Strategy into Action

In the world of executive and personal coaching, a well-regarded adage emphasizes the essence of goal setting: *"Accurately defining the objectives constitutes 80% of the coaching process."*

This insightful maxim underscores the significance of precise and thoughtful objective formulation, which is not merely a preparatory step but rather a critical determinant of the entire coaching journey's success. It highlights that the art and science of setting the right goals are fundamental to navigating the path toward personal and organizational development.

The Foundation of Effective Goal Setting

The common pitfall in defining objectives without an underlying strategy is akin to navigating without a compass. Equally detrimental is the misconception of conflating objectives with the strategy itself.

Without distinguishing between strategy and objectives, the foundation of your OKRs could be skewed. For those grappling with this distinction, it's beneficial to explore previous chapters that elucidate what strategy entails, including the nature of strategy, common strategic pitfalls, and the principles of sound strategy.

In an ideal world, effective strategy seamlessly translates into well-defined goals. Yet, reality often presents a different scenario. Teams frequently encounter inputs that are less than ideal for shaping their OKRs and roadmaps — ranging from vague growth objectives and ambiguous goals to overly concrete solutions, and sometimes, even a complete absence of guidance.

In this chapter, I will unveil five practical techniques designed to empower your product team. These strategies are crafted to help you define meaningful OKRs and an effective product roadmap, irrespective of the challenges posed by the initial input.

Whether you're grappling with unclear directives or a lack of direction, these methods will guide you in carving out a clear path towards achieving your product vision.

The Role of Strategic Themes in OKRs

Strategic themes, or guiding policies, are the vital precursors to both OKRs and the roadmap. They provide the strategic bedrock upon which OKRs are built.

For instance, a product vision such as *"to be the premier choice in our sector for premium customers"* requires an understanding of your competitive standing, capabilities, and shortcomings. Strategic themes might emerge as personalization and premium attention, which then guide the formulation of your OKRs.

Examples of strategic theme-driven objectives might include:

- For Personalization:
  - Enhance search engine optimization (SEO).
  - Streamline the checkout process.
  - Expand the range of products tailored to each customer.
- For Premium Attention:
  - Provide personalized, real-time updates on service issues.
  - Proactively propose solutions during service disruptions.
  - Offer contextual support at every step of the customer journey.

These objectives, complemented with specific Key Results (KRs), quantify the extent of their achievement, and align closely with the strategic themes.

Crafting and Refining Objectives

When defining objectives, it is recommended to use action-oriented, directional verbs such as increase, decrease, eliminate, or maximize. This method ensures that objectives are forward-moving and progress-focused. If an objective cannot be naturally expressed with such a verb, ensure that the first Key Result is a definitive measure of success.

For example, an objective like *"Offer personalized information in real time"* might be rephrased into more specific goals or complemented with KRs that clearly define success metrics, such as the number of service disruption-related calls or the average resolution time for incidents.

Definition of Objectives

A goal implies progress. It answers the question *"what progress are you trying to achieve in your life or product?"*

Therefore, it is recommended that objectives are expressed in a sentence that begins with a direction verb. For example: *increase, decrease, eliminate, improve, maximize, or minimize.*

For those objectives that we cannot express with a direction verb, it will be essential that the first Key Result (KR) be a necessary and sufficient condition to determine success.

Defining Success

When we define the objectives, a fundamental best practice is to select objectives that are within the scope of our boundaries of action, and the same for the Key Results.

It is a very common dysfunction for product teams to have business objectives such as improving revenue or reducing costs. This is a problem for many reasons, but above all because these indicators can fluctuate due to many factors outside the team's control.

The recommendation here is to identify the product objectives that will allow us to achieve the business objectives. For example: conversion, retention, CLTV, shopping cart size, etc.

But that is not all. In addition, it must be considered that in the scope of the product there will be lagging indicators and leading indicators.

It is recommended that the lagging indicator be directly associated with the objective (even in its very definition) and that the leading indicators be the Key Results (KR).

Key Considerations in OKR Development

As we delve into the specifics of OKR development, it's essential to focus on a few key considerations that can significantly impact their effectiveness and relevance. These considerations help in crafting OKRs that are not only achievable but also meaningful in driving the desired outcomes.

Scope of Objectives and Key Results

It's imperative to select objectives and KRs that fall within your team's actionable boundaries. A common pitfall is setting broad business goals for product teams, which can lead to a misalignment of efforts. Instead, focus should be placed on product-specific objectives that contribute meaningfully to the broader business goals. This approach ensures that the OKRs are directly relevant to the team's work and capabilities.

Business Metrics vs. Product Metrics

Distinguishing between business metrics and product metrics is crucial when defining product OKRs. While business metrics provide an overarching view of the company's performance, product metrics delve into the specifics of product performance and user engagement. Establish a framework of product metrics to effectively evaluate the success of roadmap initiatives and objectives. This distinction helps in aligning the product team's work with the company's broader objectives, while also providing clarity on the direct impact of product initiatives.

Lagging vs. Leading Indicators

Understanding the difference between lagging and leading indicators is vital. Lagging indicators, typically associated with objectives, reflect outcomes that have already occurred. In contrast, leading indicators, often used as KRs, are predictive and can directly influence future performance. This understanding allows teams to set KRs that are proactive and forward-looking, helping to drive the team towards achieving the set objectives.

Navigating Ambiguities and Ambitions in Goals

In setting OKRs, ambiguities and over-ambition are common pitfalls.

To clarify objectives, ask probing questions about their purpose, how you'll measure their achievement, and what changes will indicate success.

Similarly, in setting ambitious goals, ensure they are grounded in reality and achievable within your team's capabilities.

Differentiating Objectives from Roadmap Themes

A crucial aspect of OKR planning is distinguishing between objectives (what you aim to achieve) and roadmap themes (what actions you'll take). This distinction helps maintain clarity in your strategy and execution plans.

Figure 24 - Outcome-based Roadmap Theme

In the provided example, we examine a representative roadmap theme that effectively bridges the gap between the set objective and the identified opportunities. These opportunities are articulated as epics, accompanied by proposals for specific solutions.

This approach demonstrates how strategic objectives can be translated into actionable plans, aligning broader goals with detailed, implementable steps.

Turning Ambiguous Goals into Meaningful OKRs

Transforming an ambiguous or overly ambitious goal into effective OKRs might seem complex, but it becomes much more manageable with the right approach.

Consider a scenario where your product faces low user engagement, leading to churn, and you're planning the next OKR cycle. You wouldn't simply set an OKR like *'Improve Engagement.'*

As we've seen, goals shouldn't be as complex as the challenges they address. The focus should be on thoroughly understanding the challenge, diagnosing the situation, and identifying strategic hypotheses to address it. Always ask, *'What needs to be true to validate this hypothesis?'*

Using a Structured Approach

Transforming an ambiguous or overly ambitious goal into effective OKRs can be simplified with a structured approach.

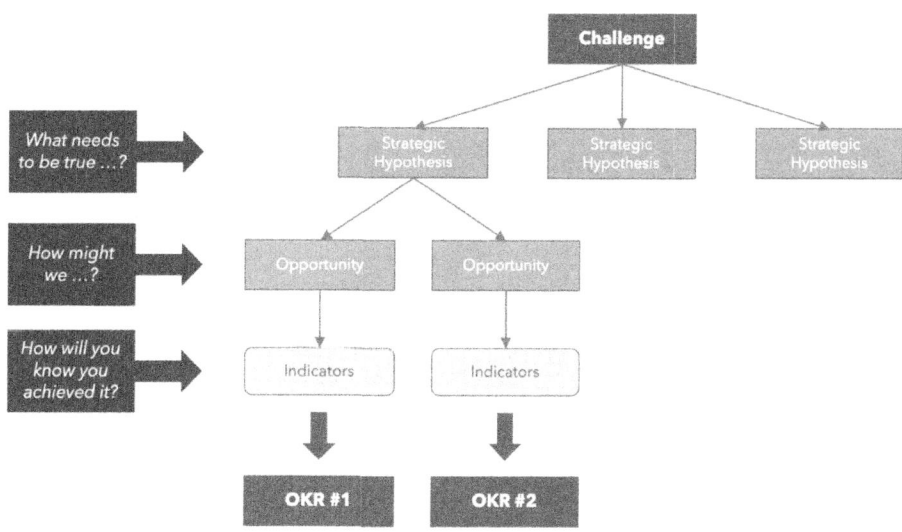

Figure 25 - Turning Ambiguous Goals into Meaningful OKRs

Adapt the Opportunity Solution Trees[21] method for this purpose:

1. Place the overarching goal at the top of the tree. Brainstorm and select significant strategic hypotheses by asking, 'What needs to be true to achieve this goal?' Place these at the second level.
2. For each hypothesis, brainstorm potential solutions with 'How might we achieve this hypothesis?' Select the most viable options and place them below each hypothesis.
3. Choose the most logical branch to start with and define an OKR for it.
4. To identify Key Results, ask: How will we know we've achieved the goal?

Identifying Key Hypotheses

For example, if your goal is to increase app engagement, start with a hypothesis like, *'Improving the interface will boost engagement.'* This question-focused approach turns vague ambitions into specific objectives.

Validating Assumptions

Next, apply the *'How might we validate this hypothesis?'* strategy. For instance, redesign the interface and measure its impact on engagement. Set an Objective like *'Create a more engaging and intuitive interface,'* with Key Results such as *'Increase average session time by 20%'* and *'Decrease bounce rate by 15%.'*

Remember, OKRs should be specific, measurable, and achievable. We're seeking tangible outcomes, not mere aspirations.

Defining Key Results

If identifying meaningful KRs is challenging, consider these questions:

- *How will we know we've achieved the goal?*
- *What visible changes will indicate success?*
- *When will we know that this goal no longer needs to be pursued?*
- *If achieved, what difference will it make for the customer and how will it benefit the business?*

Reverse Engineering OKRs

Even teams that view themselves as mere "feature factories" can develop meaningful OKRs. It's about identifying and tackling specific challenges and risks unique to your team's context, aligning with broader objectives but focused on areas where you can genuinely make a difference.

Numerous teams I've collaborated with have expressed frustration at feeling like mere 'order takers,' 'feature factories,' or 'delivery units.' This perception often transforms their OKRs into a lengthy checklist of tasks (output-focused OKRs), or leads to concocting fictional OKRs that merely resonate well with an already defined project list.

This practice, which I refer to as reverse engineering goals, is a trend I've observed in many Scrum Teams. Lacking a coherent strategy, they receive an agenda for the upcoming sprint and retrofit a sprint goal to match. It's quite an ironic situation, isn't it?

Identifying Unique Challenges

Even when your team operates in a 'feature factory' mode, it's important to concentrate on distinct challenges and objectives that fall within your realm of influence. Consider the discrepancies between assigned tasks and your team's current capabilities, such as the need to tackle technical debt or enhance delivery metrics.

Focusing on these specific areas enables your team to set impactful goals that align with broader organizational strategies while addressing directives from higher levels. This approach not only ensures compliance with top-down directives but also promotes real progress and development within your team.

Using Metrics to Define OKRs

Moving on, let's explore a practical approach from the standpoint of product metrics.

Leading vs. Lagging Indicators

It's essential to grasp the distinction between leading and lagging indicators. Leading indicators act as predictive measures, offering early insights into future performance and enabling prompt adjustments to strategies or actions. On the other hand, lagging indicators reflect outcomes after actions have already been implemented, serving as valuable tools for assessing the effectiveness of those actions.

Examples in eCommerce Business

Leading Indicators:

- **Website Traffic:** Measures the number of visitors to your eCommerce site, forecasting potential future sales.
- **Cart Abandonment Rate:** Indicates the percentage of shoppers who add items to their cart but do not complete the purchase, signaling potential issues affecting future sales.

- **Customer Engagement Metrics:** Including time spent on site and pages viewed per session, these metrics provide early insights into customer interest and potential conversions.

Lagging Indicators:

- **Monthly Sales Revenue:** Reflects the actual revenue generated, a key measure of past performance.
- **Customer Retention Rate:** Shows the percentage of customers who return for another purchase, based on past customer satisfaction.
- **Average Order Value (AOV):** Indicates the average amount spent per transaction, calculated post-purchase.

Examples in SaaS Business

Leading Indicators:

- **Free Trial Sign-ups:** The number of users signing up for a free trial, indicating potential future subscriptions.
- **Active User Count:** The number of users actively using the SaaS product, hinting at future revenue potential.
- **Feature Usage Rate:** Frequency and extent of user engagement with key features, suggesting customer engagement and future retention.

Lagging Indicators:

- **Monthly Recurring Revenue (MRR):** A fundamental indicator of actual earned revenue.
- **Customer Churn Rate:** The rate at which customers cancel their subscriptions, reflecting past customer decisions and satisfaction.
- **Customer Lifetime Value (CLV):** The total revenue expected from a single customer account, based on historical data.

Leading indicators provide a forward-looking perspective, allowing product teams to make proactive adjustments. Lagging indicators, on the other hand, offer a retrospective view, helping product teams evaluate the effectiveness of their strategies and operations.

Balancing the insights from both types of indicators is key to making informed decisions and steering the business towards success.

Practical Example: StreamlineApp

Consider a task management app where a leading indicator could be *"The percentage of daily active users using new features."* This allows for quick adjustments based on user engagement. In contrast, a lagging indicator like *"Quarterly increase in user retention"* reflects long-term impact but doesn't permit immediate adjustments.

Defining Leading Indicators

To identify direct actions and impacts, ask questions like, *"What would need to happen for the lagging indicator to improve?"* This helps in pinpointing measurable and impactful metrics.

Examples of Leading Indicators for StreamlineApp

1. **User Onboarding Completion Rate**: The percentage of new users who complete the onboarding process within their first session. This is an early indicator of how well new users are understanding and finding value in the app, which can directly influence long-term engagement and retention.

2. **Feature-Specific Engagement Metrics**: For each new feature, track metrics like the number of users who try the feature within the first week of its release, and the average number of times a feature is used per session. These metrics provide immediate feedback on the feature's acceptance and usefulness.

3. **Customer Support Interaction Rate**: The frequency of interactions between users and customer support, specifically regarding new features or common user tasks. A high interaction rate may indicate areas of confusion or difficulty, signaling a need for improvement in app usability or feature design.

These leading indicators provide immediate insights into user behavior and app performance, allowing for swift and effective modifications to enhance the user experience in real-time.

Defining OKRs for Your Team

The key lies in identifying which metrics you can directly influence and continuously measure.

Ask yourself: *"Is this metric a direct predictor of success? Can it be measured and impacted within our objective cycle?"* Avoid general indicators and consider the specific context of your team and product.

While lagging indicators provide certainty, leading indicators offer agility and the ability to respond quickly. The magic happens when we achieve a balance between the two, aligning our actions with strategic objectives and responding flexibly to changes.

Differentiating between leading and lagging indicators is essential for creating efficient building cycles and achieving product success.

Cascading Down Indicators

In this approach, leading indicators at higher organizational levels transform into lagging indicators for subordinate levels.

This cascading effect allows for a strategic navigation through the hierarchy of OKRs. By inquiring 'HOW' at each lower level, teams can understand their direct actions towards achieving these indicators. Conversely, moving upwards by asking 'WHY' aligns these actions with overarching organizational goals.

When a team is tasked with a goal represented by an indicator that's beyond their direct influence, it becomes a lagging indicator for them. Consequently, they must identify appropriate leading indicators to guide their specific discovery actions or delivery initiatives, ensuring alignment and progression towards the larger organizational objectives.

Example

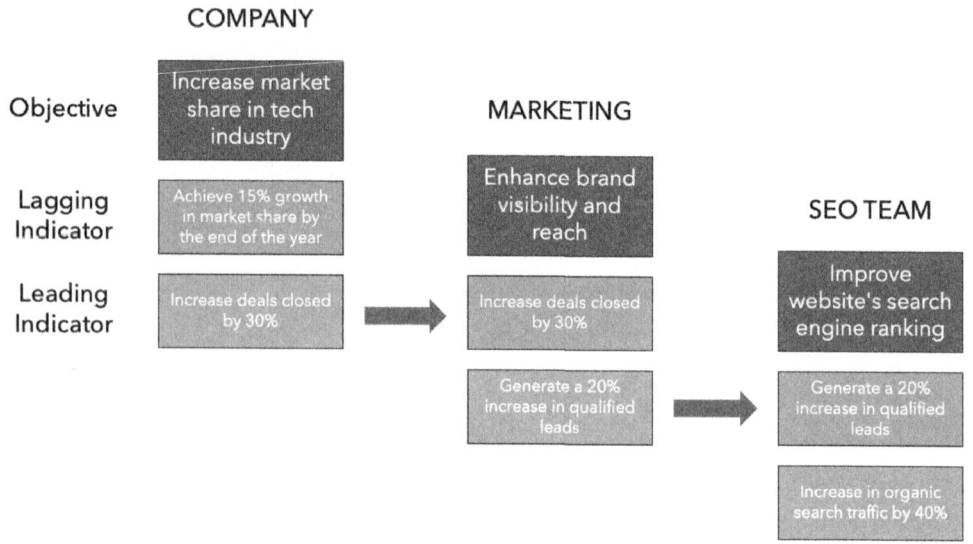

Figure 26: Leading and Lagging Indicators Cascade

In this example, the leading indicators at each higher level become the lagging indicators for the next level down. Each team or individual, therefore, focuses on their leading indicators, which contribute to achieving the lagging indicators of the level above, aligning their efforts towards the company's overarching goal.

Impact Mapping

Once you have defined your desired objectives, they will serve as the starting point in your impact map (WHY), helping you to define the product roadmap themes (HOW).

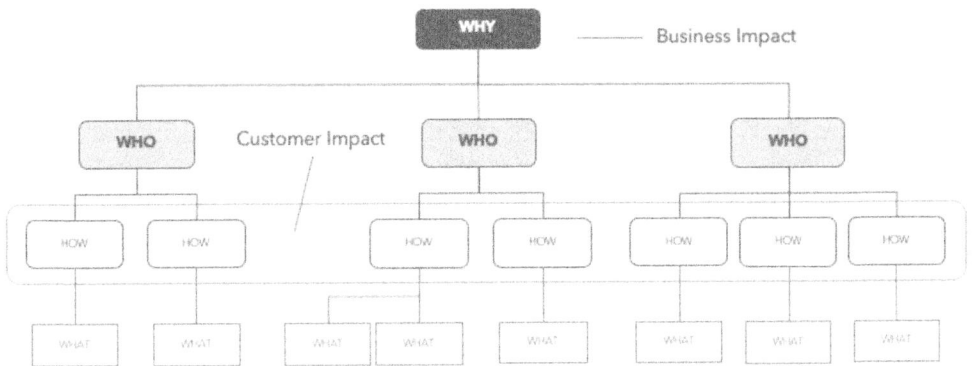

Figure 27 - Impact Mapping

Identify User Profiles

Identify opportunities for specific user profiles in your impact map, turning them into roadmap items for each outcome defined in the next step.

Identifying Desired Outcomes

Starting with your strategic objectives, use key data points to identify outcomes. For example, in an eCommerce scenario, focus on reducing operational costs by addressing high customer service call ratios or manual payment reconciliations.

Customer Experience Maps

Customer Experience Maps enable us to identify opportunities for our roadmap.

For instance, in eCommerce, we focus on the customer experience related to service information and identify specific pain points in all activities connected to our strategic objectives.

Thus, from a strategic goal, we derive various outcomes and roadmap themes for each of these pain points.

Conclusion

In conclusion, defining effective OKRs is a blend of art and science, demanding both creativity and analytical thinking.

The techniques discussed – from transforming ambiguous goals to leveraging metrics, reverse engineering, impact mapping, and customer experience journeys – provide a comprehensive toolkit for any product team.

Remember, the key is to keep your OKRs specific, measurable, and attainable, aligning them with your team's unique context and strategic vision.

Chapter 19: OKRs and Wardley Maps

In this chapter, we delve into the integration of Wardley Maps with OKRs, focusing on strategic thinking and execution, with a practical example to understand how both methods interconnect.

The process begins by identifying our strategic challenges, which involves a thorough analysis of the current situation and the formulation of a targeted policy to address these challenges effectively.

Next, we shift our attention to crafting actions that are in harmony with our strategic objectives. Richard Rumelt's concept of the "Kernel of Strategy" in his book "Good Strategy / Bad Strategy" provides a solid foundation for this process.

Wardley Maps aligns seamlessly with Rumelt's first three steps:

Kernel of Strategy	Wardley Maps
Challenge	Purpose
Diagnostic	<ul><li>Maps</li><li>Climatic Patterns</li><li>Types of Inertia</li></ul>
Guiding Policy	Gameplays
Coherent Actions	N/A

However, it's in the fourth step, Coherent Actions, that OKRs prove to be invaluable.

Using the insights derived from Wardley Maps and our guiding policies, we can establish effective OKRs. This approach not only follows Rumelt's model but also adds depth to it.

We collaboratively create a decision tree that originates from our map's guiding policy and leads directly to tangible OKRs. This process involves:

1. Determining the Guiding Policy as per the identified Challenge
2. Developing Strategic Hypotheses
3. Identifying Opportunities
4. Establishing relevant Indicators.

From this point, we select the most impactful OKRs, ensuring each decision tree branch is interconnected and directly contributes to our strategic vision.

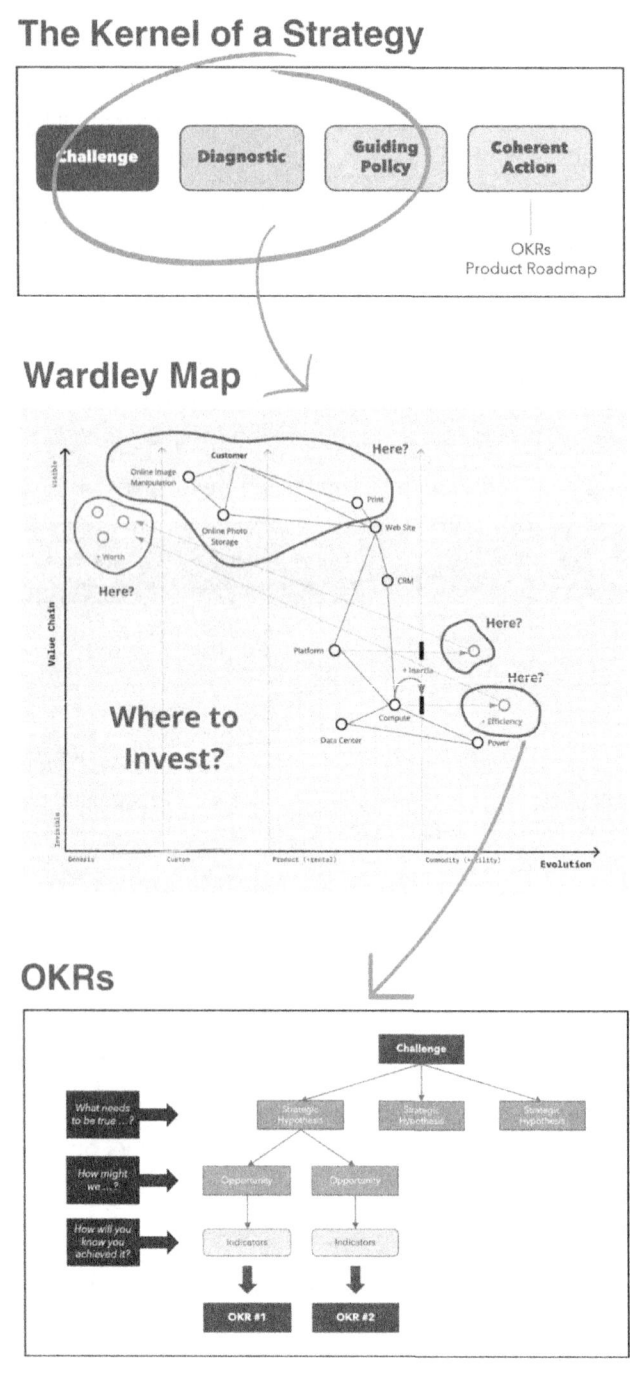

Figure 28 - OKRs and Wardley Maps

Integrating OKRs with Wardley Maps

Integrating Wardley Maps with OKRs for strategic thinking and execution is a powerful approach that combines the strengths of both methods to create a comprehensive strategy development and implementation plan. Here's how the process unfolds:

1. **Identifying Strategic Challenges**:
    - Begin by conducting a thorough analysis of the current situation.
    - Formulate a targeted policy to address these challenges effectively.
    - This step aligns with Richard Rumelt's concept of the "Kernel of Strategy" from "Good Strategy / Bad Strategy", focusing on diagnosing the problem and creating a guiding policy.

2. **Using Wardley Maps for Diagnostic and Policy Formulation**:
    - Use Wardley Maps to visualize the landscape and identify leverage points.
    - Conduct a diagnostic analysis using climate patterns and understanding types of inertia.
    - Formulate a Guiding Policy through strategic gameplays, drawing insights from the map's layout and the relationships between different elements.

3. **Translating Guiding Policy into Coherent Actions with OKRs**:
    - Use the insights and guiding policy from Wardley Maps to establish effective OKRs.
    - Create a decision tree that stems from the map's guiding policy, leading to tangible OKRs.
    - This process involves determining the guiding policy based on the identified challenge, developing strategic hypotheses, identifying opportunities, and establishing relevant indicators.

4. **Selecting Impactful OKRs**:
    - Choose OKRs that are most impactful and aligned with the strategic vision.
    - Ensure each decision tree branch is interconnected, contributing directly to the strategic objectives.
    - Focus on creating OKRs that are specific, measurable, achievable, relevant, and time-bound (SMART).

Example

Spain's market leader in lunch book delivery, let's call it EatBox, faces an increasingly competitive landscape. Numerous competitors are emerging, targeting not only EatBox' core customer base but also exploring new segments. This intensifying competition warrants a close examination of the evolving market dynamics.

The early-stage nature of this market signals vast growth potential, but it also means the battle for customer retention is intensifying as the space becomes more crowded.

In this context, EatBox's leadership position hinges on its ability to stay agile and responsive. The company needs to keep a close watch on the market, especially considering the rapid changes fueled by the COVID-19 pandemic, the shift towards remote work, and broader digitalization trends.

To maintain its edge, EatBox must not only monitor these evolving market conditions but also act swiftly to adapt. This could involve innovating in product offerings, exploring new customer segments, or enhancing customer experience. With the market evolving rapidly, EatBox's ability to anticipate changes and respond proactively will be crucial for its continued success.

Diagnostic

Now, let's explore the main opportunities for strategic advantage that EatBox might pursue, indicated with numbers 1 to 6 in the map below.

LUNCH BOXES DELIVERY (ex. EatBox)

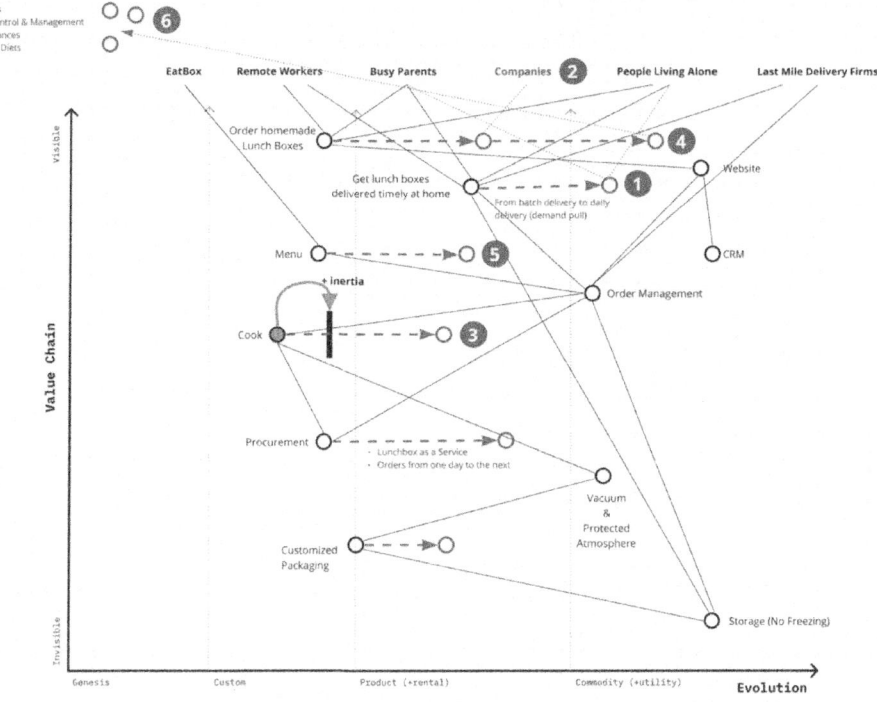

Figure 29 - Wardley Map for EatBox

1. **24-48 Hour Delivery and Quality Considerations:** Expanding into rapid delivery requires operational changes, like freezing and stocking meals, which might affect product quality. This could lead to differentiating product lines – one for premium quality (current model) and another for faster, potentially lower-quality offerings. This bifurcation caters to diverse customer preferences. A strategic acquisition of smaller competitors could also be a way to quickly adapt to these operational changes.
2. **New Customer Segments and Acquisition Channels:** The emergence of B2B customers, like businesses offering employee perks, suggests a shift in both product offering (like lunch boxes) and acquisition strategies. Moving from B2C-focused paid ads to B2B-focused outbound sales efforts could be more effective in reaching HR departments. Integrating subscriptions with added value services like diet control aligns with evolving market needs and can enhance customer retention.
3. **Culinary Approach Adaptation:** The company's high-cuisine cooking style may face challenges as market demands shift towards more productized offerings. Competitors are moving in this direction, so there's a need for a strategic decision on whether to adapt to these market changes or maintain the current culinary approach.

This decision has significant implications for brand positioning and customer perception.
4. **Normalization of Lunch Box Delivery:** The future trend towards regular lunch box orders for home or business use suggests a market shift. This could lead to new service models beyond the current offerings of companies like Just Eat. However, it's unclear how this will unfold, especially considering the potential overlap with existing fast food delivery services.
5. **Product Offer Variation:** The quality and variety of offerings might need to vary based on the delivery model. Competitors with dual business lines (weekly and on-demand) suggest a possible strategic move. The on-demand model, in particular, will likely face intense competition, necessitating distinct strategies for different service models.
6. **Opportunities in Commoditization and Higher Order Systems:** As the market commoditizes, there's potential for higher-order systems offering new value sources. This includes specialized diet services, health apps, or tailored offerings for specific groups like athletes or schools. Such differentiation could be crucial for retention and standing out in a crowded market.

Guiding Policy

Following a comprehensive analysis and collaborative discussions, the leadership team has crystallized their focus into two pivotal strategic directions:

1. Recognizing the increasing trend of remote work, they see a valuable opportunity to keep growing their current model. They aim to capitalize on the rising demand for home-style cuisine by offering weekly home delivery services.
2. In parallel, they're venturing into the adjacent market of corporate employee benefits. They see potential in developing a range of business perks tailored for employees. This new avenue not only diversifies their portfolio but also taps into the growing corporate focus on employee well-being and satisfaction.

With these strategic guidelines set, it's now up to their two dedicated product teams – the existing team for their home cuisine model and the new team for business perks – to take the lead. They will craft their OKRs to ensure these strategies are effectively translated into actionable goals and measurable outcomes, paving the way for our next phase of growth.

Defining OKRs

The team dedicated to exploring the new market segment has established a strategic hypothesis map to guide their efforts. They've pinpointed three critical assumptions essential for success in this venture: market demand exists, the company can scale production to meet the demands of potentially thousands of new users, and current operating profits can be maintained during this expansion.

To confirm the presence of market demand, the team has decided to develop a Minimum Viable Product (MVP) and initiate a series of outreach campaigns targeted at the existing customer base. The effectiveness of these approaches will be measured by the number of new subscriptions generated, serving as key indicators for each initiative.

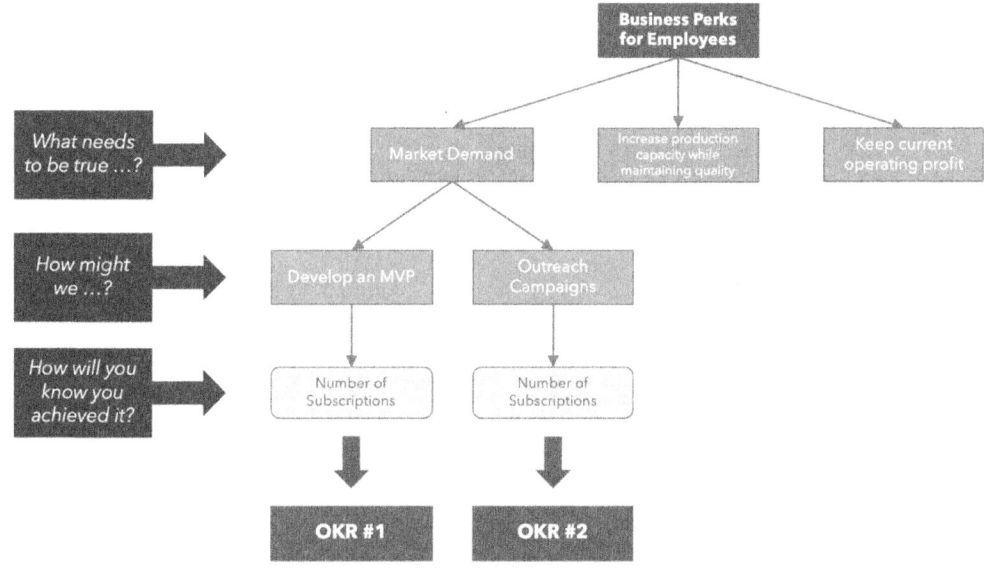

Figure 30 - Defining OKRs

When considering OKRs, teams have two main approaches to choose from.

The team might opt for a separate OKR for each path, as illustrated above. While some argue that these should be outcome-based objectives rather than output-based, it's important to remember that arbitrary OKRs are unhelpful. Given the unpredictable nature of this process, setting a definitive outcome goal may not be practical. Nonetheless, it's crucial that the KRs clearly define what constitutes the experiment's success. For example, a KR could be *"Attain X number of subscriptions with a 10% conversion rate"*.

Developing a Minimum Viable Product (MVP) involves extensive product discovery and assumption validation, making arbitrary goals impractical. However, it's still necessary to determine whether the experiment succeeds. The same principle applies to the second path involving campaigns.

Alternatively, the team may set an overarching objective based on a strategic hypothesis, measured through subscriptions, conversion rate, and Customer Acquisition Cost (CAC).

For instance:

- *Objective: Break into the business market segment.*
    - KR1: Gain 1,000 subscriptions within 6 months.
    - KR2: Achieve a 10% conversion rate.
    - KR3: Keep CAC below $200 per client.

In this scenario, the team could incorporate both initiatives into their outcome-focused product roadmap.

Regardless of the chosen approach, the key is to ensure strategic alignment and clear decision-making guidance.

Conclusion

In conclusion, this chapter has delved into the powerful synergy between OKRs and Wardley Maps, highlighting their role as vital tools in contemporary strategic planning and execution.

We've seen how Wardley Maps provide a unique perspective, enabling organizations to map out their competitive landscape, understand market dynamics, and anticipate technological evolution. This insight is instrumental in identifying strategic challenges and formulating guiding policies.

On the other hand, OKRs come into play as a transformative framework for turning these policies into actionable, measurable goals.

Together, OKRs and Wardley Maps create a robust structure for businesses to not only strategize effectively but also to implement these strategies in a way that drives tangible progress and success.

Chapter 20: OKRs vs KPIs

Sometimes, clients come to us ready to try out OKRs, but they're already using KPIs. They often ask us if they should keep their KPIs, what exactly sets KPIs apart from OKRs, and how they can switch to OKRs without causing disruption.

In this chapter, we'll clear up the confusion between KPIs and OKRs. We'll show you what makes each one unique, and we'll walk you through the best ways to use them both effectively.

Key Differences Between KPIs and OKRs

To put it simply from the start, comparing KPIs to OKRs is like comparing apples to oranges; they are different, with varied purposes and applications.

OKRs act as a tool for strategic implementation, designed to set key objectives and ensure that the organization stays aligned towards a common direction. They also aid in coordinating adjustments in direction, fostering continuous improvement and autonomy.

Conversely, KPIs focus on metrics that indicate the current performance, serving as tools to monitor the well-being of your organization.

For example, if we consider a high-performance athlete, an OKR could be to win the world championship by achieving the best mark of the year in their discipline, whereas KPIs would be factors such as weight, resting heart rate, or VO2MAX.

It's true that on certain occasions KPIs are integrated into OKRs through Key Results, since these are nothing more than metrics and, in some cases, OKRs rely on these to assess success and progress. However, as a general rule and for those who prefer a brief explanation without reading the full article, it's important to recognize that a KPI is simply another way to refer to a metric. Therefore, if you wonder about the difference between a strategic system based on objectives and metrics, the answer is quite straightforward.

Among all the metrics that might be essential to monitor in a business, KPIs are crucial and vary according to each organization. For instance, while weight may be a relevant KPI for anyone, muscle mass would only be so for an athlete.

To provide a more detailed analysis of the differences, in case it's not yet clear:

OKRs	KPIs
OKRs set milestones within strategic direction, aiming for progress and improvement.	KPIs are used to monitor the 'business as usual' activities.
Key Results are typically expressed with metrics of progress and success.	KPIs are metrics measuring the health status of a system or process.

Understanding KPIs

Key Performance Indicators (KPIs) are essential metrics that reflect the current state of an organization's performance. These indicators are crucial for assessing the effectiveness of various aspects of business operations, including project outcomes, product performance, and employee productivity.

KPIs are invaluable for providing immediate feedback on performance levels, indicating whether results are satisfactory or require attention. However, they primarily offer snapshot evaluations without detailing the broader context or suggesting future actions for improvement.

Exploring OKRs

Objectives and Key Results (OKRs) serve as a strategic framework for goal setting, bridging the gap between overarching strategies and their practical execution, thereby ensuring organizational alignment around shared goals.

Unlike KPIs, OKRs supply the necessary context and direction, outlining the ambitions (Objectives) and the measurable outcomes (Key Results) that signify progress and achievement.

OKRs encourage strategic planning and execution by defining clear goals and metrics for success.

KPIs vs OKRs: A Synergistic Relationship

The relationship between KPIs and OKRs is not competitive but complementary. Each serves a distinct purpose within the organizational framework.

KPIs quantify performance in specific areas, offering benchmarks for ongoing operations. In contrast, OKRs provide a structured approach to goal setting, aiming for growth and strategic achievements. Together, they create a comprehensive view of both current performance and future objectives.

For instance, in a SaaS business, maintaining a churn rate below 10% might be a critical KPI, indicative of business health and customer retention. However, while essential, such KPIs do not directly translate into OKRs, which are designed to drive significant changes or improvements. Nevertheless, a KPI can evolve into an OKR when there's a strategic need to improve or transform a specific metric, such as reducing a churn rate that exceeds the desired threshold.

The Interplay of OKRs and KPIs

While KPIs remain vital for monitoring key business aspects, OKRs play a significant role in setting and achieving transformative goals. KPIs reflect the current state, maintaining focus on the "business as usual" activities, whereas OKRs aim to outline and achieve future aspirations. This dynamic allows for the strategic elevation of certain KPIs into OKRs when significant improvements are targeted, offering a flexible framework for both maintaining operational standards and pursuing ambitious goals.

Consider a finance team struggling to meet the KPI of timely contract filings. Transforming this challenge into an OKR for a specific period can sharpen focus and drive improvements. Once the objective is consistently met, it can revert to being monitored as a KPI, allowing management to maintain oversight while freeing up resources to focus on new strategic objectives. This cyclical approach ensures that KPIs and OKRs work in tandem to sustain operational excellence and foster strategic growth.

Can You Have Both KPIs and OKRs?

Integrating KPIs and OKRs is not only feasible but also beneficial for businesses. KPIs serve as indicators of current operational health, showing where your business stands today. OKRs, on the other hand, outline your key strategic goals and the benchmarks for future success, acting as navigational beacons toward achieving these aims. While KPIs track the ongoing performance and operational metrics, OKRs set the strategic direction and milestones to strive for.

Consider the analogy of an airline pilot to understand how to blend OKRs for strategic objectives with KPIs for operational efficiency. If an airline aims to enhance its punctuality, a pilot might adopt an OKR to "Achieve punctuality for flights under two hours." Success could be defined by a Key Result such as "Achieving 90% on-time departures," complemented by KPIs like "Maintaining fuel consumption below industry average" to ensure operational efficiency supports the strategic goal.

The Synergy Between OKRs and KPIs

The question isn't whether to choose OKRs or KPIs but rather how to use them in tandem for optimal effect. OKRs are a framework for setting and pursuing systemic goals, while KPIs are specific metrics that monitor the health and performance of various aspects of the business.

For instance, maintaining a 99% uptime for a patient registration platform is a crucial KPI, indicative of the system's reliability. However, KPIs alone might not drive significant strategic changes. They are vital for operational health but may not always align with the transformative goals captured by OKRs.

A KPI can evolve into an OKR when there's a strategic intent to improve that metric significantly. If improving the uptime of a registration portal from 50% to 99% becomes a strategic objective, then stabilizing uptime not only serves as a Key Result but also doubles as a critical KPI, demonstrating how achieving specific outcomes can elevate operational metrics to strategic importance.

Transitioning from KPIs to OKRs

For organizations transitioning from KPI-focused management to adopting OKRs, several steps are crucial:

1. Ensure a clear strategy is in place.
2. Review all current KPIs to identify any that need enhancement.
3. Determine which KPIs could effectively measure progress or achievement of objectives.
4. Identify if any existing KPIs can act as North Star Metrics (NSMs).
5. Differentiate KPIs into leading (predictive) and lagging (outcome) indicators and understand the metrics leading to these indicators.
6. Categorize KPIs into those measuring quality and those measuring progress.

This preparatory work lays the foundation for setting meaningful OKRs across the organization.

A potential challenge is the shift from managing a large array of KPIs to focusing on a limited number of objectives (1 to 3) per team or business unit, which requires a more streamlined approach to goal setting and performance management.

Conclusion

Integrating KPIs with OKRs in your organization offers the advantage of capturing both the current operational health and the ambitious strides toward future achievements. KPIs measure the here and now, showing how well the business is doing today, while OKRs help map out and measure your goals for tomorrow. They are two sides of the same coin, providing a comprehensive view of where your company stands and where it's headed.

While OKRs are about setting and reaching for strategic objectives, KPIs keep track of performance against the benchmarks you've set. In fact, it's common to use KPIs as the Key Results in your OKRs, marrying your current performance metrics with your strategic objectives. This way, your OKRs are not only ambitious but also rooted in the reality of your business's current operations.

However, a KPI on its own doesn't become an OKR. OKRs require an objective and key results — a KPI can become a key result, but the objective is what turns a metric into a strategic tool.

Regular reviews are essential. Typically done quarterly, these check-ins ensure that you are on the right track towards achieving your strategic goals while staying true to your operational performance. Your organization's specific rhythm might vary, but the principle remains: keep your eyes on both the horizon and the path beneath your feet.

In conclusion, utilizing both OKRs and KPIs is crucial. OKRs give you the strategic framework for setting and reaching long-term goals, while KPIs offer a precise measure of your current performance. Together, they enable your organization to aim high with its strategic objectives while ensuring you're grounded in the solid reality of day-to-day operations. This dual approach is the key to balanced and sustainable success.

Chapter 21: OKRs and North Star Metrics

North Star Metric (NSM) and Objectives and Key Results (OKRs) are both vital concepts in strategic planning and performance management, but they serve different purposes and functions within an organization. Understanding their relationship, whether teams need both, and how they can be used independently or together, is crucial for effective strategic execution.

Relationship Between NSM and OKRs

The North Star Metric is a single, overarching metric that captures the core value that a company delivers to its customers. It is the key measure of a company's success and is closely aligned with its vision and mission. The NSM is meant to be a guiding light for the entire organization, ensuring that all efforts are aligned towards achieving this central goal.

OKRs, on the other hand, are a framework for setting and tracking goals and outcomes. An OKR consists of an Objective, which is a clearly defined goal, and Key Results, which are specific measures used to track the achievement of that goal. OKRs are used to create alignment and engagement around measurable goals, typically set quarterly or annually.

The NSM provides a high-level focus point for the organization, while OKRs break down this focus into specific, actionable, and measurable goals. Ideally, OKRs should be aligned in such a way that achieving them moves the organization towards its NSM.

While the NSM offers a broad, singular focus, OKRs provide a structured way to achieve that focus through specific objectives. OKRs can be seen as the steps or milestones needed to reach the NSM.

Do Teams Need Both?

Some organizations may focus solely on an NSM to maintain a broad strategic focus, while others may find OKRs alone sufficient for setting and achieving specific goals. However, using both can create a powerful synergy between strategic direction (NSM) and tactical execution (OKRs).

Utilizing both NSMs and OKRs can provide a clear direction (through the NSM) and a pathway to get there (through OKRs). This can be particularly effective in ensuring that all team efforts are aligned with the overall strategic intent of the organization.

Working with Only NSM or OKRs

Some teams might operate effectively with just a North Star Metric, especially if their work is highly focused on a singular, overarching goal. In such cases, the NSM provides sufficient guidance.

Teams may also function well with just OKRs, particularly if they require a more structured and detailed approach to goal setting and measurement. OKRs allow for flexibility and adaptability in setting and achieving a variety of specific goals.

My Approach

I advocate for a balanced approach. While an NSM provides a clear, unifying goal that everyone in the organization can rally around, OKRs offer a practical and systematic method for achieving that goal. The use of both, when aligned properly, can drive not only strategic alignment but also operational efficiency and effectiveness.

In summary, while NSM and OKRs serve different purposes, they are not mutually exclusive and can be highly complementary when used together. The choice to use both, one, or the other depends on the specific needs, structure, and strategic objectives of the organization.

Example

Let's consider a fictitious technology company, "InnovateTech," which specializes in developing productivity software for small businesses. InnovateTech aims to enhance workplace efficiency and collaboration through its innovative software solutions.

North Star Metric (NSM)

For InnovateTech, a suitable North Star Metric might be: *"Number of active daily users on the platform."* This NSM aligns with their core mission of improving productivity for small businesses. The rationale is that more active users indicate greater reliance on and engagement with their software, which correlates with increased productivity in their customers' workplaces.

OKRs

To support this NSM, InnovateTech could develop several OKRs. These OKRs are designed to drive progress towards increasing the daily active user count.

Q1 OKRs

1. **Objective: Enhance User Engagement and Satisfaction**
   - KR1: Achieve a user satisfaction score of 90%.
   - KR2: Increase daily active users by 15%.
   - KR3: Reduce churn rate to less than 5%.

2. **Objective: Improve Product Features Based on User Feedback**
   - KR1: Implement 5 major feature updates requested by users.
   - KR2: Decrease average customer support response time to under 2 hours.
   - KR3: Increase feature awareness through bi-weekly educational webinars, targeting 500 attendees per session.

3. **Objective: Expand Market Reach to New Small Business Segments**
   - KR1: Acquire 300 new small business accounts.
   - KR2: Launch a targeted marketing campaign reaching 10,000 potential users.
   - KR3: Establish partnerships with 5 industry associations for cross-promotion.

Q2 OKRs (Subsequent Quarter, with Adjusted KRs)

1. **Objective: Enhance User Engagement and Satisfaction**
   - KR1: Increase user satisfaction score to 92%.
   - KR2: Increase daily active users by 20%.
   - KR3: Introduce a customer loyalty program and enroll 30% of existing customers.

2. **Objective: Introduce AI-Driven Productivity Features**
   - KR1: Launch 3 AI-driven tools within the software.
   - KR2: Conduct a user feedback survey on the new AI features with a 70% response rate.
   - KR3: Publish 10 case studies showcasing the impact of AI features on user productivity.

3. **Objective: Strengthen Brand Presence in the Business Community**

- KR1: Host a virtual summit on small business productivity with 1,000 attendees.
- KR2: Increase social media followers by 25%.
- KR3: Secure 5 speaking engagements at industry events.

Combining NSM and OKRs

InnovateTech's NSM of increasing active daily users serves as the guiding light for all their strategic efforts. The OKRs, with their specific objectives and measurable key results, provide a structured path towards achieving this NSM. Each OKR is crafted to contribute directly to enhancing user engagement and market reach, which in turn drives the NSM upwards.

For example, the OKRs for improving user satisfaction and expanding market reach are expected to directly impact the number of active daily users. The launch of AI-driven features and hosting a virtual summit are strategic moves to not only improve the product but also to amplify InnovateTech's market presence, thereby attracting more users to the platform.

This strategic framework, where the NSM provides the overarching goal and the OKRs lay out the pathway to achieve it, ensures that every team and individual at InnovateTech is aligned and working cohesively towards the common objective of enhancing productivity for small businesses.

NSM and OMTM

By combining both North Star Metrics and The One Metric That Matters you can also effectively define and continuously review meaningful OKRs for your team.

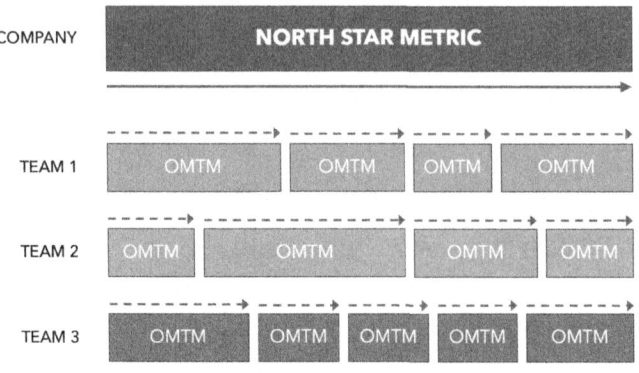

Figure 31: NSM and OMTMs

The North Star Metric (NSM) is a company-wide metric for long-term growth.

- It's the number that best reflects the value you bring to your customers.
- It's a single customer-centric metric used by the entire company.
- It serves as the leading success indicator for team alignment.

Examples of NSM:

- *Spotify = 'Time spent listening'*
- *Airbnb = 'Number of nights booked'*
- *Facebook = 'Monthly active users'*

The One Metric That Matters (OMTM) is a team metric for short-term growth that changes every few months.

- It's the number that has the most impact on growth in the next 2-4 months.
- It's a specific metric one team focuses on to achieve rapid growth.
- It supports and contributes to NSM to achieve faster results.

Examples of OMTM:

- *Number of website visitors per month*
- *Retention of new customers after 7 days*
- *Avg. click-through percentage from homepage to checkout*

Chapter 22: OKRs and Roadmaps

Effective product management hinges on having a clear strategy to guide development and achieve goals. Two crucial tools in this process are OKRs and roadmaps. Yet, there's often confusion about their usage - whether to use one, the other, or both in tandem.

In this chapter, we'll clarify these questions, demonstrating the importance of integrating both OKRs and roadmaps for successful outcomes.

Despite OKRs gaining popularity recently, misconceptions about their relationship with roadmaps persist. Some believe that OKRs can replace roadmaps, while others see roadmaps as obsolete. Contrary to these views, OKRs and roadmaps fulfill different, yet complementary roles in product strategy.

We'll explore the advantages of employing both OKRs and roadmaps together, with practical examples illustrating their combined effectiveness.

What is a Product Roadmap?

Product roadmaps serve as a bridge between strategic decisions and concrete actions, offering clear guidance to development teams and other stakeholders. They ensure that everyone involved in the product's success has a shared understanding of its projected growth and the impact on their roles.

Today's product roadmap is a visual representation, encapsulating the strategy and objectives of a product. It outlines key future milestones and achievements.

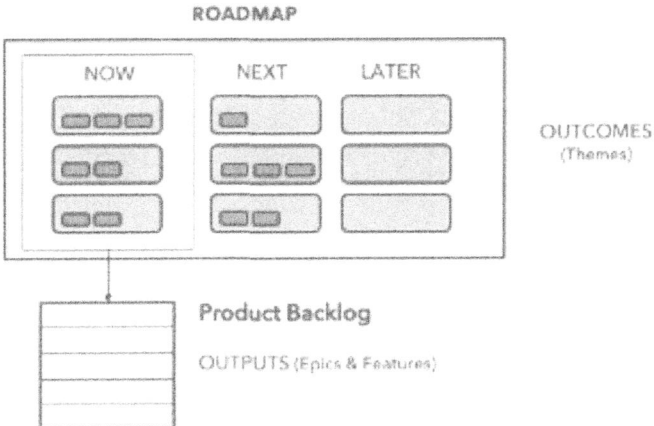

Figure 32 - Outcome-based Roadmap

Roadmaps evolve over time; they're no longer just static blueprints for future builds. Modern product roadmaps emphasize delivering customer value swiftly, adapting based on rapid customer feedback and iterative development.

Can OKRs replace Roadmaps?

Can roadmaps be replaced by OKRs? The answer, unequivocally, is a resounding no. Conversely, suggesting that OKRs can be substituted by roadmaps is equally misguided. These misconceptions, unfortunately, stem from a fundamental misunderstanding of product strategy and its essential tools.

Both OKRs and roadmaps are integral to a well-rounded product strategy, each playing a distinct yet complementary role. The burgeoning popularity of OKRs in recent years, coupled with some negative experiences surrounding product roadmaps in various organizations, has led to some confusion about the necessity and relevance of roadmaps.

However, it's crucial to recognize that OKRs and roadmaps are not interchangeable. They are, in fact, synergistic elements that, when effectively utilized together, can significantly enhance the clarity and effectiveness of a product strategy.

The roadmap serves as a crucial component of a strategic framework. It acts as the tangible embodiment of coherent actions stemming from a thorough diagnostic process. It outlines the strategic direction determined by the guiding policy and is informed by the capabilities needed to achieve set objectives.

Simply put, while OKRs help define what the goals are (the 'what' and the 'why'), roadmaps provide the 'how' and the 'when'. They offer a visual and strategic plan that guides the development process, setting out the steps and timelines for achieving the objectives outlined in the OKRs.

Thus, asserting that OKRs can replace roadmaps, or vice versa, is not just a misunderstanding of their functions but also an underestimation of their collective value in driving effective product management and strategy. Both OKRs and roadmaps are not only necessary but also indispensable in their harmonious coexistence within a robust product strategy framework.

Strategic Planning

The strategic process is divided into two main phases: design and planning.

- **Design Phase**: This involves identifying strategic challenges, diagnosing problems, and defining a strategic guide.
- **Planning Phase**: This is where OKRs (Objectives and Key Results) and the roadmap (action plan) are identified.

Effective strategy begins with a precise diagnosis of the challenge's structure. The next step is selecting a broad policy to address this situation, leveraging existing advantages or creating new ones. The final step involves crafting a detailed plan of actions and allocating resources to execute the chosen policy.

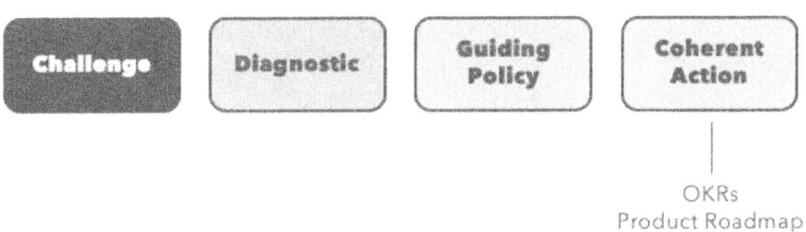

Figure 33 - The Kernel of a Good Strategy from the book "Good Strategy/Bad Strategy."

As a result, both OKRs and the product roadmap are instrumental in simplifying the planning and execution of a product strategy.

Decision Levels

Let's delve into the various layers of decision-making in product development: vision, strategy, objectives, roadmap themes, and releases.

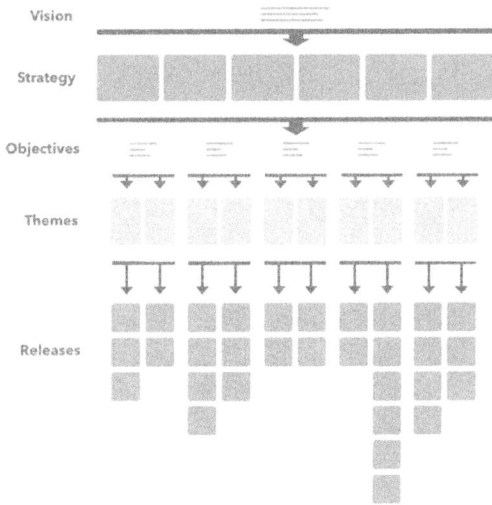

Figure 34: Decision Levels

Strategic Guidelines

The strategic guidelines represent the guiding policies to follow in order to achieve the product vision.

It could be about developing new capabilities, positioning yourself in a particular segment, entering a new market or using a new technology.

Product Objectives

Each product team has goals to pursue. These goals define what each team has to achieve to bring the product closer to the vision by following the guiding policy.

Roadmap Themes (Initiatives)

By connecting strategy with execution themes (or initiatives) are the main information units of a roadmap. They connect the product goals with the concrete solutions to be implemented.

How to Effectively Integrate OKRs and Roadmap?

OKRs and product roadmaps collaborate to establish alignment within teams, while also offering autonomy for teams to develop their own solutions. This ensures that their efforts are in sync with the product's vision and strategic guidelines.

While OKRs can be integrated with traditional roadmaps, their greatest potential is realized when combined with an agile product roadmap.

What is an Agile Roadmap?

The agile product roadmap is a prototype of the product strategy, differing significantly from the traditional timeline-based roadmap.

Unlike traditional roadmaps that prioritize dates and specific deliverables, the agile roadmap centers on the goals and objectives to be achieved. It is structured around themes that link product goals with potential solutions, highlighting problem-solving as a pathway to business growth.

How OKRs and Agile Roadmaps Work Together?

Under our approach to designing an agile product roadmap, OKRs are a fundamental element of the product plan.

	Q1	Q2	2H	Next Year
Goal 1	Theme 1.1	Theme 1.2		
Goal 2		Theme 2.1 Theme 2.2	Theme 2.3 Theme 2.4	Theme 2.5
Goal 3	Theme 3.1 Theme 3.2		Theme 3.3	Theme 3.4 Theme 3.5

Each theme (or initiative) in an agile roadmap comprises three key components:

- **Product Objectives**: These define the targets that product teams aim to achieve.
- **Product Metrics**: These are used to track progress towards the objectives and signal when adjustments might be needed.
- **Opportunities**: These represent potential areas for growth or improvement.

Therefore, by integrating OKRs with the agile roadmap, we ensure both alignment with the overarching strategy and autonomy for product teams in their execution.

For a comprehensive understanding of this topic, refer to my previous book, *'Product Roadmapping in Practice'*.

OKRs and Roadmaps - The Best of Two Worlds

OKRs and product roadmaps can effectively synchronize with each other, each bringing its own advantages to the table.

Let's delve into a side-by-side comparison of the benefits that OKRs and roadmaps offer.

OKR Benefits	Roadmap Benefits
Setting direction, boundaries and KPIs	Providing visibility on how the product is likely to grow within the guidelines provided by product strategy and towards the goals.

OKR Benefits	Roadmap Benefits
Maximize focus by describing the most important strategic challenges to overcome	Maximize focus by describing the strategic initiatives which are likely to get you closer to your goals. Everything else should be left out of the roadmap.
Align everyone to business goals and product goals	Cross-team alignment to the strategic initiatives to be pursued to achieve the product goals.
Frequent review and update of strategic direction	Frequent review and update of strategic plan based on insights from product discovery efforts, customer feedback, research, and delivery outcomes.
Help establish a modern product mindset by helping everyone focus on strategic outcomes rather than revenue goals and deliverables.	Help product teams move from output-oriented to outcome-oriented by providing strategic guidance and problem orientation rather than solution orientation.

Chapter 23: OKRs for Product Launch

In my experience with new product development, a common scenario is teams focusing primarily on launching their product by a certain deadline post-product discovery. This approach seems practical given the high levels of uncertainty involved. However, I've developed a more nuanced strategy that I've been successfully employing with my clients.

A comprehensive product discovery process, if executed correctly, reveals the critical components of your value proposition essential for success. These insights should be the focal point of your go-to-market strategy, ensuring that your efforts are not just about meeting a launch deadline, but about genuinely addressing the needs and preferences of your target market.

Furthermore, there's often an overarching business goal that needs to be integrated into this strategy.

Case Study: Crafting OKRs for a Novel Food Delivery Service

Imagine embarking on the journey of developing a groundbreaking food delivery service. The initial phase of product discovery unveils pivotal insights: our primary customer segment not only craves a plethora of healthy food choices but also places immense value on rapid delivery. Concurrently, our strategic business objective is ambitious yet clear - to establish a significant presence in the three major capital cities within our country.

With these crucial findings at the forefront, we meticulously craft our Objectives and Key Results (OKRs) for the inaugural year of operation. These OKRs are not mere goals; they are the beacon that guides our venture towards tangible success and measurable growth.

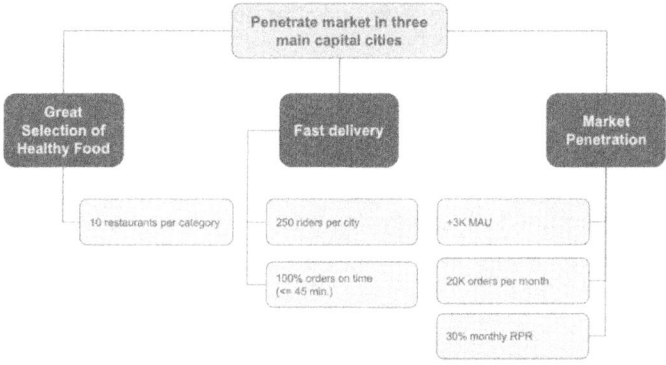

Figure 35: OKRs for Food Delivery Service Launch

In orchestrating these OKRs, we align our product's trajectory with the needs and desires of our customers while staying true to our overarching business ambitions. These objectives not only focus on launching the product but also on establishing a solid market presence and delivering tangible value to your customers.

Release Strategy

Now, you can align your release strategy with your OKRs. The key to an effective release strategy is to segment your comprehensive solution into smaller, impactful releases.

Consider this process as dividing your solution into phases, with each one delivering concrete value. In doing so, specify the release name, identify the target customers, outline the customer outcomes or needs being addressed, and determine the metrics for each phase.

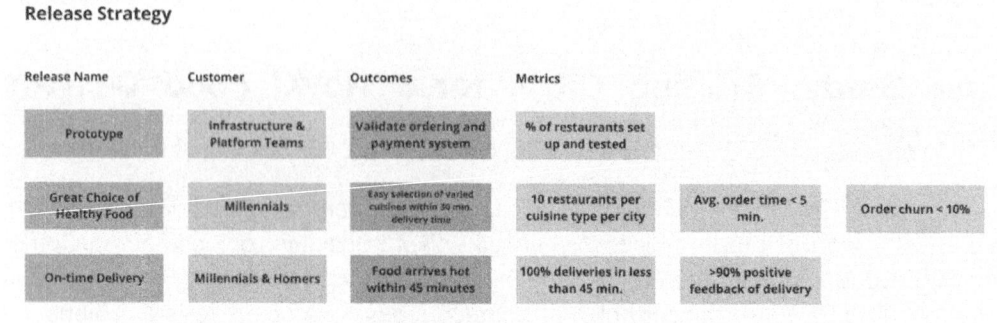

Figure 36: Release Strategy

Detailing your Feature List

User Story Mapping[22] stands as a cornerstone technique, pivotal in delineating a feature-rich release plan that aligns perfectly with user needs and business goals.

The essence of User Story Mapping is to dissect and arrange your proposed feature list into a coherent, user-centric story. This methodical approach doesn't just catalogue features; it weaves them into the user's daily experiences, ensuring each feature resonates with their needs and enhances their interaction with the product.

User Story Mapping purpose is to identify the smallest successful release. This approach ensures maximum value with minimal risk, ensuring a positive outcome for both your business and users.

Figure 37: User Story Mapping Example

Story mapping is a powerful tool in this endeavor.

Here's how it works:

- **Break It Down:** Segment your comprehensive solution into a series of smaller releases identified in your release strategy ('Prototype', 'Great Choice of Healthy Food', 'On-time Delivery'). Each should offer a positive outcome and impact for both your customers and the business.

- **Visualize the Breakdown:** When plotted on a story map, your solution gets divided into release blocks. For instance, the top actions might be categorized under the 'Prototype Release', followed by the 'Great Choice of Healthy Food', and so on.

- **Maximize Value, Minimize Risk:** The goal is to deliver maximum value at every stage while mitigating risks. Pre-planning your release strategy ensures you consistently offer high value throughout the product's lifecycle.

User Story Mapping ensures that your product's initial release, no matter how small, is a powerhouse of value. It's about striking that delicate balance between what's essential for success and what can be developed with minimal risk. This approach not only safeguards your investment but also guarantees a product that resonates deeply with your users, fostering satisfaction and loyalty.

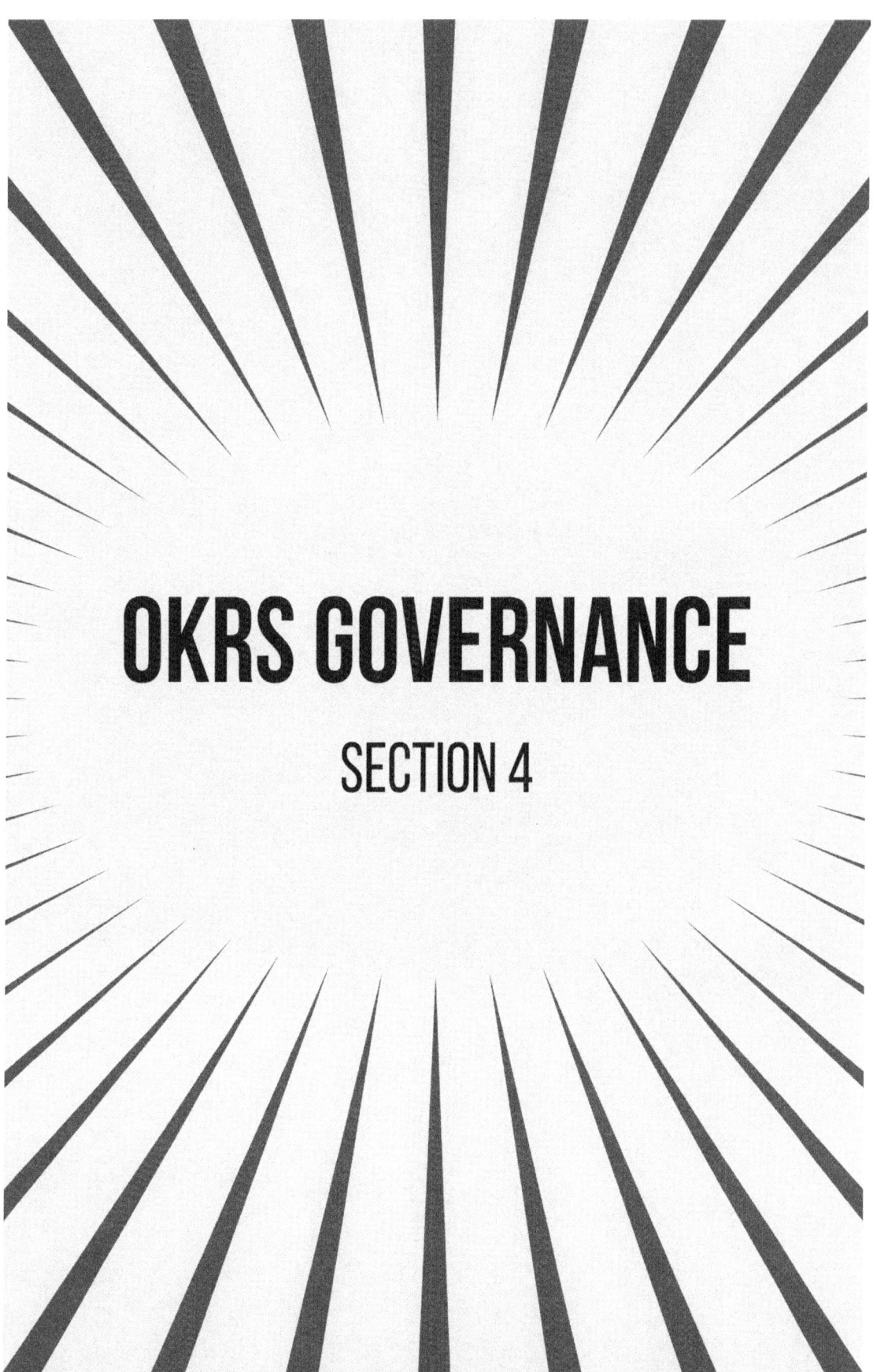

OKRS GOVERNANCE

SECTION 4

Chapter 24: Managing Frequently Changing OKRs

The stability of Objectives and Key Results is pivotal for sustained focus and strategic direction. However, a prevalent challenge that many product teams face is the frequent alteration of these OKRs.

This chapter explores the underlying reasons for this instability, its impacts on teams, and best practices to mitigate the issue.

The Core of the Problem

The root causes of frequently changing OKRs can be multifaceted.

Firstly, an absence of strategy at higher management levels often leads to arbitrary goal-setting, where OKRs lack a long-term vision and are subject to whimsical changes. This issue is particularly acute in core product, innovation, and platform teams, where strategic stability is crucial.

Secondly, too fine-grained goals can lead to a hyper-focus on specific, narrow objectives. This approach often overlooks broader, more stable strategic goals, like North Star Metrics (NSMs), leading to frequent shifts in focus.

Lastly, the problem of task-list OKRs arises when OKRs resemble a checklist rather than outcome-focused objectives. This converts the strategic tool into a mere operational list, triggering constant adjustments as tasks are completed or priorities shift.

Understanding the Absence of Strategy

At the heart of unstable OKRs often lies an Absence of Strategy.

Well-structured goals stem from a robust strategy. In its absence, organizations find themselves grappling with random or arbitrary goals, subject to frequent change.

This is especially detrimental for core product teams, innovation teams, and platform teams, where stability in goals is key for motivation and focus.

In contrast, growth teams may experience more frequent goal changes due to their focus on driving immediate growth, using metrics like North Star Metrics (NSMs) and One Metric That Matters (OMTMs) for shorter-term objectives.

The Issue with Too Fine-Grained Goals

Another challenge is the setting of too fine-grained goals at higher levels.

When goals are overly specific, such as improving a particular checkout dropout rate, they tend to change more often.

A more effective approach is to align these specific goals with broader objectives like increasing monthly orders for certain user profiles by a defined percentage. This ensures that all teams are working towards a common, overarching goal, thus reducing the frequency of goal changes, and promoting strategic alignment.

The Pitfall of To-Do List OKRs

To-Do list OKRs represent a fundamental misunderstanding of the OKR framework.

When managers or stakeholders request a list of tasks, they are essentially creating a shopping list, not setting goals. This often leads to frustration and non-strategic work as these 'goals' change too frequently.

The recommendation in such cases is to gradually shift the focus towards outcome-driven roadmaps, moving away from a task-oriented approach to one that is aligned with the company's strategic objectives.

The Importance of Stability

Stable OKRs are the bedrock of effective long-term planning and team alignment. They provide a clear direction and enable teams to channel their efforts towards consistent objectives. The frequent change of OKRs not only disrupts workflow but also erodes trust in the strategic direction, undermining the integrity of the OKR framework itself.

The Detrimental Impact of Changes

The consequences of constantly shifting OKRs are far-reaching. Teams become demoralized, as their efforts seem to contribute to a moving target. This lack of stability can lead to frustration, decreased motivation, and a feeling of aimlessness, ultimately impacting the overall productivity and effectiveness of the team.

Strategies for Balancing Flexibility and Stability

To counteract the challenges of frequently changing OKRs, several strategies can be employed:

- **Seeking Strategic Context**: Product teams should proactively seek strategic clarity from higher management. Understanding the long-term vision helps in aligning OKRs accordingly and defending them against unnecessary changes.

- **Alignment with Overarching Goals**: Emphasizing the alignment of team goals with broader company objectives, such as NSMs, can ensure a more stable and consistent focus for OKRs.

- **Promoting Outcome-Driven Goals**: Transitioning the mindset from task completion to outcome-driven objectives can lead to more meaningful and stable OKRs. This shift helps teams focus on impact rather than just activities.

- **Roadmap Integration**: Gradually embedding the concept of outcome-driven roadmaps can align daily tasks with strategic OKRs. This integration ensures that team efforts are consistently contributing to larger company goals.

- **Regular Strategic Reviews**: Implementing periodic strategic reviews can help adjust OKRs when genuinely necessary, rather than on an ad-hoc basis. These reviews should be an opportunity to reassess and realign, not to overhaul.

- **Empowering Teams**: Allowing teams some autonomy in defining how they contribute to broader goals can foster a sense of ownership. This empowerment can often lead to more stable and internally motivated OKRs.

Optimal Duration of an OKRs Cycle

The inaugural cycle of implementing Objectives and Key Results can span from a brisk one-month pilot to an extensive full-year period. It's generally advisable to steer clear of a one-month cycle due to the challenges in crafting meaningful OKRs within such a brief timeframe. It's beneficial to standardize the cycle duration at the outset.

Commencing with a uniform cycle time facilitates synchronized completion and shared learning experiences across all teams. Although a quarterly basis is commonly preferred for defining OKRs, some organizations opt for a four-month cycle to circumvent the pressures of holiday seasons and end-of-quarter rushes.

After a year or more of utilizing OKRs, organizations often find that a single, fixed cycle time for all teams is not mandatory. While many teams adhere to the initial cycle timing, others, particularly those in areas like research and development, might find value in adjusting their cycle duration after a few cycles to accommodate the need for more substantial progress measurement time.

Furthermore, the standard cycle length may vary depending on the organizational hierarchy. Higher-level OKRs, which are more strategic, are typically set for longer periods. Conversely, OKRs at lower organizational levels, which are more operational, are often slated for shorter durations.

Consistency and Adaptation in OKR Cycles

Maintaining consistency in top-level objectives throughout a year can be advantageous. This steadiness allows lower-level teams ample time to comprehend and integrate these top-level objectives into the context of their team-specific OKRs.

At the team level, OKRs are generally set on a quarterly or four-month basis, although this is not a strict requirement. Some organizations introduce multiple layers of team-level OKRs, each with distinct cycle durations.

For instance, consider organizing these into distinct 'Layers.' Teams in Layer 1 set objectives for the entire year and review their key results every quarter. Layer 2 teams, while also focusing on annual objectives, aim to achieve their key results within a six-month timeframe, with progress reviewed quarterly. On the other hand, Layer 3 teams are dedicated to quarterly objectives and key results, including mid-quarter evaluations to facilitate continuous monitoring and prompt adjustments.

Conclusion

The challenge of managing frequently changing OKRs requires a balanced approach that combines strategic understanding, alignment with overarching company goals, and a shift towards outcome-driven objectives.

Product managers and their teams, through the application of these strategies, can effectively navigate the challenges of instability. This approach fosters a focused, motivated, and strategically aligned methodology, essential for the successful attainment of their objectives.

Chapter 25: Alignment with OKRs

In a large organization, the shift to OKRs can reveal the complex web of interdependencies between teams. It's common to hear teams express concerns about their inability to achieve outcomes independently, as they rely on others to fulfill their objectives. This is where the true power of OKRs lies—not just in setting goals, but in forging alignment across various functions of the company.

Dependencies

When large companies adopt OKRs, a frequent complaint I hear from teams is their inability to deliver specific outcomes independently due to dependencies on other teams.

This challenge often manifests in various forms, such as reliance on multiple departments for a single initiative or the need for sequential input from different teams.

Such dependencies highlight the interconnected nature of tasks and goals within larger organizations and underscore the necessity for a more collaborative and integrated approach to achieving objectives.

While restructuring organizational design and incentives is a broader challenge, OKRs lay the groundwork for acknowledging and tackling crucial inter-team dependencies.

Unmasking Dependencies with OKRs

OKRs don't dissolve dependencies in large organizations. Instead, they expose them, highlighting often unspoken constraints that slow down value delivery. For instance, when a team embraces an outcome as a KR, understanding its placement in the customer journey is crucial. This realization brings to light the interdependence among teams.

Breaking the Silo Mentality

Teams quickly realize that they're not as autonomous as they might believe.

Consider a marketing team tasked with increasing brand awareness through social media. Their success is not solely dependent on their creativity and campaign execution. It also hinges on the quality and appeal of the product, managed by the product development team, and the customer service experience, overseen by the support team.

If the product isn't well-received or customer issues are not efficiently resolved, the marketing team's efforts may not translate into the desired brand image enhancement, regardless of the effectiveness of their social media strategies.

This scenario underscores the interdependence and need for alignment across different departments in achieving shared objectives.

Forcing a New Perspective

Traditionally, teams would develop features in isolation, measuring success solely by deployment. However, OKRs have illuminated the need for closer inter-departmental collaboration to build a cohesive user journey.

Success is no longer an isolated affair; it requires understanding and cooperation across departments.

OKRs as Catalysts for Organizational Transformation

OKRs not only highlight inter-team dependencies but can also trigger a shift towards a product-oriented organization structured around empowered, end-to-end product teams or value streams.

This transformation is rooted in the realization that achieving objectives often requires cross-functional collaboration and a more integrated approach.

OKRs encourage breaking down traditional silos, prompting teams to align around shared goals and customer-centric outcomes.

This shift fosters a more agile, responsive organizational structure, where teams are empowered to deliver complete product experiences, from inception to delivery, enhancing overall efficiency and value creation.

Aligning for Impact: A Practical Guide to OKRs in Multi-Team Environments

The art of aligning Objectives and Key Results across various teams is akin to conducting an orchestra—each section must harmonize with the others to create a symphonic masterpiece. This section delves into the intricacies of collaborative goal setting, its profound benefits, and a practical guide to fostering a cohesive environment where all department's efforts resonate with the company's strategic symphony.

In multi-team environments, crafting goals collaboratively across product teams and then seeking feedback from supporting departments ensures a harmonious pursuit of organizational objectives.

Common Scenarios

In the journey of aligning organizational efforts with strategic goals, OKRs play a pivotal role.

Let's delve into three typical scenarios as illustrated in the attached diagram: shared, complementary, and conflicting OKRs.

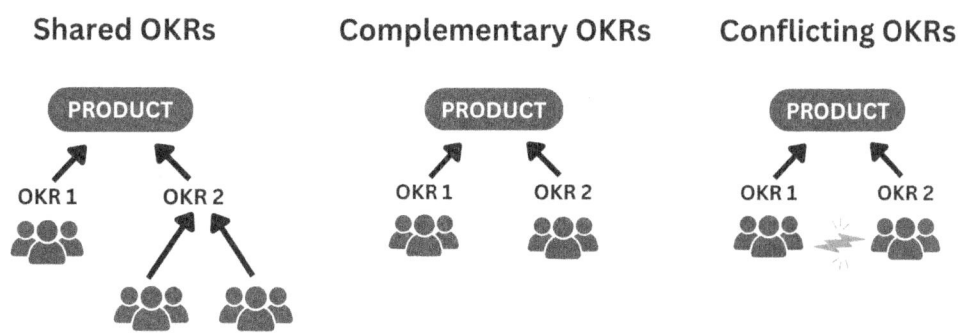

Figure 38: Shared, Complementary and Conflicting OKRs

Shared OKRs

Shared OKRs occur when multiple teams collaborate on a shared objective, combining their resources and expertise. For example, the product and marketing teams might jointly pursue an OKR like *'Increase product sign-ups by 20% in Q2.'* In this scenario, the marketing team would concentrate on generating leads, while the product team would work on improving the sign-up process.

Complementary OKRs

Complementary OKRs occur when different teams set distinct but interrelated OKRs that support each other's goals. If the customer service team's OKR is to *'Reduce call resolution time by 30%'*, it complements the product team's OKR to *'Improve user self-service tools'*, as both aim to enhance customer satisfaction.

Conflicting OKRs

Conflicting OKRs arise when teams have objectives that inadvertently obstruct each other's goals, leading to organizational misalignment. For example, if one team's OKR is to *'Expand feature set to attract new users'* while another's is to *'Minimize product complexity for user retention'*, the disparity can create tension and inefficiency.

Conflicting OKRs can introduce dissonance. If one team's objective inadvertently hinders another's, it's akin to two instruments playing in different keys. To resolve this, teams need to engage in a dialogue, re-evaluate their priorities, and sometimes, seek a mediator—perhaps a leader or a cross-functional group—to help tune their strategies into harmony.

Resolving Conflicting OKRs

Let's delve into strategies designed to effectively address and resolve conflicting objectives among teams. The goal of these methods is to align OKRs across various teams with the overarching company strategy, fostering a cohesive approach to achieving shared goals:

1. **Cross-functional Review**: Organize a cross-functional meeting to review conflicting OKRs and understand the rationale behind each team's objectives.
2. **Strategic Intent**: Use the company's strategic priorities to decide which OKRs should take precedence.
3. **Integration**: Where possible, integrate conflicting OKRs into a unified approach that satisfies both parties' intents.
4. **Iteration**: Adjust OKRs in iterative cycles, allowing teams to realign and recalibrate based on feedback and changing company direction.
5. **Mediation**: If conflicts persist, a neutral party or executive team may need to mediate and provide a decision that aligns with the broader company strategy.
6. **Checksum**: my concept of a 'checksum' from network communications can be translated into a mechanism for resolving conflicting OKRs by establishing control Key Results (KRs) or a control OKR.

Checksum OKR Technique for Addressing Conflicting OKRs

Often times two teams may find themselves stepping on each other's toes, their OKRs pulling in opposing directions. It's a common predicament where one team's push for enhanced user conversion clashes with another's mandate to bolster retention.

Such conflicts can cause friction and impede the collective drive toward product success. Enter the concept I coined as *'checksum OKRs'*—a reconciliatory technique borrowed from the principles of network communications.

This approach introduces a system of control OKRs that operate like a checksum, validating that the pursuit of individual objectives does not compromise the integrity of the overall product strategy.

Let's explore how this technique can harmonize the OKRs of two fictitious product teams, ensuring their efforts collectively amplify, rather than undermine, the product's success.

Scenario:

A fictitious company, AppTech, has two product teams with seemingly conflicting OKRs. Team A focuses on *'Improving Conversion Rates'* while Team B works on *'Enhancing User Retention.'*

Conflicting OKRs:

- *Team A's OKR: Increase the conversion rate of free trial users to premium subscribers by 25%.*
- *Team B's OKR: Increase the retention rate of existing premium subscribers by 30%.*

Resolution with Checksum OKR:

To resolve this, AppTech introduces a control OKR that acts as a checksum:

Control OKR:

Ensure overall user satisfaction improves by 20% without negatively impacting either conversion or retention rates.

Control KRs:

1. *User satisfaction score among new subscribers > 80%.*
2. *User satisfaction score among existing subscribers > 90%.*

Through the checksum approach, teams can align their strategies to achieve their individual OKRs while simultaneously enhancing the user experience, the collective checksum goal. This method ensures that efforts to enhance one metric do not unintentionally negatively impact the other. It promotes a balanced strategy for product development and user satisfaction.

Step-by-Step Guide for Building Alignment

Aligning OKRs involves all teams. It starts with collaborative goal-setting sessions where teams draft their OKRs together, ensuring they align from the outset. Then, socializing these goals across the organization invites feedback and brings to light any overlooked conflicts or dependencies.

Here's a step-by-step guide for multi-team alignment with OKRs:

1. **Inter-Team Workshops**: Conduct workshops with product teams to define overarching goals.

2. **Cross-Functional Feedback Sessions**: Invite supporting departments to provide input on the proposed OKRs, ensuring alignment with wider company objectives.

3. **Alignment Mapping**: Visually map out how individual team OKRs contribute to higher-level goals to identify overlaps and gaps.

4. **Regular Alignment Check-ins**: Schedule periodic meetings to ensure ongoing alignment and to address any emerging conflicts.

5. **Transparent Communication**: Maintain open channels of communication across all teams for continuous feedback and updates on progress.

6. **Socializing Goals**: Share finalized OKRs company-wide to foster transparency and collective responsibility.

Adhering to these steps enables organizations to build a network of teams where OKRs are not only aligned but also reinforce the company's strategic direction. This approach ensures a unified and successful path forward.

Chapter 26: Navigating Shared OKRs Across Teams

Shared Objectives and Key Results are instrumental in aligning various teams towards common organizational goals. The success of shared OKRs largely depends on establishing clear ownership, ensuring effective communication, and utilizing appropriate tools for documentation and tracking.

Setting Up Shared OKRs for Success

This section delves into these critical aspects to set up shared OKRs for success.

Establishing Clear Ownership and Responsibilities for Shared OKRs

- **Assigning Ownership:** Clearly designate ownership of each shared OKR. While these OKRs span multiple teams, having a specific owner or lead for each ensures accountability and focus.

- **Defining Roles and Responsibilities:** Explicitly outline the roles and responsibilities of each team involved. This includes specifying who is responsible for which aspects of the OKR and how contributions will be measured.

- **Collaborative Goal Setting:** Involve representatives from all relevant teams in the goal-setting process. This collaborative approach ensures that shared OKRs are realistic, achievable, and aligned with the capabilities and resources of each team.

- **Regular Cross-Team Meetings:** Schedule regular meetings involving members from all teams working on the shared OKR. These meetings should focus on progress updates, addressing challenges, and coordinating efforts.

- **Transparent Information Sharing:** Create a system for transparent information sharing. This could include a shared digital workspace where updates, data, and feedback are accessible to all relevant stakeholders.

Tools and Methods for Documenting and Tracking Shared OKRs

- **Choosing the Right Tools:** Utilize project management and OKR tracking tools that allow multiple users to update progress, share data, and communicate.

- **Real-Time Progress Tracking:** Implement systems that provide real-time tracking of key results. This enables all teams to see the current status of shared OKRs at any given time.
- **Documentation Best Practices:** Maintain thorough documentation of all aspects of the shared OKRs. This includes initial objectives, key results, metrics for success, and any changes or adjustments made over time.

Monitoring and Evaluating Progress

Monitoring and evaluating the progress of shared OKRs is vital to ensure alignment and successful execution. This section outlines effective techniques for tracking progress, addresses the unique challenges in evaluating shared OKRs, and emphasizes the importance of regular cross-team meetings.

Techniques for Tracking Progress on Shared OKRs

- **Centralized Tracking System:** Use a centralized platform or tool where all involved teams can update and monitor the progress of shared OKRs. This could be a specialized OKR software or a project management tool with OKR tracking features.
- **Visual Dashboards:** Create visual dashboards that display real-time progress. This can include charts, graphs, and progress bars, making it easier for all team members to quickly grasp the status of shared OKRs.

Addressing Challenges Unique to Shared OKR Evaluation

- **Aligning Differing Team Priorities:** In cases where team priorities differ, it's crucial to establish a common ground and align the OKRs with the overarching goals of the organization. Regular discussions and adjustments may be required to keep all teams aligned.
- **Cross-Functional Dependencies:** Identify and manage cross-functional dependencies early in the OKR cycle. Establish clear communication channels to ensure that dependencies are addressed promptly and do not impede progress.

Regular Cross-Team Meetings and Updates to Assess Progress

- **Scheduled Progress Meetings:** Hold regular meetings with representatives from all teams involved in the shared OKRs. These meetings should focus on discussing progress, obstacles, and collaborative solutions.

- **Update and Review Sessions:** Use these meetings for detailed update and review sessions where teams can share their achievements, challenges, and learnings. This helps in maintaining a comprehensive view of the shared OKRs' progress.

- **Action Planning:** Based on the discussions and evaluations during these meetings, jointly plan actions for the next period. This may include reassigning tasks, addressing resource gaps, or re-prioritizing efforts to stay on track with the shared OKRs.

Resolving Conflicts and Realigning Goals

In the implementation of shared or complementary OKRs, conflicts may arise due to differing priorities, resource limitations, or varied interpretations of objectives. Effectively resolving these conflicts and realigning goals is crucial to maintain the integrity of the OKR process and ensure collective success.

This section explores strategies for conflict resolution, methods for realigning divergent objectives, and the role of leadership in these processes.

Strategies for Resolving Conflicts Arising from Shared or Complementary OKRs

- **Early Identification of Potential Conflicts:** Proactively identify areas where conflicts might arise. This could be related to resource allocation, timelines, or differing team priorities.

- **Structured Conflict Resolution Process:** Implement a structured process for conflict resolution. This can include discussions facilitated by a neutral party, structured brainstorming sessions, or formal mediation.

- **Focus on Common Objectives:** Encourage teams to focus on the overarching goals of the organization. Remind all parties involved of the shared vision and how each team's contribution is vital to achieving this vision.

Methods for Realigning OKRs When Teams' Objectives Diverge

- **Assess and Reevaluate Objectives:** When objectives between teams begin to diverge, take time to assess and reevaluate these objectives. Determine if the original OKRs still align with the overall strategic goals of the organization.
- **Collaborative Goal Resetting:** Engage all relevant teams in a collaborative process to reset goals. This should be a consensus-driven process, ensuring that all voices are heard and that the revised OKRs are mutually agreed upon.
- **Flexible Approach:** Maintain a flexible approach to OKR management. Be willing to make adjustments to OKRs as needed, while still keeping the focus on the larger organizational objectives.

The Role of Leadership in Mediating and Facilitating Alignment

Leadership plays a critical role in facilitating these processes, ensuring that teams remain focused on the collective objectives of the organization.

- **Active Mediation:** Leadership should take an active role in mediating conflicts. This involves understanding the perspectives of each team, identifying common ground, and guiding teams towards a resolution.
- **Clear Communication:** Leaders must ensure that communication channels are open and effective. Clear, transparent, and frequent communication can prevent misunderstandings and keep all teams aligned.
- **Support and Guidance:** Provide support and guidance to teams as they work through conflicts and realign goals. Leaders should be seen as facilitators of collaboration and alignment, helping teams navigate through challenges.

Celebrating Joint Successes

The achievement of shared Objectives and Key Results is not just a milestone for the teams involved but also an opportunity to reinforce collaboration and unity within the organization. Celebrating these joint successes is crucial for acknowledging hard work, sharing key learnings, and strengthening inter-team relationships.

This section outlines how to effectively recognize and celebrate shared OKR achievements, disseminate learnings, and leverage these successes to foster a collaborative culture.

Recognizing and Rewarding the Successful Achievement of Shared OKRs

- **Formal Recognition:** Implement formal recognition programs or events to celebrate the successful achievement of shared OKRs. This could include award ceremonies, public acknowledgments in company meetings, or features in internal communications.
- **Personalized Appreciation:** Ensure that recognition is personalized and specific. Acknowledge individual contributions as well as team efforts, highlighting how each person's work contributed to the overall success.

Sharing Learnings and Best Practices Across Teams

- **Debriefing Sessions:** Conduct debriefing sessions where teams can share their experiences, challenges faced, and strategies that led to success. This is an opportunity to extract and document best practices.
- **Knowledge Sharing Platforms:** Utilize internal platforms, such as intranets or newsletters, to share stories and insights from the successful OKR journey. This not only celebrates achievements but also serves as a learning resource for other teams.
- **Workshops and Training Sessions:** Convert the learnings into actionable insights by organizing workshops or training sessions. These can be led by members of the successful teams, fostering a culture of peer-to-peer learning.

Using Shared Successes to Build Stronger Inter-Team Relationships for Future Collaborations

- **Building a Narrative of Collaboration:** Use the success stories as narratives that underscore the importance and effectiveness of collaboration. Highlight how different teams working together can achieve greater results than working in silos.
- **Networking and Relationship Building:** Create opportunities for networking and informal interactions between teams. Celebratory events, team-building activities, or casual meet-ups can facilitate relationship building.
- **Planning for Future Collaborations:** Leverage the goodwill and positive momentum generated by the success to plan future collaborative initiatives. Encourage teams to explore new possibilities for working together, using the learnings from the shared OKR experience as a foundation.

Celebrating joint successes is not just about acknowledging achievements; it is essential to reinforce a collaborative culture, share valuable insights, and strengthen inter-team relationships.

Personal Experience as a Product Coach

As a Product Strategy Coach, I encountered a challenging situation at a mid-sized tech company, which was struggling to synchronize its product and marketing teams. Each team operated in silos, with distinct OKRs that lacked alignment, leading to missed opportunities and inefficiencies.

The Challenge:

The product team was focused on innovating and rolling out new features for their flagship software. Meanwhile, the marketing team was concentrated on broadening market reach. However, without shared objectives, the marketing team was often unaware of the new features being developed, resulting in misaligned marketing strategies and a failure to capitalize on the product innovations.

Intervention:

As their Product Strategy Coach, I stepped in to bridge this gap. The first step was to facilitate a joint workshop with both teams. The goal was to identify areas where their objectives overlapped and could be transformed into shared OKRs.

Establishing Shared Objectives:

Through collaborative discussions, we identified a mutual goal: *'Improve Conversion by 30% for Retail Customers.'* This shared objective was broken down into complementary OKRs, with each team responsible for specific key results that supported the common goal.

Action Taken:

1. **Product Development:** Implement user feedback mechanisms to guide the development of new features.
2. **Marketing Team:** Develop marketing campaigns that specifically highlight new features and user-driven improvements.
3. **Regular Cross-Team Meetings:** We established bi-weekly cross-functional meetings for progress updates and collaborative planning. These sessions

allowed for real-time feedback and adjustments, ensuring both teams were aligned and responsive to each other's needs.

4. **Conflict Resolution:** Conflicts arose initially, particularly in resource allocation and prioritizing tasks. To address this, we set up a conflict resolution protocol that involved transparent communication and finding middle ground solutions, always keeping the shared objectives in focus.

Outcome:

In just a few months, the results were impressive. Innovations from the product team were seamlessly integrated into marketing campaigns. This synergy led to a 40% increase in conversion rates for retail customers, a 25% boost in customer engagement, and a significant expansion of market reach.

Learning and Reflection:

The power of shared and complementary objectives was vividly illustrated through this experience. It brought to light the importance of cross-team collaboration for achieving broader organizational goals, and the need for regular communication to align efforts and resolve conflicts.

Moreover, it underscored the vital role of leadership in fostering a collaborative environment. Reinforcing my belief in the transformative impact of shared objectives, the experience clearly showed that when teams align their goals and work together, they can drive significant success and innovation, going far beyond what they could achieve individually.

Chapter 27: Evaluating OKR Progress

The essence of OKRs lies not just in their formulation but significantly in their evaluation. This chapter delves into the critical process of evaluating OKR progress, an essential practice that bridges the gap between aspiration and reality.

OKRs combine ambitious objectives with concrete, measurable key results, providing a clear roadmap for teams and organizations. They serve as a compass, guiding efforts towards strategic goals while allowing flexibility and adaptation.

This dual nature of aspiration and measurability makes the evaluation of OKRs a nuanced yet powerful exercise. It's not merely about ticking off completed tasks; it's about assessing progress towards strategic objectives, understanding the impact, and learning from the journey.

This chapter aims to equip managers, teams, and leaders with effective methods and best practices to assess and enhance their journey towards achieving key organizational goals.

Setting the Stage for Effective Evaluation

The Foundation of Clarity

The first step in evaluating OKRs effectively is to ensure their initial formulation is crystal-clear. Clear OKRs set the stage for accurate and meaningful evaluation. They should be concise, unambiguous, and easily understandable, leaving no room for varied interpretations. This clarity helps in making the evaluation process straightforward and objective, focused on actual progress rather than perceptions or assumptions.

Alignment with Organizational Timelines

OKRs should be in harmony with the rhythm of the organization. Whether they are set on a quarterly, bi-annual, or annual basis, aligning them with the organizational timelines ensures that they are relevant and that their evaluation coincides with other critical business processes. This alignment fosters a sense of timeliness and urgency, making OKR evaluation a regular and integral part of organizational life.

Establishing Benchmarks and Success Criteria

To evaluate progress, one must first define what success looks like. Setting benchmarks and criteria for success at the outset provides a target to aim for and a standard against which to measure progress.

These benchmarks should be realistic yet challenging, pushing the boundaries of what's possible while remaining achievable. They should also be quantifiable, providing a clear metric for evaluation.

Establishing these parameters upfront turns the evaluation of OKRs from a subjective judgment into an objective analysis, empowering teams to assess their progress accurately and make informed decisions for future strategies.

In the following sections, we will explore the mechanisms of regular check-ins, methods for measuring key results, and strategies for adapting OKRs to changing circumstances, among other critical aspects of OKR evaluation.

Creating an OKRs Working Agreement

As a product coach, one key observation is the gap between teams expressing interest in OKRs and their actual integration into daily work. This phenomenon, known in the OKRs community as "set-it-and-forget-it," occurs when teams define their OKRs but fail to embed them in their routine tasks.

To counter this, initiating a working agreement at the outset proves beneficial. This working agreement, which teams fill out and sign, serves as a commitment device. While customizable, it typically includes elements like the team's name, mission, OKRs review cadence, attendees of review meetings, and methods of celebrating OKR achievements.

This process ensures that each team not only creates but also commits to regularly reviewing their OKRs throughout the cycle, thereby circumventing the *"set-it-and-forget-it"* pitfall.

Addressing the Issue of Too Many Meetings

Conversely, another challenge encountered is the tendency of some teams to overcompensate with excessive OKRs-specific meetings. It's not uncommon to find organizations scheduling two meetings per week solely for OKR reviews, which can transform the OKRs program into an unwelcome burden.

Integrating OKRs Check-Ins into Existing Meetings

The most effective approach is to incorporate OKR check-ins into existing team meetings. A practical strategy is to start weekly or biweekly team meetings with a brief OKR review. This integration is particularly advantageous when beginning with top-level OKRs, as executives often lead these sessions, providing a template for success that can be replicated at the team level.

Advising on Team-Level OKRs Implementation

For clients eager to implement team-level OKRs from the onset, it is advisable to start small. Coaching a pilot group of three to five teams through a complete OKR cycle allows for focused guidance and learning. Emphasize prioritizing learning about OKRs in the first cycle and considering scalability in subsequent cycles.

Regular Check-Ins and Reviews

To navigate the path towards achieving OKRs successfully, consistent monitoring and reviewing are indispensable.

Regular check-ins and reviews are more than just a procedural requirement; they are a crucial opportunity for teams to align, adjust, and learn.

This section outlines the strategies for regular check-ins and reviews, which are pivotal in maintaining momentum and ensuring alignment with set goals.

Scheduling and Conducting Regular OKR Review Meetings

The cadence of OKR review meetings should align with the rhythm of the OKR cycle. For most organizations, this means conducting reviews either monthly or quarterly. The key is to find a balance that allows enough time for meaningful progress while still maintaining a sense of urgency and focus.

These meetings should have a clear structure. Begin with a review of each key result, followed by an assessment of the progress made towards the objective. This should be both quantitative (looking at the metrics) and qualitative (discussing the challenges and successes).

Encourage active participation from all teams. Each team should have the opportunity to report on their OKRs, share insights, and provide updates on challenges and breakthroughs. This not only fosters a sense of ownership but also promotes transparency and collective responsibility.

Methods for Tracking Progress

There are numerous software tools designed specifically for tracking OKRs. These tools often offer features like dashboards for real-time progress tracking, integration with other business tools, and facilities for regular updates.

For teams not using specialized software, customized spreadsheets or documents can be effective. These should be structured to clearly outline objectives, key results, and progress indicators.

Using visual tools such as charts, graphs, and progress bars can make the tracking process more engaging and understandable. Visual representations of data can help teams quickly grasp their progress and identify areas needing attention.

The Role of Managers in Facilitating Progress Discussions

Team leads and managers should guide the OKR review discussions, ensuring that they stay focused and productive. This involves steering the conversation towards strategic insights, problem-solving, and planning for the next steps.

They are also responsible for providing the necessary support and resources to their team members. This might include helping to remove roadblocks, offering guidance, or reallocating resources where needed.

An important aspect of these discussions is to encourage reflection on what's working and what isn't. It's not just about assessing progress, but also about learning from the process and applying those learnings to future cycles.

Measuring Key Results

Tracking the progress of Key Results (KRs) is a crucial component of the OKR framework, offering teams an objective way to evaluate their advancement towards set goals. This section will explore two important facets of measuring KRs: the different scoring systems and strategies for handling KRs that are either partially achieved or in a state of evolution.

Using a Scoring System

- **0-1 Scale or Percentage Completion:** A common method for measuring progress in OKRs is using a scale from 0 to 1, where 0 means no progress and 1 signifies complete achievement of the KR. Alternatively, a percentage scale (0% to 100%) can serve the same purpose. These scales provide a simple, straightforward way to gauge how far the team has come in achieving its KRs.

- **Setting Thresholds for Success:** It's crucial to define what success looks like on these scales beforehand. For instance, a score of 0.7 or 70% might be considered a success in some cases, depending on the level of challenge and ambition inherent in the KR.
- **Consistency in Scoring:** Ensure that scoring is consistent across all KRs. This means having a uniform understanding across the team of what each point on the scale represents.

Handling Partially Achieved or Evolving Key Results

It's not uncommon for KRs to be partially achieved. In such cases, assess the extent of achievement and the impact it has had towards reaching the overall objective. Reflect on the factors contributing to the partial achievement and how they can be addressed in the next cycle.

Any changes in KRs, whether in their definition or in their measurement criteria, should be thoroughly documented and communicated to all stakeholders. This ensures transparency and maintains the integrity of the OKR process.

Measuring Key Results (Revised with Alternative Approach)

While traditional scoring systems for evaluating Key Results (KRs) are widely used, they can sometimes lead to conflicts, subjective interpretations, and unproductive discussions. An alternative approach, focusing on defining success upfront and assessing the quality of achievement, can provide a more nuanced and effective way of measuring progress.

Redefining the Measurement of Key Results

When setting OKRs, it's crucial that the first KR explicitly defines what success looks like. This involves establishing a clear, specific target at the outset. This target should be ambitious yet achievable, providing a clear goal for the team to aim for.

The remaining KRs should be designed to assess how well the goal was achieved. This involves looking beyond just whether the target was hit and delving into the quality, impact, and sustainability of the results. This approach encourages teams to think more deeply about the implications and long-term effects of their efforts.

Example Illustrating the Alternative Approach

- **Traditional Scoring System:** Suppose a sales team has an OKR to *"Increase sales revenue."* A typical KR might be, *"Achieve a 20% increase in sales revenue by the end of Q2."* Using a traditional scoring system, the team might rate themselves 0.8 if they achieve a 16% increase.

- **Alternative Approach:** In the alternative approach, the first KR could be, *"Achieve a 20% increase in sales revenue, with a focus on long-term customer relationships."* Additional KRs could include, *"Secure at least 30% of the increased revenue from repeat customers"* and *"Achieve a customer satisfaction score of over 85% for new sales."* This approach not only targets the quantitative aspect (20% increase) but also emphasizes the quality and sustainability of the sales (repeat customers, high customer satisfaction).

Advantages of the Alternative Approach

Emphasizing the quality of goal achievement, this approach motivates teams to prioritize long-term value over merely achieving short-term targets. By setting clear objectives from the start and concentrating on quantifiable success factors, it aims to minimize subjectivity in evaluations.

Teams are encouraged to reflect on the wider implications of their work, ensuring a stronger alignment with the business's overall objectives and values.

This revised method for measuring Key Results in the OKR framework is designed for a more thorough and significant assessment of progress, spotlighting not just what is achieved but also how well it is achieved.

Adjusting OKRs Mid-Cycle

The dynamic nature of business often necessitates adjustments to OKRs mid-cycle. Being adaptable and responsive to change is as important as setting ambitious goals at the outset.

This section focuses on how to identify the need for such adjustments, balance ambition with realism, and ensure that changes are well-documented and communicated.

Identifying When and How to Adjust OKRs

- **Monitoring External and Internal Factors:** Regularly review external market trends, internal business changes, and team performance. Significant shifts in any of these areas may necessitate a reassessment of your current OKRs.

- **Assessing Progress and Roadblocks:** If the progress on a particular KR is consistently behind schedule, or if unforeseen roadblocks have emerged, it may be time to re-evaluate and adjust your objectives or key results.
- **Collaborative Decision-Making:** Adjustments should ideally be made in consultation with the team members involved in the OKRs. This encourages ownership and ensures that changes are grounded in the team's practical experiences and insights.

Balancing Ambition and Realism in Mid-Cycle Adjustments

- **Reassessing Ambition Levels:** If an OKR is found to be unrealistically ambitious, recalibrate it to a more attainable level without losing sight of the drive to challenge and improve.
- **Maintaining Alignment with Overall Goals:** Ensure that any adjustments made mid-cycle continue to align with the overall strategic goals of the organization. Adjustments should not derail the OKR from its intended purpose.
- **Incremental Adjustments:** Prefer incremental adjustments over radical changes unless there's a strong strategic reason to do otherwise. This approach minimizes disruption and maintains focus.

Documenting Changes and Communicating Them to the Team

- **Clear Documentation:** Document any changes made to the OKRs, including the rationale behind these changes. This not only provides a record for future reference but also helps in understanding the evolution of your strategy.
- **Effective Communication:** Communicate changes clearly and promptly to all stakeholders. This can be done through team meetings, email updates, or through the OKR tracking tool being used.
- **Soliciting Feedback:** After communicating the changes, solicit feedback to ensure that everyone understands and is on board with the new direction. This can also provide valuable insights for future adjustments.

Adjusting OKRs mid-cycle is not a sign of failure but a reflection of agility and responsiveness to the ever-changing business environment.

Identifying the need for change with precision, striking a balance between ambition and realism, and upholding clear documentation and communication are crucial for organizations to keep their OKRs relevant and effective throughout the cycle.

Mid-term Check-Ins

For an effective OKRs cycle I recommend standard set of tools. In Chapter 11 I provided a template for quarterly strategy review meeting.

Now, let's see a proposed template for mid-term check-in[23]:

---

1 – Progress
- Evaluate recent initiatives contributing to Key Results.
- Document both the current value and the target for each KR.

2 – Scoring
- Present both current and predicted scores or confidence levels.
- Utilize the predetermined scoring system.

3 – Impediments
- Identify factors hindering progress.
- Assess any unforeseen negative impacts.

4 – Plan
- Outline initiatives and actions to advance KRs.
- Update the product roadmap and product backlog accordingly.

Teams typically document progress in a unified format and location, which varies based on their comfort level.

OKR Check-in Coaching Questions

Facilitating check-in sessions is more structured with specific questions:

- If on track to achieve the key result, what instills this confidence? If not, what has affected our confidence, and where are the obstacles?
- Explore alternatives to get back on track.
- Seek recommendations and decisions needed from the team.

With key results marked "green" considered on track, the focus during check-ins usually shifts to the "red" items, enhancing efficiency.

Agreeing on the check-in frequency at the start of the cycle, as part of the working agreement, is crucial. This could be weekly, biweekly, monthly, or even ad-hoc.

Multi-Team Check-Ins

When facilitating a mid-cycle review with multiple teams, avoid having each team recite their entire set of OKRs. Focus instead on sharing two key results per team:

- **Progress:** A key result that is on track. This moment is about celebrating progress.
- **Learning:** A key result that isn't on track, focusing on what the team is learning about the business or the OKRs process. This isn't for assigning blame but for reinforcing that OKRs are as much about learning as they are about making measurable progress.

Common Challenges and Solutions

Effective OKR evaluation is not without its challenges. Recognizing and addressing these challenges is crucial for the success of the OKR process.

This section outlines some common pitfalls in OKR evaluation and provides practical solutions, supplemented with case studies to illustrate how organizations have successfully navigated these issues.

Addressing Common Pitfalls in OKR Evaluation

- **Overemphasis on Task Completion:** One common mistake is equating the completion of tasks with the achievement of key results. This focus on mere task completion can overshadow the actual impact of the work done.
    - *Solution:* Shift the focus from tasks to outcomes. Encourage teams to look at the broader picture of how their tasks contribute to achieving key results and the overall objective.
- **Lack of Flexibility:** Rigid adherence to OKRs without considering changing circumstances can lead to irrelevant or unattainable goals.
    - *Solution:* Foster a culture of adaptability where revisiting and adjusting OKRs in response to new information or changes in the environment is seen as a positive and proactive strategy.

Case Studies: Examples of Effective OKR Evaluations and Adjustments

In my experience as a coach working with various companies, I've witnessed firsthand the dynamic nature of Objectives and Key Results in practice.

A crucial aspect of successfully implementing OKRs is the ability to adapt and adjust them mid-cycle, based on emerging insights and changing circumstances.

Below, I present some case studies from my coaching tenure. These examples highlight how different organizations effectively evaluated and adjusted their OKRs, demonstrating the importance of flexibility and responsiveness in achieving strategic goals.

1. **Tech Company Embraces Flexibility:** A burgeoning tech startup had initially set aggressive growth targets for its innovative product. However, user feedback in the first quarter revealed a significant need for product enhancements. Responding promptly, the company revised its OKRs to prioritize product feature enhancements and user experience improvements. This pivot not only led to heightened customer satisfaction and retention but also laid the groundwork for sustainable long-term growth.
2. **Retail Chain Focuses on Customer Service:** A well-established national retail chain originally had its OKRs centered around ambitious sales targets. Mid-cycle, an emerging need to uplift customer service - crucial to their brand image - became apparent. The chain adapted its OKRs to incorporate employee training programs and customer satisfaction metrics. The outcome was twofold: a noticeable improvement in sales and a substantial enhancement in customer experience, bolstering their brand reputation.
3. **Manufacturing Firm Moves Beyond Task Completion:** A manufacturing firm was initially focused on meeting production quotas, using these as their sole success metric. This approach led to a concerning pattern of last-minute rushes and compromised product quality. Recognizing this, they restructured their OKRs to include process efficiency and product quality measures. This shift encouraged a more balanced and sustainable production approach, resulting in notable improvements in product quality and heightened employee satisfaction.

These case studies illustrate how addressing common challenges in OKR evaluation and being willing to make thoughtful adjustments can lead to more effective and meaningful outcomes.

Focusing on the quality of achievements, maintaining flexibility, and transcending beyond mere task completion are essential steps for organizations to ensure their OKRs stay relevant, achievable, and in alignment with their overarching strategic goals.

OKR Retrospectives

OKR retrospectives are critical in closing the loop of an OKR cycle. They provide an opportunity to reflect on the achievements and learnings of the past cycle, fostering continuous improvement in the goal-setting and achieving process.

This section outlines how to conduct effective retrospectives, gather feedback, and learn from both successes and failures.

Conducting End-of-Cycle Retrospectives

- **Scheduling the Retrospective:** Plan the retrospective at the end of each OKR cycle, ensuring all team members can participate. This should be a dedicated session separate from regular meetings.
- **Structured Discussion Format:** Follow a structured format such as 'What went well?', 'What didn't go well?', and 'What can be improved?'. Encourage open and honest discussions, focusing on both the process and the outcomes.
- **Reviewing OKR Achievements:** Evaluate the extent to which each OKR was achieved. Discuss factors that contributed to the success or shortfall, going beyond mere numbers to understand the context and the journey.

Gathering and Incorporating Feedback from Team Members

- **Creating a Safe Space for Feedback:** Establish a comfortable and non-judgmental environment where team members feel safe to share their honest feedback.
- **Diverse Perspectives:** Encourage input from all team members, regardless of their role. Different perspectives can provide valuable insights.
- **Actionable Takeaways:** Aim to extract actionable takeaways from the feedback. Identify specific changes that can be made in the next cycle to improve the OKR process.

Learning from Successes and Failures to Refine Future OKRs

- **Analyzing Successes:** Understand what led to successful outcomes. Was it effective planning, team effort, external factors, or a combination of these? Consider how these success factors can be replicated or enhanced in future cycles.
- **Learning from Failures:** Similarly, analyze the failures or shortfalls. Was it due to unrealistic goal-setting, external challenges, lack of resources, or execution issues? Use these insights to make more informed and realistic OKR planning in the future.
- **Documenting Learnings:** Keep a record of the lessons learned and insights gained during the retrospective. This documentation will be invaluable for future reference and for onboarding new team members.

OKR retrospectives are not just about evaluating past performance but are a crucial step in the cycle of continuous improvement. They provide invaluable learnings that can refine the OKR process, making it more effective and aligned with the organization's evolving needs and challenges.

Conducting thoughtful retrospectives, gathering comprehensive feedback, and learning from both successes and failures empowers teams to refine their approach to OKRs. This leads to more meaningful and impactful outcomes in future cycles.

Best Practices for Continuous Improvement

Continuous improvement in the OKR process is key to achieving long-term success and maintaining alignment with evolving organizational goals.

This section highlights best practices for cultivating a culture of accountability and continuous improvement, fostering open communication, and effectively integrating learnings into future OKR cycles.

Cultivating a Culture of Accountability and Continuous Improvement

- **Empowering Ownership:** Encourage teams to take ownership of their OKRs. This means being responsible not just for achieving key results but also for actively seeking solutions and improvements.
- **Regular Reflection:** Promote a habit of regular self-reflection and team reflection on progress and challenges. This shouldn't only occur at the end of a cycle but should be an ongoing process.
- **Learning-Oriented Mindset:** Foster a culture where learning from both successes and failures is valued. Encourage teams to view challenges and setbacks as opportunities for growth and learning.
- **Celebrate Progress and Learning:** Recognize and celebrate achievements and progress, even if they are incremental. Acknowledging effort and learning encourages a positive attitude toward continuous improvement.

Encouraging Open Communication and Transparency

- **Transparent Sharing of OKRs and Progress:** Make OKRs and their progress visible to all relevant stakeholders. This transparency helps in aligning efforts and fosters a sense of shared purpose.
- **Creating Safe Spaces for Discussion:** Ensure that team meetings and one-on-ones are safe spaces where team members can openly discuss challenges and seek support without fear of judgment.

- **Feedback Mechanisms:** Implement regular and structured feedback mechanisms. This can include surveys, suggestion boxes, or regular check-in meetings.

Integrating Learnings into the Next OKR Cycle

- **Documenting Insights:** Systematically document the insights and learnings from each OKR cycle. This documentation should be easily accessible for reference in future planning sessions.
- **Iterative Learning:** Apply the learnings from each cycle to refine the OKR setting process. This includes setting more realistic KRs, adjusting timelines, or redefining objectives to better align with the organization's strategy.
- **Training and Development:** Based on the retrospectives and feedback, identify areas for training and development that can enhance the team's capacity to achieve OKRs.

Conclusion

The journey through the intricacies of setting, evaluating, and refining Objectives and Key Results is both challenging and rewarding.

This comprehensive exploration has provided a roadmap for navigating the OKR process, emphasizing the importance of clarity in setting OKRs, regular check-ins, effective measurement techniques, the agility to adjust mid-cycle, learning from retrospectives, and the continuous improvement of the OKR process.

NOTES

[1] https://youtu.be/OqmdLcyES_Q?si=fLUTiKZKVminM42D

[2] https://www.amazon.com/Good-Strategy-Bad-difference-matters-ebook/dp/B005331U7Q/

[3] https://www.amazon.com/Strategy-Design-Sprint-How-Designing-ebook/dp/B0BR5ZVGVH

[4] https://www.strategyzer.com/library/the-business-model-canvas

[5] https://aktiasolutions.com/getting-started-with-wardley-maps/

[6] https://www.amazon.com/Competing-Future-Gary-Hamel-ebook/dp/B004OC070S

[7] https://www.amazon.com/Strategy-Design-Sprint-How-Designing-ebook/dp/B0BR5ZVGVH

[8] https://aktiasolutions.com/blue-ocean-strategy-navigating-beyond-traditional-competition/

[9] https://aktiasolutions.com/introduction-to-jobs-to-be-done-introduction-to-jtbd/

[10] https://aktiasolutions.com/harnessing-the-seven-powers-strategies-for-dominant-product-leadership/

[xi] https://www.amazon.com/Good-Strategy-Bad-difference-matters-ebook/dp/B005331U7Q/

[xii] https://www.amazon.com/Art-Action-Leaders-between-Actions-ebook/dp/B01HPVHLHG

[13] https://www.amazon.com/Blue-Ocean-Strategy-Expanded-Uncontested-ebook/dp/B00O4CRR7Y

[14] https://www.amazon.com/Product-Roadmapping-Practice-Growth-Strategy-ebook/dp/B0BGPJP7QY

[15] https://www.amazon.com/Product-Roadmapping-Practice-Growth-Strategy-ebook/dp/B0BGPJP7QY

[16] https://aktiasolutions.com/blog-aktia-solutions/

[17] https://www.hbs.edu/faculty/Pages/item.aspx?num=3460

[18] https://www.cambridge.org/core/journals/industrial-and-organizational-psychology/article/breaking-engagement-apart-the-role-of-intrinsic-and-extrinsic-motivation-in-engagement-strategies/A277714CC7A3FE3E94DE80F4EEBBC2EF

[19] https://www.amazon.com/Drive-Surprising-Truth-About-Motivates-ebook/dp/B0033TI4BW

[20] https://www.amazon.com/OKRs-Field-Book-Step-Step/dp/1119816424

[21] https://www.producttalk.org/2023/12/opportunity-solution-trees/

[22] https://www.amazon.com/User-Story-Mapping-Discover-Product/dp/1491904909

[23] Adapted from 'The OKRs Field Book' by Ben Lamorte

Printed in Great Britain
by Amazon